South Pacific Oral Traditions

Voices in Performance and Text

John Miles Foley, General Editor

South Pacific Oral Traditions

Edited by Ruth Finnegan and Margaret Orbell

INDIANA UNIVERSITY PRESS

Bloomington and Indianapolis

The paper used in this publication meets the minimum
requirements of American National Standard for Information
Sciences—Permanence of Paper for Printed Library
Materials, ANSI Z39.48-1984.

Manufactured in the United States of America

Library of Congress Cataloging-in-Publication Data

South Pacific oral traditions / edited by Ruth Finnegan and Margaret Orbell.
        p.   cm. — (Voices in performance and text)
        Includes bibliographical references and index.
      ISBN 0-253-32868-3 (cloth : alk. paper). — ISBN 0-253-20958-7 (pbk. : alk. paper)
      1. Oral tradition—Melanesia. 2. Oral tradition—Polynesia. 3. Folklore—
Melanesia—Performance. 4. Folklore—Polynesia—Performance. I. Finnegan, Ruth H. II.
        Orbell, Margaret Rose. III. Series.
        GR380.S68 1995
    398'.0995—dc20   95-4830

        1 2 3 4 5 00 99 98 97 96 95

CONTENTS

Preface   1

I.   Introduction; or, Why the Comparativist Should Take Account of the South Pacific   *Ruth Finnegan*   6

II.   "My Summit Where I Sit": Form and Content in Maori Women's Love Songs   *Margaret Orbell*   30

III.   Wry Comment from the Outback: Songs of Protest from the Niua Islands, Tonga   *Wendy Pond*   49

IV.   Sex and Slander in Tikopia Song: Public Antagonism and Private Intrigue   *Raymond Firth*   64

V.   Wept Thoughts: The Voicing of Kaluli Memories *Steven Feld*   85

VI.   Profile of a Composer: Ihaia Puka, A *Pulotu* of of the Tokelau Islands   *Allan Thomas and Ineleo Tuia*   109

VII.   Fiction, Fact, and Imagination: A Tokelau Narrative *Judith Huntsman*   124

VIII.   "That Isn't Really a Pig": Spirit Traditions in the Southern Cook Islands   *Christian Clerk*   161

IX.   "Head" and "Tail": The Shaping of Oral Traditions among the Binandere in Papua New Guinea *John D. Waiko*   177

X.   Every Picture Tells a Story: Visual Alternatives to Oral Tradition in Ponam Society   *James Carrier and Achsah Carrier*   195

XI.   Winged Tangi'ia: A Mangaian Dramatic Performance *Marivee McMath and Teaea Parima*   215

Contributors   256

Index   258

South Pacific Oral Traditions

Preface

The oral traditions of the South Pacific have much to tell us. Their sophisticated and artful commentary on the human condition is demonstrated in the studies included here, the more striking in that the performance and composition of oral forms represent a still vibrant tradition in the Pacific, new as well as old. As is explained in the Introduction, they contribute too to widely-discussed issues about the nature of tradition and of human creativity, illuminating current theoretical debates through the detailed cases they present. Above all, this volume comes out of the interplay of voices among people who themselves live in the South Pacific region or have worked there over many years, so that the boundaries between the once-separate categories of native and outsider, theorist and practitioner, are rightly crossed and recrossed.

The comparative and theoretical interest of the South Pacific is clearly brought out in the directions taken in recent scholarly analysis (including work that has appeared since the first publication of these papers in 1990—for which see select references following this Preface). This recent work strongly reinforces the wider relevance of these Pacific examples—only too often ignored in comparative discussion of the issues.

The theorists continue to argue, for example, about the nature of oral composition and style, or the implications of oral as against literate communication (Lord 1991, Foley 1991 and 1995, Finnegan 1992, Street 1993, Keller-Cohen 1994). Several of the papers here make a lively contribution to these questions, challenging once again some older generalizing presuppositions through their detailed attention both to the *variety* of oral traditions and to the practical processes actually observed, rather than speculatively surmised.

The verbal *texts* documented here are clearly one essential element in our understanding of South Pacific oral traditions. But scholars are now increasingly also drawing our attention to the poetics of extra-textual, nonverbal, and performance features (Bauman 1992, Brady 1991, Howes 1991, Classen 1993, Schechner and Appel 1990, Sherzer 1990). Here too the impressive Pacific performances—including several of those presented here—have an important contribution to make to our expanding appreciation of the multifaceted nature of both art forms and human culture more generally.

The early 1990s have also seen many publications reanalyzing the concept of "tradition." The focus has often been on tradition in the sense not so much of product as of process: *how* traditions are maintained, molded, developed, or, indeed, created. Sometimes the concern is with how verbally articulated traditions are constructed, as artistic genres (say) or oral historical narratives developed through the dynamic interaction between culturally recognized conventions, personal creativity, and the varying voices of differing individuals or groups (Sienaert *et al*. 1991, Finnegan 1992, Tonkin 1991). Other influential work has revolved round a critique of the concept and practice of "tradition" in more general terms. Particularly intense controversy has been generated by a series of writings on the so-called "invention of tradition" in Pacific culture (Hanson 1989, Jolly and Thomas 1992—among many others). Some contenders hold that such approaches harmfully and unjustifiably challenge accepted cultural traditions, through the apparent implication that these are "made up," even "fabricated." Others retort that rejecting an "essentialist" view of tradition should enable a clearer appreciation (rather than an undermining) of the processes at work, and provide furthermore the opportunity to "include, rather than exclude, non-scholarly voices" (Linnekin 1992:250).

The present volume in one sense bypasses the more polemical aspects of these recent controversies about the *general* constitution of "tradition." This is because it focuses in the main on empirically-based micro-studies of verbal genres which clearly already exist and are practiced—rather than speculating overmuch on the macro-politics of how they came to be as they are, or on tradition in the more generalized meaning of that term. In another way, however, the papers here make a crucial contribution to the debate. For it is precisely through such micro-studies that we can test out what the more general claims and counterclaims might actually mean in practice, and illuminate the question of what actually *are* the active roles of individuals and groups in shaping and creating their oral productions.

And whose are the voices that should be heard? Much has been written over recent years questioning the presumed "authority" of the scholar or stressing the importance of hearing contending interpretations and otherwise "submerged" viewpoints. There has been a backlash too, querying whether some of all this "reflexivity" has not just been an excuse for an abdication of scholarly responsibility or even for mere self-indulgent navel-gazing. This volume to an extent straddles the gap. Its studies are based on the traditionally accepted canons of detailed scholarly analysis and careful fieldwork; and it certainly avoids lengthy postmodernist discoursing. But it does also implicitly reject the notion of the foreign authoritative scholar as producing *the* definitive version (it will be noticeable how many of the cases here involve joint authorship) and reveals the often multi-layered meanings of differing voices, often ones hitherto relatively unheard outside their own settings. It is our belief, too, that it is in part through such oral forms, and not just through the enunciations of scholars or of politicians, that people formulate and convey their own verbally realized interpretations of the world. Would it not be right to conclude that the theoretical interpretations formulated in oral traditions of the kind presented in this volume are no less "real" than those produced by the academics? And that they too demand their own recognition?

All these issues—and more—are illuminated by the firsthand and detailed studies here. They are studies, furthermore, that have the virtue of not being obscured in high theoretical wrappings, but expressed through close attention to the words and doings of the active participants themselves. Far from being outdated the oral traditions here, both new and old, speak with a fresh and relevant voice for both admirers of South Pacific cultures and for comparative scholars throughout the world.

Finally we should like to thank John Miles Foley for encouraging and supporting the first appearance of these papers in the journal *Oral Tradition*, and to express our heartfelt appreciation not only to all the writers in this volume but also to the manifold authors and performers whose voices these papers represent.

Ruth Finnegan and Margaret Orbell
July 1994

References

Bauman 1992

Richard Bauman, ed. *Folklore, Cultural Performances, and Popular Entertainments: A Communications-Centered Handbook*. New York: Oxford University Press.

Brady 1991

Ivan Brady, ed. *Anthropological Poetics*. Savage, MD: Rowman and Littlefield.

Carrier 1992

James G. Carrier. *History and Tradition in Melanesian Anthropology*. Berkeley: University of California Press.

Classen 1993

Constance Classen. *Worlds of Sense: Exploring the Senses in History and Across Cultures*. London and New York: Routledge.

Finnegan 1992

Ruth Finnegan. *Oral Traditions and the Verbal Arts: A Guide to Research Practices*. ASA Research Methods Series. London: Routledge.

Foley 1991

John Miles Foley. *Immanent Art: From Structure to Meaning in Traditional Oral Epic*. Bloomington: Indiana University Press.

Foley 1995

_____. *The Singer of Tales in Performance*. Bloomington: Indiana University Press.

Hanson 1989

Allan Hanson. "The Making of the Maori: Culture Invention and its Logic." *American Anthropologist*, 91, 4:890-902.

Howes 1991

David Howes, ed. *The Varieties of Sensory Experience: A Sourcebook in the Anthropology of the Senses*. Toronto: University of Toronto Press.

Jolly and Thomas 1992

Margaret Jolly and Nicholas Thomas, eds. "The Politics of Tradition in the Pacific." *Oceania*, 62, 4 (special issue):241-354.

Keller-Cohen 1994

Deborah Keller-Cohen, ed. *Literacy: Interdiscplinary Conversations*. New York: Hampton Press.

Linnekin 1992

Jocelyn Linnekin. "On the Theory and Politics of Cultural Construction in the Pacific." In Jolly and Thomas 1992:249-63.

Lord 1991

Albert Bates Lord. *Epic Singers and Oral Tradition*. Ithaca: Cornell University Press.

Nicholas 1992

Nicholas Thomas. "The Inversion of Tradition." *American Ethnologist*, 19, 2:213-32.

Schechner and Appel 1990

Richard Schechner and Willa Appel, eds. *By Means of Performance: Intercultural Studies of Theater and Ritual*. Cambridge: Cambridge University Press.

Sherzer 1990

Joel Sherzer. *Verbal Art in San Blas*. Cambridge: Cambridge University Press.

Sienaert *et al.* 1991

Edgard Sienaert, Nigel Bell, and Meg Lewis, eds. *Tradition and Innovation: New Wine in Old Bottles?* Durban: University of Natal.

Street 1993

Brian Street, ed. *Cross-Cultural Approaches to Literacy*. Cambridge: Cambridge University Press.

Tonkin 1991   Elizabeth Tonkin. *Narrating our Pasts: The Social Construction of Oral History.* Cambridge: Cambridge University Press.

I

Introduction; or, Why the Comparativist Should Take Account of the South Pacific

Ruth Finnegan

This volume is devoted to oral traditions in the South Pacific and reports the results of a series of twentieth-century and mainly field-based studies. Since this region may be unfamiliar to some readers, these opening comments give a very brief introduction to this vast area, followed by some discussion of the significance of its oral traditions and their study for the wider comparative study of oral tradition.[1]

The Cultural Background and Central Theoretical Issues

The scattered islands and land masses within the huge Pacific Ocean make up a fascinating and too little known portion of the globe—and of our human culture. It is one that, with its evocation of the noble savage and the life of nature, has for long had a romantic appeal for Westerners. But despite this (or even perhaps because of it?), the international scholarly literature outside the Pacific has taken surprisingly little account of the study of Pacific cultural forms. In particular, informed references to Pacific oral tradition are rare in comparative literary analyses or in theories of oral literature and tradition.

This relative neglect of the Pacific in the comparative literature is both unfortunate and paradoxical, for as will become clear from the papers that follow this region is rich in oral literature and tradition. There is a great deal already available in the voluminous collections—both published and archival—which

---

[1] Although I am responsible for this Introduction (and therefore for all its deficiencies), I would like to express my sincere gratitude to Margaret Orbell both for all her constructive suggestions and for saving me from many errors, also for her valuable comments reproduced in the next note.

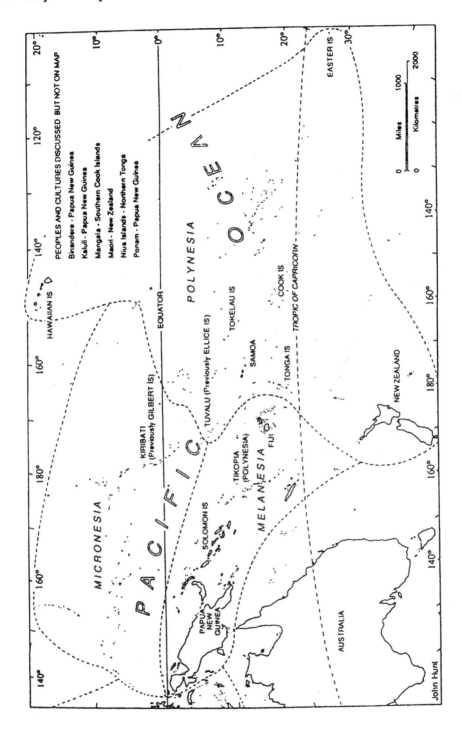

PEOPLES AND CULTURES DISCUSSED BUT NOT ON MAP

Binandere - Papua New Guinea
Kaluli - Papua New Guinea
Mangaia - Southern Cook Islands
Maori - New Zealand
Niua Islands - Northern Tonga
Ponam - Papua New Guinea

John Hunt

resulted from the long tradition of scholarship in the Pacific[2] and yet more is, like many of the examples in this volume, known from more recent field studies. In the form of spoken narratives, of chorally performed and often danced songs and dramas, and of emotive and wept laments transmitting the sorrow of individuals, these—and other—oral formulations from the Pacific are interesting and often moving in their own right, deserving to take their place among the world's treasury of literature and tradition. In addition, these traditions manifest important features for the scholar, not least because of their exemplification of a living tradition, often still open to study by field researchers. These features are of the greatest potential interest for comparative research on oral literature and tradition, and yet for the most part are relatively little noticed by non-Pacific specialists.

The cultures of the South Pacific are usually divided into Polynesian and Melanesian (still commonly used, if in the last analysis somewhat inexact, terms), each category represented by several papers in this volume[3] (see map on page 7). In very general terms, it can be said that Polynesia is characterized by its closely linked set of languages (some nearly mutually intelligible) and its tradition of chiefly and hierarchical rule, whereas Melanesian societies are more heterogeneous both linguistically and socially, usually with a more egalitarian and individualistic ethic and social structure. Not that these generalities correctly sum up all the specifics of each of these many cultures, or indeed dictate the thought patterns and artistic expressions of individuals within them in any simple

---

[2] In fact, as comes out particularly clearly in Margaret Orbell's analysis of the earlier Maori *waiata* songs, there are huge collections, both published and unpublished, of nineteenth-century Maori and other Pacific texts. As she comments more generally (personal communication), one of the noteworthy points about the history of scholarship in the South Pacific is "the existence, especially in Polynesia, of voluminous early collections of texts and historical records, and the potential significance also of this material for comparative research—for example, I hope my article may do something to show that it is possible to contribute to general, theoretical issues by drawing upon this material (*which is so much more extensive and comprehensive, as regards to social contexts as well as texts, than that which is available to, for example, the students of the earliest, orally composed, European literatures*). In some parts of Polynesia, most especially New Zealand, Hawaii, and the Societies, there have been for a good 150 years very considerable local traditions of (written) scholarship in this field—these have had varied fortunes, but they have *existed*, the continuity has been there, just as, for example, there have been continuous traditions of scholarship in Irish, Finnish, English (etc.) folklore/oral tradition. My work in New Zealand, and John Charlot's in Hawaii, are among the contemporary manifestations of these local traditions. Hopefully we are more aware of the comparative dimension, and international scholarship in this field, than some of our predecessors (although the work of such early writers as Fornander, Emerson, Krämer, Gifford, Collocott, Te Uira Henry, Gill, Smith, Best, Taylor, Grey, Wohlers, Ngata, and Te Hurinui was the product, in its time, of formidable scholarship: they were very aware of their European contemporaries and did, in their own styles, interpret and analyze as well as collect; in fact, they could hardly have collected so widely if they had not done so). Of course, different questions now need to be asked and also a greater rigor brought to the kind of things that they did do. But it is important to note the resources in the valuable written records which do already exist, and which contain material which provides opportunities for further research (as do early books on, say, Celtic tradition)."

[3] The small islands making up what is usually called Micronesia to the north do not, as it happens, appear directly in this collection, although the Tokelau poet Ihaia described in "Profile of a Composer" has close connections with Kiribati culture through his foster mother.

way; as appears in Wendy Pond's paper, for example, a hierarchical and apparently tradition-bound Polynesian culture may offer all the more incentive for individual and poetic voices to enunciate a differing viewpoint through the "safe" medium of art. However, even for the unexpected ways in which people can manipulate the cultural patterns, some knowledge of this general background as well as of the specificities of each culture is helpful for appreciating the nature and use of these traditions.

These are small-scale cultures. Apart from the Maori on the "mainland" of New Zealand, most island populations are extremely small, often separated from their neighbors by many hundreds of miles of ocean. Even independent nation-states within the Pacific, for example Kiribati (the previously named Gilbert Islands) or the Cook Islands, sometimes contain only a few thousand people in all—hence their appropriate designation by political scientists as "micro-states." It has to be remembered too that most of these nations consist of archipelagoes rather than single islands, adding yet more to the small-scale and remote existence of the dispersed islands. Papua New Guinea provides a larger land mass, but there too there have been physical and cultural barriers to travel and the size of the traditional communities was very small; thus the Melanesian Kaluli, Binandere, or Ponam whose oral traditions are discussed here number only a few thousands or less each.

In one way Pacific life and culture has thus been isolated and independent, but in another way their traditional seafaring skills and, in recent times, their use of modern transport opportunities have led to interaction and mutual contact, especially among the closely cognate Polynesian languages (the Tokelauan poet Ihaia Puka described by Thomas and Tuia, for example, can and does compose in three languages). There have also been continuing interactions with other areas around the Pacific and—for two centuries or so for Polynesia, from earlier this century for the interior of Papua New Guinea—with Europe. This history of contact has been varied, although it usually included some form or another of colonial experience (in most cases now constitutionally in the past)[4] with perhaps the single most important aspect of that history being the influence of the Christian church on—indeed in some senses incorporation into—earlier and contemporary Pacific culture. As will become clear in the later papers, these interactions are reflected and exploited in local oral arts, for which they form part of the background and context.

Although each paper stands independently and the authors represent a number of different disciplines (anthropology, ethnomusicology, folklore, literature, history) as well as different personal backgrounds, there is one important characteristic shared among the studies in this issue: they are by authors who live or have carried out long-term fieldwork in the areas of the South Pacific that they

---

[4] Hence the changed names in recent years of several of the countries mentioned here. The unfamiliar reader may wish to know that these include the Kiribati (old name Gilbert Islands), Tuvalu (Ellice Islands), and Vanuatu (New Hebrides); most other names have remained the same or near enough to recognize.

describe. This already makes this collection of interest through its presentation of new empirical material—in itself both intriguing and enjoyable—by scholars steeped in the traditions of an important area of the world which is as yet too little known outside the Pacific itself. But it is also worth commenting on two more theoretical implications of the mainly contemporary, local, and field-based nature of the papers here.

First, unlike many earlier accounts and collections of "oral traditions" from non-literate or colonized peoples, the discussions here are not the outcome of brief forays into the "field" by foreign collectors from a self-styled "superior" culture, concerned only to complete some rapid recording then get back to their capitals with their hoards: to be regarded as a collection of museum "specimens," as it were, from a radically different and probably somewhat despised stratum of society—at best one to be condescended to. The research reported here, by contrast, no doubt reflecting wider changes in both intellectual concerns and political realities, arises rather from long and intensive local interaction either by scholars themselves living in the region or through research visits continuing through many years of friendship and contact. In several cases the authorship is a joint one, combining the insights of academic researcher and local native-speaking scholar (in the case of John Waiko with both roles united in the same person). It is clear not only from the explicit salutation at the outset of Wendy Pond's paper ("I ask leave from the poets and orators of Tonga...") but also from the comments and acknowledgments in paper after paper that scholars now, far more than in the past, are rightly conscious that the subjects they seek to communicate and analyze are owned neither by the researchers nor by some outside academic community but represent the authentic voices of people and cultures rich in their own dignity and achievements.

One corollary of this more "equal" and humane approach is a much greater appreciation than in many earlier studies of the aesthetic and (often) personally creative quality of these oral forms. No longer can they be assumed to be the generalized passive products of some far-away or long-ago stage in society (a lesson for some historians too here, perhaps?), but rather can be seen for what they indeed often are: the living processes through which thinking and feeling individuals interweave their own insights, experiences, and interests with the cultural traditions of their times.

Second, this spotlight on recent field studies of living traditions intentionally complements one of the foci in many scholarly studies of oral tradition on forms which, however "oral" in their earlier composition or circulation, have basically come down to us in the form of written texts. What comes out of the distinctive approach here, then, is not only the chance to extend our experience of human expression through encountering traditions from a culture that may be unfamiliar to many readers, but also a rather different range of questions and issues from those raised in the study of historical texts—an unsurprising result of its main reliance on fieldwork in continuing literary traditions rather than on written texts. Thus there are many more references than is usual to ideas drawn from anthropology, folklore, ethnomusicology, or, to some extent, literary theory (not all will necessarily be familiar—or even perhaps congenial—for all readers, but the editors have endeavored to ensure that the ideas are generally presented accessibly and not in specialist jargon). The particular issues stressed here should provide not only new insights but also perhaps a challenge to engage in new ways of approaching older material—or, if this kind of investigation is not wholly practicable with some of the historical texts studied elsewhere, at least to raise questions to ponder.

The issues raised in this collection that can, I hope, feed directly into comparative scholarship on oral tradition will only emerge in detail from the later papers themselves. Let me start however by summarizing the main issues quickly, before going on to discuss them more generally in this introduction. They are questions about:

(1)   The nature and view of what is meant by "tradition" (both controversies among outsiders, and the question of how tradition is conceived and practiced by local poets and their audiences themselves).

(2)   The significance of extra-textual elements in oral tradition, in particular of *performance* attributes, of the *visual and non-verbal* aspects, and of the *context* (in the widest sense of that term).

(3)   Composition and its relation to performance, the interaction of individual and tradition, and the relevance for wider comparative theories.

These issues in one way or another run through the otherwise differing papers in this collection, and are also taken up for some further comment below (not always in the order given above). They add a fresh light that can complement, challenge, and sometimes confirm the work that has already been done for rather different sources and contexts. In some cases too they can perhaps alert the students of written textual forms and traditions in archival or historical sources to new questions or interpretations that they can try to pursue with their sources. In others (or perhaps this is the same point put more negatively!) they can point up previously unappreciated areas of ignorance that scholars working with older sources may at the least need to take account of and perhaps face up to explicitly. Above all perhaps, it can draw on the well-known rewards of a comparative perspective—familiar already, no doubt, to readers of the journal *Oral Tradition*, which draws its inspiration directly from this ideal of comparison. For it can stimulate us to look anew at our own traditions within a wider scale of things, and, having looked (whether from elsewhere in the Pacific or from the viewpoint of a Western outsider), to turn our eyes back to instances within our own culture and history with greater perspective and a clearer eye for distinctive characteristics that we might otherwise take for granted (and, in taking for granted, project too easily onto others) and perhaps then to detect patterns before unnoticed.

"Tradition" and "Oral Tradition" in the Pacific

Perhaps the single most striking conclusion from the papers here is the continuing vitality and interest of oral forms in the Pacific. This presents a marked contrast to some other oral traditions in which the prime scholarly focus often seems to be founded in the urgency of recording them (or their fragments) now before they die out.[5] Any perusal of the accounts here must surely lead to the conclusion that unwritten songs, dances, narratives, and laments, all drawing primarily (if not necessarily exclusively) on oral media and native cultural forms, are still being performed, transmitted, and newly created throughout the islands of the South Pacific.

There is more to be said than that, however, for the concept of "tradition" (or of "traditional," or of "traditionality") is a controversial one. It is true that it is often used as a key concept, for example in many discussions about oral literature and the verbal arts—indeed is sometimes taken as a defining characteristic marking out a field of study or a specific set of verbal forms. But it is also of course more elusive and controversial than it sometimes seems on the surface and its problematic nature is now being increasingly discussed (see in particular Henige 1988, also Hobsbawm and Ranger 1987, Ben-Amos 1985, Honko 1988:9-11). This is not the place to enter into such controversies in detail, but they cannot be totally ignored, and it is at the least worth flagging the way that the evidence on the South Pacific presented in this volume can feed into some of this discussion.

How far and in what sense are examples in this volume "traditional" and/or "oral"? Some may wish to query whether the label of "tradition" or "oral tradition" is appropriate at all (at least for some of the examples), on the grounds that only some primal stage or some form untouched by the written word or by Western influences should count. Some Pacific scholars in the past (though fewer in the present) would have taken that attitude too.

That would be a possible—though surely rather extreme—line. But against it one must point out that it does not, in the first place, accord with many of the local perceptions of these oral forms—regarded as a form of continuity from the past, hence in at least one sense "traditional" and local as against what are regarded as outside or Western education-based forms. Secondly, although I would certainly hold that the term "oral" is a much more problematic and relative one than is often assumed (see, e.g., Finnegan 1977, 1988), the preponderance of the songs, laments, and narratives discussed here are at least on the face of it oral in that they are essentially based in spoken or sung—that is *performed*—rather than written formulation, often orally composed in at least some sense of that term, and located within oral conventions. So scholars recording these forms

---

[5] For example, one recurrent theme in the recent special issue of *Oral Tradition*, Hispanic Balladry (2/2-3, 1987). Of course in the Pacific as elsewhere fashions change, so certain genres (e.g., those discussed in Margaret Orbell's paper) are no longer being composed, whereas others have risen in popularity.

now would surely wish to accept them alongside other comparable forms which *have* been defined as "oral" or as examples of "oral tradition."

The common (if unstated) association of the idea of the "collective" with tradition is harder to deal with. Some scholars may indeed wish to argue that because individual poets often apparently play a significant role in Pacific oral forms, their products should not after all be treated as "tradition" or "traditional." But it has to be said that if the empirical evidence (rather than merely questions of logic or definition) is to play a part, then the findings in this volume certainly suggest that this common association of "tradition" with "the collective" may need to be queried. Thus while many of the Pacific forms discussed here might on superficial study appear to be instances of collective or inert tradition (and so to qualify in the same sense as other examples of "oral tradition"), detailed analysis reveals the complex individual/tradition interaction that lies behind them, where established conventions of content or form do not after all preclude individual creativity. So pure collective "tradition" seems to constantly recede and elude us—does this, therefore, not present some challenge to comparative scholars to look in more detail at other cases, perhaps to modify some earlier definitions and assumptions?

There are certainly problems of interpretation and nomenclature here. But despite such problems it would seem unreasonable to reject at least a preliminary case for provisionally bringing these Pacific examples within the same comparative discussion as the other apparently comparable forms normally included within the scope of "oral tradition," even if in the last analysis we are still left with the challenge of investigating how far and in what sense these—and indeed the other apparently unambiguous examples elsewhere—are indeed rightly termed instances of oral tradition.

Part of the reason for our difficulty in just asserting that these examples are "oral" and/or "traditional" and leaving it at that is the complexity and elusiveness of so many of the forms being discussed here (in practice perhaps not so unlike other forms widely accepted as falling under the head of "oral tradition"?). Indeed, perhaps the main virtue of the largely field-based and in-depth studies here is precisely that this enables us to glimpse these complexities in a more vivid way than is possible in the case of much archive-based research: long-term observation, direct questioning of poets and narrators, or lengthy experience over many years and changes can all sometimes lead to the discovery of unanticipated insights. In this connection it is interesting how many of the papers in this volume seem to agree in questioning the once taken-for-granted search for old and inert Tradition—the "authentic" survival from a primal and "natural" past. Instead, while starting in other respects from independent stances, they almost all end up in stressing the dynamic and creative processes inherent in "traditional" narratives and songs—sometimes precisely, as Margaret Orbell demonstrates, because they *are* traditional—and the complex and not always predictable roles played by individuals within particular traditions, and by ongoing historical and political events.

However "old" a particular theme or genre may actually or reputedly be in one sense, it seems that its contemporary usage can give it a new meaning and reception. Examples are the old Tokelau song-types described by Thomas and Tuia where composers rework older texts with new music and choreography to put them in a new light and "remind listeners of their contemporary relevance," or the new twists given to traditional themes and formulaic expressions in Maori song composition as described in Orbell's article, where part of the effect and originality lies in the clever way the composer plays on these older themes. Firth comments on Tikopia songs (in a conclusion that could be applied much more widely) that even where the conventions of a traditional genre remain the same, "the *content* was continually changing" as different songs (including newly composed ones) moved in and out of the repertoire according to their popularity at a given time. Individual creativity building on established themes and audience expectations is part of contemporary tradition ("tradition" here being understood—as it would be in the context of written literature surely—in the sense of the established conventions about genre form and content), and thus is itself as authentic as earlier practices—of which it probably represents a continuation. Certainly such processes seem to be a not uncommon part of the present-day local scene and to be regarded locally as currently relevant manifestations of ongoing and valued native cultural tradition.

As well as this deliberate drawing on older themes and conventions, it is also clear that some of the content, genres, or performance techniques are also in one sense new, even if already thoroughly established in the local and—by now—"traditional" repertoire. In other words, texts and performances recorded in the twentieth (or even the nineteenth) century have *not* necessarily come down unchanging from the remote pre-Christian or pre-colonial past, even if they are sometimes assumed to be such by outsiders (or even in some cases by their own native exponents).[6] Taking the remote Tokelau Islands again, Thomas and Tuia point to some of the changes in genres and performance styles by quoting the octogenarian composer Ihaia's comment on the way compositions and performances by the younger singers are moving away from what *he* considered the more authentic tradition in action songs—that authentic tradition being, in his eyes, that of relying mainly on "Bible stories"! Christianity, in fact, has become so much a part of Pacific life in many areas that it would in most cases be impossible—and probably unproductive—to try to disentangle it to deduce the properties of some postulated primal stage beforehand. Indeed, Biblical stories have for long now been among the favored themes of Pacific oral arts and feature frequently in locally composed songs and dance dramas.

The South Pacific material illustrates strikingly well (if we still need to remind ourselves of this) that "tradition," in the sense at least of the established conventions of composition and performances and the accepted themes and

---

[6] For a discussion of how even the nineteenth-century classic collections of Pacific "myths" and "traditions" were themselves affected by individual participants and by specific historical circumstances, see Finnegan 1988:ch. 6.

content of oral literary forms, need not be archaic and unchanging—indeed its continued vitality and dynamic in an oral situation, as here, almost guarantees that it will not be. There are the lively and continuously creative Cook Islands ghost stories described in Clerk's paper, the complex re-creation of older narratives explored by Huntsman, the newly forged songs of the Tongan underdogs in witty and ironic protests against their rulers, or the processes, described so faithfully by John Waiko, by which the clan traditions are successfully filtered and codified as generation succeeds generation.

If oral tradition does not remain all of a piece in historical terms, but rather changes and develops over time, neither is it homogeneous or simple at any one time either. The term "oral tradition" is sometimes used with a very realist connotation, as if it represented one monolithic or always uncontested corpus. But it emerges very clearly from many of the accounts here that at any one time there are likely to be many different recognized oral genres, each with its own conventions as regards content, style, purpose, and expected modes of composition and performance (for example, the very different conventions for composition in different Kaluli genres described in Feld's paper). In addition, there are also often different expectations and pressures among different sections or age groups among the local community. Political pressures and outlooks vary, there are contradictory and competing traditional accounts of events, young people prefer song genres that appeal less to their elders, and rival poets or groupings contend with each other.

It is not only outside scholars who puzzle about the processes of tradition and its transmission or seek ways to represent this process in words, for there are also differing local notions about such matters. John Waiko's account is particularly illuminating here, with its explanation of the vivid local metaphor of the "fishtrap" through which the Binandere picture the past and its transmission to the present. Again, both Wendy Pond's account of Tongan views of the past as something just *ahead* of us (a similar view, incidentally to that in the Columbian Andes, see Rappaport 1988:721) and Thomas and Tuia's discussion of the Tokelauan combination of both anonymity *and* personal reputation for their poets in the light of local ideas about the relation between individual and community contrast interestingly with some Western views of these subjects. They can thus provide a useful challenge to otherwise taken-for-granted and ethnocentric views of how "tradition" works and is locally regarded. So too do the instances of the complex and varied interactions between the triad of what Huntsman aptly terms "fact, fiction, and imagination." In her analysis of Tokelau traditions and their formulation, as well as in Cook Islands spirit narratives, the Binandere sifting of clan traditions, or even the Ponam visual representation of genealogical traditions, we encounter interesting comparative issues about how people in other cultures represent to themselves the reality of their past and present experience. Such examples stimulate the recognition that there is clearly much here for us still to investigate both in field study and in new perusal of the existing sources.

It is interesting that these points come out so strongly in these accounts of South Pacific tradition. For of all the areas of the world, it might have been expected that it would be in the South Pacific, with its long-standing image in Western eyes of standing for "natural" humanity, that we could find access to the "authentic" and quintessential traditions of the long-distant past. But—even if one accepts such a chimera as worth searching for (something now increasingly queried by modern folklorists, social historians, and anthropologists)—much of what is now regarded and practiced as native tradition and enunciated in oral forms at the local level turns out to be intimately interrelated with the dynamic of nineteenth- and twentieth-century historical changes and to depend for its existence on the creative enterprise of individuals as well as the conventions of both old and developing traditions.

"Tradition" in both theory and practice thus turns out to be interestingly complex and elusive rather than a simply identifiable and concrete phenomenon—so much so that there are times when I am doubtful how far this idea really helps rather than hinders analysis. But one message at least we can draw from the Pacific examples here is that the concept does alert us to a range of questions and controversies which the continuing vitality of *something*—whether we wish to call it "oral tradition" or "verbal art" or "oral literature"—in the Pacific can help to illuminate. At the very least these Pacific instances can disabuse us of some simplistic assumptions about the automatic existence of frozen or sacrosanct "Tradition" from the past, and point to yet further questions about the dynamic interaction of individuals, historical specificity, and established conventions at any one point in time.

Composition: Individual and Tradition

The experience of "tradition"—with all its complications—in the context of the investigation of living traditions can also throw further light on the processes of composition. These processes may still be elusive indeed (even the composers themselves may not be fully aware of what takes place, it seems), but—from Parry and Lord's eye-opening work on South Slavic epic to more recent research in Africa, Asia, or, as here, the Pacific—it is clear that field-based studies can usually provide more opportunities and insights into this process than are easily open to those working with archival and historical material. This is all the more interesting since it is clear that new songs and poems are being composed in the Pacific—often within the framework of older traditions—and several of the papers comment directly or indirectly on the compositional processes underlying these or the way they become translated into performance.

One of the striking features of the forms from the Pacific that are illustrated here is the *variety* of modes of composition. Steven Feld's paper shows this particularly well when he explains the composition-in-performance mode of the soloistic Kaluli laments and contrasts this phenomenon with the different—and themselves varying—forms of composition in Kaluli songs where (depending on the precise genre) there can be memorization, prior composition, separation from performance, or the concept of a fixed text. Again, even within the same general category of song, different processes may be at work depending on the occasion, as with the Tikopia sexual taunting songs described by Firth, with some composed and worked up beforehand, some uttered in a trance (one common Pacific pattern), and some made up on the spot as a clever response to a song by an opposing group. Again the dance-drama described by McMath and Parima was largely prepared and planned beforehand, but still included some scope for improvisation by participants in certain of the elements of the performance. Even a single composer—like the admired Tokelau composer Ihaia—could use a series of different strategies, it seems: sometimes collaborating with his wife (joint composition being another common Pacific pattern), sometimes composing on his own (or with an assistant to memorize the words for him to be ready for the later group rehearsal—again not unparalleled), and varying between reworking old songs with new meanings and performances and composing anew and often with an intensely personal touch but within the established conventions.

We also encounter interesting variants on what at first sight look like familiar patterns. Margaret Orbell's paper provides a detailed explanation of how Maori women used formulaic expression in their love songs not in the context of composition-in-performance but as an effective mode, building on their own tradition of *prior* composition, to make witty play on accepted formulaic expressions and themes and startle their audiences with their unexpected new twists—a subtle example of the interaction of individual and tradition in composing.

Much of the scholarly literature on oral composition concentrates on poetic forms, and so it is interesting to consult analyses of prose. Judith Huntsman's discussion of variants of a particular narrative and their background makes fascinating reading, with her detailed description of the personal experiences (including indirect interaction with written forms) that lay behind the renderings, and her interesting contrast of the differing constraints on individual variation within the "true" (*tala*) and the "fictional" (*kakai*) accounts respectively. A fresh light is also thrown on the whole subject of the creation of traditions in John Waiko's analysis of the filtering of clan and other narratives among the Binandere, where these accounts are not formulated by expert narrators but are generated in the sifting of traditional accounts through the successive generations.

An interest in the interaction between individual creativity and the demands of traditional or collective conventions of style, theme, or occasion runs through most of the accounts here. The exact nature of this balance seems to vary not only between different cultures but also with genre, historical setting, and even individual composer and performer, and thus clearly demands specific investigation in its own right rather than generalized prediction. In this connection there seem to be some interesting variations in the attribution of authorship and ownership. In some cases (as described by Firth of the Tikopia, Pond for Tonga), names of the composers are known and remembered, perhaps over several generations. By contrast, as Thomas and Tuia bring out in their intriguing account of the interaction between collectivity and individuality, Tokelauan composers are anonymous—and yet may have high personal reputations. This is obviously a complex topic on which it is impossible to draw definitive conclusions. What does emerge is the possibility that in the past we may have placed too much emphasis on the tradition and the collective side of the interaction, and not enough on the scope for individuality and creativity. It is of course too easy just to take poets' own interpretations of what they do as the final word, but Judith Huntsman has a point when she stresses the value of asking the composers themselves—they can sometimes give us "answers unimagined"—just as the poet Ihaia's own words can give us new insights into the creative process (Thomas and Tuia):

> When I begin a *fatele* [action song], I don't think or worry about it, it will come naturally. No guessing or uncertainty, I will just pick it up. For the words: a bit here, a bit there, a bit here, a bit there, and... got one!... Once the words are in my head the tune is also already there.... More words, more ideas keep coming into my mind. It is a gift of God, there is nothing about it which is difficult for me. It is quite simple to create a *fatele*, the more you do the easier it is.

None of the examples discussed in this volume are of the lengthy poetic form that would make them comparable with the epic and heroic songs discussed in some of the classic literature on oral tradition, such as Lord's *The Singer of Tales* (1960). And it is in any case misleading to draw exact or generalizing analogies from one culture or genre to another (in *either* direction). But if direct feedback into a single theory about composition is not possible, nevertheless the Pacific evidence can highlight certain very relevant—and sometimes overlooked—points for a comparative perspective on the subject. First, there is the existence of a *number* of patterns within and around the process of composition in the Pacific. One of these patterns is indeed some version of the rather broad (and itself sometimes a touch elusive) pattern known as "oral-formulaic." But there are also others which, perhaps, may be of wider occurrence than has been appreciated in the past and which are therefore worth being alerted to. The second point worth stressing is the occurrence of *differing* combinations and permutations in actual usage (even for a given composer there may not just be one mode in which he composes) and the way both individuals and cultures can play on and with these forms. Once again we meet that well-worn interaction between individual and tradition—but an interaction in which not only are individuals sometimes more personally creative and self-conscious than has often been recognized, but also— equally importantly—in which the tradition is not a passive and inert mass but itself part of the dynamic.

Texts and Extratextual Features: Performance, Nonverbal Representation, and Visual Features

Another notable feature of many of the traditions discussed here is the way texts seldom stand alone as verbal formulations. As will be clear from most papers in this volume, they almost always form part of a wider communication context, often of music, song, dance, or visual representation.

Some texts on the surface look very short and "simple," and it is especially important to bear in mind the complexities and (sometimes) intensity of emotion carried in performance—for these are all performance texts rather than designed to be taken in and assessed through the reader's eye alone. To ignore this element of performance would be to seriously misunderstand their actual meaning and purpose in practice. This is well exemplified in, for example, the accounts by Pond and by Orbell, where the richness and originality inherent in what looks on the face of it like extremely simple wording or the passive rendering of unchanging "tradition" only come through with an understanding of the circumstances of performance. Thomas and Tuia similarly comment on a brief six-line Tokelauan song:

> It must be remembered too that this short text is appreciated in actual performance rather than through reading. [It] begins with the text sung slowly, unadorned by the dance. As the text is repeated dance movements are added (some of which highlight aspects of the text), the tempo accelerates, and other music and dance intensification creates an exhilarating experience. The repetitions of the text provide opportunities for enjoyment and contemplation of its message and craftsmanship.

The Mangaian dance drama described in the final paper illustrates particularly vividly the complex interaction of the many performance processes—in which the verbal text is only one element—that make up this complex art form; but something of this composite contribution of many modes is evident to one extent or another in practically all the oral forms described here. Discussing the interpretation or nature of these oral traditions without taking account of these other aspects would be to miss their reality: such aspects are not just optional extras but essential. Thus to focus on verbal *text* only is too narrow. (Is there perhaps a wider message here for other studies of oral tradition and, indeed, of forms which it can perhaps be misleading, as well as illuminating, to call "oral literature"—for far more than just literature [in a textual sense] is involved?)

An emphasis on the processes of performance thus runs through most of the reports here. South Pacific oral traditions are designed as performance-based rather than to-be-read texts, with performance characteristics as much as purely verbal style or content often constituting the basis of genre attribution. So this is an aspect which we obviously must take seriously. This approach also fits with recent theoretical concerns in folklore and anthropology with their emphasis on the central (not just additional) role of performance in the study of oral literature or verbal art,[7] an approach to oral forms that is likely to become of increasing importance in the study of oral tradition.

---

[7] See particularly the work of the so-called performance-oriented folklorists/anthropologists (such as Roger Abrahams, Richard Bauman, Dell Hymes, and similar writers—for summary and reference see, e.g., Bauman 1977, 1989; Finnegan 1977:ch. 4.)

Field-based studies like those recorded here provide researchers with particular opportunities to become alerted to the significance of performance (one of the fruits also of Parry and Lord's fieldwork in Yugoslavia). Performance may take place before their very eyes, and can be investigated further by questioning and observing both performers and audience at first hand—an opportunity clearly not so open to researchers on historical or archival texts and no doubt one eminently intelligible reason why such researchers have paid so much less attention to questions of performance. It does not follow, however, that performance features were therefore unimportant in the case of such texts. Perhaps they cannot be satisfactorily investigated in any direct way—if so, that is sad and we may indeed need to concentrate on other more amenable questions. But we do need to be wary of just concluding automatically from our own lack of access to the evidence that performance aspects were *therefore* of secondary significance in such texts, as is sometimes implied (e.g., in Lord's incisive paper on the nature of oral poetry, 1987:326, 345): that would be to let the argument from silence take us too far. On a more positive note, it is also possible that as questions about performance become more recognized as potentially important in the study of oral tradition it may turn out that their indirect investigation may sometimes be more feasible than used to be assumed when such aspects were considered of little interest anyhow (this possibility is well demonstrated in Margaret Orbell's re-analysis of historical Maori texts or by the way in which Pond, McMath, and Parima are able to draw from historical sources as well as field research).

At any rate, the papers here, and the experience of South Pacific oral traditions, point us in the direction of emphasizing the significance of performance. They can provide not so much direct evidence to generalize from but some suggestive indications of the *kinds* of performance features—and the possible questions—that we might be able to investigate in other traditions: for example, the often-structuring role of music (both vocal and instrumental); different modes of delivery (whether recited or sung, group or solo); repetitions; delivery techniques through, for instance, voice modulation, gesture, mime, or dramatization; dance and display; specific occasions; and audience interaction. All these are aspects where, as Foley cogently argues, information from the study of living traditions can provide us with some indirect "comparative assistance... for literatures whose original form and context are lost to us" (1988:110).

The *visual* representation of tradition is another particularly challenging facet of traditions in the South Pacific. This goes further than just the visual way in which gestures enliven performance, or costume, dance, and mime provide vehicles for communication as well as heard words—although these are all noteworthy elements of performance. But it also extends to the way in which, for example, particular string figures are associated with stories (in a sense stand for them), and tradition and memory are enshrined not in words alone but in plastic art or in statements through self-decoration (see, e.g., Küchler 1987, Sillitoe 1988). This element comes out with particular force in the Carriers' striking paper where they argue—and provide detailed evidence in support—that for the Ponam people in Papua New Guinea non-verbal and visual modes played a crucial part in the transmission and formulation of certain of their traditions and that the verbal accompaniments to these played a secondary role only (rather than, as we would perhaps conclude for any form of verbalizable tradition, forming the essential constituent). This conclusion perhaps throws a new and challenging light on what we conceive as "oral tradition," with the implication that writing is not the only alternative to spoken verbal communication for the encapsulation of unwritten traditions. As the Carriers point out, to assume that the *verbal* elements are necessarily central here would be to "unthinkingly reproduce and impose on the people we study the Western valuation of verbal communication."

At first sight this may seem a strange emphasis to outsiders. Indeed on the basis of this (and similar) evidence from the Pacific it could be suggested that one distinctive characteristic of many cultures in the South Pacific is a particularly developed sense of the visual representation of art and communication (a feature, incidentally, that makes the inclusion of the photographs in this volume especially appropriate). This aspect is apparently less developed in Western culture and as such will be of particular comparative interest for Western scholars.

A further step in this argument, however, could also be the suggestion that a visual element, combined perhaps with an emphasis on the verbal and textual, has formed a more important element in Western culture than is often explicitly recognized by scholars—or maybe even by the participants themselves (masked even from them perhaps by the powerful intellectual focus on the force of the alphabetically written word), and that it is therefore only when Western scholars look at *unfamiliar* cultural forms that this aspect stands out clearly. If so, greater awareness of how the visual and verbal mutually interact in Pacific contexts may stimulate more work on such aspects for Western tradition (both oral and perhaps written) to complement the relatively few but increasing number of historians and others who are now drawing on interdisciplinary insights to call our attention more forcibly to the role played by, for example, woodcuts and other visual propaganda even in contexts where in the past the conventional wisdom took the *written* texts and sources to be central (e.g. Scribner 1981).

Either way, this visual emphasis in Pacific culture is clearly an aspect where Western scholars have much to learn from Pacific experience. It can open their eyes to new and different ways of embellishing oral tradition or—at the least—sensitize them to an aspect of their own culture to which they may in the past have paid too little attention.

Significance of Cultural Context in Interpreting Oral Traditions

The evidence from the papers here bears out the point made by Foley and others (e.g., Foley 1988:109f.) that the study of oral traditions needs to take account of differences not just generalities—a point that would certainly be congenial to most anthropologists. In other words, for a full understanding we have to know the specifics of particular traditions and genres—the Pacific emphasis on performance or visual representation, for example, or the many differing genres within Maori, Tikopian, or Kaluli oral forms—for it turns out that we cannot just assume in advance that because some form has been labelled "oral" or even "traditional oral" that we already know all about its likely characteristics.

The same point also applies to other aspects of the forms discussed here, in particular to the whole cultural context in which they are performed and transmitted, and to the elusive question of their uses or purposes. There are many examples in these papers of the way in which the songs or narratives (or at least their meanings) cannot be grasped without some knowledge of the historical or contemporary background as experienced by those who compose, deliver, or listen to them. For example, appreciating the layers of meaning, complex metaphors, and witty word-play in the Tongan protest songs described by Pond is only possible with some understanding of the current power relations and their history in Tongan society, just as modern experience as well as traditional verbal forms give the context for the Cook Islands ghost stories, while Kaluli laments are informed by both the gender differences and the interplay between the individual and the collective within their basically egalitarian society. Such understanding can only come with the in-depth study of particular cultures, and renders by now unacceptable the older practice of the rapid collection of texts without full background information.

The wider context that gives the traditions meaning may also include not just the historical background but also the immediate delivery and setting (in the sense of the occasion in its historical and social specificity), as well as the local resonances of the content and themes of the genre, and the performance in all its rich musical and choreographic setting (see above). There are also occasions where one needs to know about the actual or intended audience (important, for example, in the cleverly concealed meanings in Tongan songs) or, as the paper by Thomas and Tuia illustrates, the known personality and reputation of an individual composer.

All these factors can thus be relevant for a full understanding of the meaning of songs or narratives. Such aspects, however, are too often neglected in the interpretation of texts. The kinds of examples provided here are thus not just of interest for their own sake (though they are that), but can also suggest insights and questions worth exploring in other cases of oral traditional forms and in a wider comparative framework.

If meanings are not always self-evident from the texts alone, the related question of the interpretation of their uses or purposes is perhaps even more knotty. It is easy to substitute speculation for evidence here—the scholarly literature is full of examples. This is not just a characteristic of text-based historical disciplines, for, despite its emphasis on firsthand field observation, it must be confessed that anthropology too has been far from exempt from this tendency. Earlier this century, for example, a generalized and simplistic functionalist interpretation was the fashionable one among many anthropologists, depending on the assumption that oral formulations, whether in the form of "myths," tales, or songs, were ultimately to be analyzed in terms of their support for the status quo: institutions which thus upheld the current social and power structure and (implicitly at least) inhibited change.   This kind of crude reductionism is now less acceptable as a general theory in anthropology, although paradoxically it is now sometimes being echoed by scholars in other disciplines drawing on the earlier anthropological work. It is increasingly being replaced by a more differentiated interest in the specific roles and dynamics of particular oral genres (perhaps varying on different occasions or as used by different personalities) which—as well exemplified in the papers here—can only be investigated by close study of particulars.

The modern tendency in much anthropology and folklore is now far more to envisage and investigate the possibility that oral traditions may be locally regarded and valued as forms of artistic or emotional expression—works of the human imagination with more, or less, space for the age-old and probably worldwide dynamic between the individual and the tradition. This possible set of roles is never exactly easy to prove definitively (is it in literate contexts either?), and dogmatic assertions on these lines may themselves face later reassessment. But it certainly seems from many of the papers here that something of this kind is often very definitely to the fore in the local perceptions and practices of many of the Pacific oral forms. As comes out in most of the discussions—especially though not exclusively of the poetic forms—these forms express, and are intended to express, not just simple "content" or passive tradition, but subtle and often reflective comment (irony, protest, surprise, lament), created and interpreted by individuals within continuing (or new) local traditions. They can carry intense connotations or metaphorical associations (through their images of place-names, of flowers, or of winds and mountains, for example), representing the imaginative and aesthetic side of human culture in a way which makes it wholly suitable to interpret one facet of these as constituting forms of expressive art whatever their other additional roles within the culture.

There is now also more awareness of another aspect that comes out very clearly in several of the papers here: the way in which oral forms can be used not only by the powerful or educated, but also by those whom otherwise we might not hear or might too easily ignore: the poor, the non-literate, the members of apparently isolated or marginal islands in the "Third World," or, within particular communities, those who, like the women discussed by Orbell, Firth, or Feld, or the underprivileged groups expressing their views in song in the remoter Tongan islands, might seem at first sight not to have a voice. But once we start to pay attention, they turn out to have their own effective ways in which they can express their interests and emotions in artistic form and so interpret and thus in a sense form their own identity and the world around them.

This recent emphasis on the artistic and personal roles of oral forms is something which perhaps could only come out of the kind of fieldwork and long experience reported here, with its opportunities for seeing how these oral forms are actually *used*. It is from this firsthand observation that we can gain an impression of the subtle, clever, sophisticated ways in which people play with and within their traditions. The picture we end up with is very different from the literal-minded and even mechanical generalized view of "oral tradition" given in some older publications. We can now aspire instead to investigate issues having to do with active human processes of artistry, reflection, creative manipulation of established conventions, and even—as with any of us—of human suffering or fallibility.

Postscript: Order and Preview of the Papers

A brief preview of the papers severally may help the reader to appreciate some of the other themes that can feed into wider discussion. The collection starts from the more "poetic" or musically based forms—in particular the songs for which the South Pacific is rightly so famous and which tend to attract particular local prestige and expertise. After a brief portrait of one of the poets, it then moves to discussions (and examples) of more "prose"-based narrative, followed by the provocative exploration of some visually and materially based forms of transmitting and exemplifying unwritten tradition. Finally, the collection is concluded by McMath and Parima's magnificent account of an art form that, even more than all the others (although there are traces of this breadth in all of them), unites the various strands, not only of the "old" and the "new," but also of both "prose" and "verse," visual display and verbal elaboration, as well as the interplay of composer, performer, and audience in a live tradition.

The brief overviews of each paper that follow are not intended to serve as definitive abstracts, but rather to indicate the genres and areas discussed, the main lines of interpretation and the kinds of questions of potential comparative interest that are being pursued. Although these comprise only an illustrative set of cases, and certainly not a comprehensive account of the findings or scholarship from this great area of the globe, it will, I hope, emerge yet more clearly from this introduction—and, best, from the detailed papers that follow—that oral tradition in the South Pacific and its study has much to offer to the comparativist.

The collection opens with Margaret Orbell's discussion (which, unlike the later papers, is based on early archival and historical sources) elucidating the form, mode of composition, and use of traditional themes in Maori women's love songs. Relating her analysis to the wider literature, she emphasizes that composition-in-performance has indeed been established as one process through which poets make use of set themes and formulaic expressions (as in Lord's study of South Slavic oral epic poetry). But familiar themes and formulae can also, she explains, be used in an alternative way: as a basis for prior-composed songs that are later performed as fixed texts. She illustrates this situation from the example of Maori women's love songs and shows among other things how the cluster of well-known themes and set expressions—a tradition—and the audience's familiarity with these could in itself lead to poetic creativity, for example in the way a poet could produce witty play on conventions in her compositions or cleverly take unexpected liberties with these traditional forms. Poets thus used set expressions with great freedom, in fact needed to do so to introduce their individual voices within these short and otherwise somewhat predictable songs. This form of composition thus produces a subtle balance between tradition and personal originality while at the same time making extensive use of formulaic expression. Various texts of love songs are quoted to illustrate and support the argument and some of their related roles for the culture and individuals discussed.

The protest songs from three isolated northern islands in the kingdom of Tonga described in Wendy Pond's paper ("Wry Comment From the Outback") exhibit one of the common roles of poetry—a mode of expression employed by people who are otherwise poor and powerless in opposition to their powerful rulers. They convey their ideas and experience through the subtle medium of their songs, where the inner meaning is veiled from outsiders, to be understood only by those for whom it is intended. The islanders also use their songs as an artistically wrought poetic medium to comment on their own lives with wit, irony, and skillful imagery. As well as illustrating the argument with examples and analyses of these local songs, the paper also provides a telling example of the impossibility of grasping the complexities of meaning from the texts alone, without having some understanding of the political and historical background and of the varied local interpretations of a multiplicity of meanings.

Raymond Firth's account of taunting songs between the sexes in Tikopia takes up something of the same theme of the power given through song to what in other respects might be a submerged group—in this case women in the mainly male-oriented public life of Tikopia. It becomes clear in this vivid account of the processes of taunting sung interchanges between young men and women that the women too demonstrate remarkable freedom and independence of thought. These choral dance songs are set in the wider framework of Tikopian song, and numerous texts are used to illustrate their wit and metaphorical expression, in particular their rich floral metaphors, and how they are performed and composed, with both old songs being repeated and new ones composed drawing on the traditional images.

Steven Feld's "Wept Thoughts" is a commentary on one of the most basic genres in South Pacific life (and perhaps also, as he suggests, basic to human poetic development more generally): the lament. The women's ritual wailing known as *sa-yalab* among the Kaluli of Papua New Guinea provides an illustration of the interplay between individual emotion and collective forms so typical of the lament. This is a complex interplay that, as Feld demonstrates, can throw new light on the particular form of composition-in-performance characteristic of this lament form (but not, it appears, of Kaluli *song* genres, which are characterized by different compositional conventions). For a full appreciation the laments also need to be seen against the background of their mode of performance and creation (soloistic but collaborative) and of local views about gender differences and about personal autonomy and experience within the wider egalitarian ethos of the Kaluli; a verbal text alone could in no way convey their richness.

The paper by Allan Thomas and Tokelauan scholar Ineleo Tuia gives us a personal portrait (in photographs as well as words) of an individual "maker of songs" in the Tokelau Islands, one who composes both the words and the music and—since these are performed songs to be danced as well as sung—is also often the choreographer as well. His various modes of composition are discussed and illustrated, supplemented by some thought-provoking comments on the complex relationship between individuality and community in Tokelauan culture as regards the ownership, composition, and performance of songs. Contrary to the impression often given in collections of music or texts, composers are unique individuals whose known background and personality form part of the context—and hence meaning—of their songs as actually performed and appreciated in the local community.

We are then introduced to prose narrative through Judith Huntsman's presentation and analysis of three different versions that she recorded of the "same" Tokelau narrative. Although the basic story was an older one, the actual renderings can be regarded as examples of creative art rather than inert "tradition." The analysis uses detailed consultation with individual narrators to illuminate the quite specific (and unexpected) ways in which they both molded the narratives they had heard and manipulated the notions of fact and fiction within the local narrative genres of *kakai* (entertaining fictional story) and *tala* (true account)—a far more personal and firsthand account of the processes of oral transmission than we can normally reach. Huntsman concludes by reminding us of the insights that can be gained from leaving aside generalized speculation in favor of consulting the experience of the narrators themselves.

The interplay of narrative and experience is also a theme in Christian Clerk's analysis of ghost stories in the Cook Islands. This lively and creative tradition, both directly located within the realities of contemporary local life and also founded in the structure and themes of older forms, provides a striking illustration of the processes of continuity and adaptation within local traditions. As well as the distinctive local themes and references (building, for example, on animal imagery and on specific associations with places, fragrances, and bodily sensations), many features of these tales will also be of interest within the wider comparative study of urban legends.

John Waiko's unique account of how oral traditions are shaped and transmitted by members of the small Binandere group in Papua New Guinea combines the perspective of the academic historian with the firsthand insights of the insider reflecting on the processes inherent in the oral traditions of his own people. He explains the native Binandere concepts of the nature and formulation of oral tradition, drawing on their imagery of the conical fishtrap through which the traditions are filtered and stored. He also illustrates the complex developing ways in which these traditions are created and codified in sophisticated oral art forms at various levels—both narratives and sung poetic genres—and how a spontaneous individual expression of emotion is taken up and shaped by the gifted poets and singers to become a work of art. He concludes by emphasizing that even in this egalitarian society, which on the face of it has no specialists to take responsibility for creating and transmitting oral traditions, there are nevertheless established mechanics and concepts through which these traditions are developed as part of an ongoing cultural process.

The paper by James and Achsah Carrier is the joker in the pack—for it concentrates on *non*-verbal forms of tradition. The Ponam people of Papua New Guinea portray and transmit important elements of their tradition through visual and material forms, in particular through their complex sytem of gift displays. At first sight the ethnography of Ponam gift interchange may seem far from the concerns of students of oral tradition, but, as the authors make clear, their approach raises a challenge for all those concerned with the study of oral tradition: can the centrality almost always given to *words* in our analyses of unwritten traditions be justified? Even where words do play a part, do they need to be regarded in a wider framework in which visual and material modes of communication may give them additional meaning—or even somehow consitute much of their primary meaning? And are there ways other than spoken transmission through which unwritten but cognitively meaningful traditions can be symbolized and transmitted, and if so, should this make us reassess the quality of the "oralness" in "oral tradition" that we tend to take for granted without questioning?

To conclude, McMath and Parima give us a text, translation, and description of a remarkable dance-drama performed during one of the regular festivals in a village in the small island of Mangaia in the southern Cook Islands in 1973, together with some description of its composition, performance, and audience responses. Far from "dying out," as some commentators earlier predicted of oral tradition in the Pacific islands, this performance—apparently one of many similar ones—represents a notable blend of traditional Mangaian art forms and legends, Christian themes, and reflections of modern society. The paper demonstrates well the ongoing creative processes in this striking—and entertaining—synthesis of new and old. It also gives us some vicarious experience of a rich and flexible art form which, in some ways reminiscent of classical Greek drama, deploys not only the arts of words (both spoken dialog and sung chorus), but also of music, dance, mime, the visual display of costume and special effects, and the heightened atmosphere created by the artful and emotive beat of the drum—thus reminding us yet again of the significance of the complex and often many-faceted processes of performance that in one way or another underlie so many forms of Pacific oral traditions.

References

Barnouw et al. 1989   Eric Barnouw et al., eds. *International Encyclopedia of Communications*. New York and Oxford: Oxford University Press.

Bauman 1977   Richard Bauman. *Verbal Art as Performance*. Rowley, MA: Newbury House.

Bauman 1986   _____ . *Story, Performance, and Event: Contextual Studies of Oral Narrative*. Cambridge: Cambridge University Press.

Bauman 1989   _____ . "Performance." In Barnouw et al. 1989:III, 262-66.

Ben-Amos 1985   Dan Ben-Amos. "The Seven Strands of *Tradition*: Varieties in its Meaning in American Folklore Studies." *Journal of Folklore Research*, 21:97-131.

Finnegan 1977   Ruth Finnegan. *Oral Poetry: Its Nature, Significance and Social Context*. Cambridge: Cambridge University Press.

Finnegan 1988   _____ . *Literacy and Orality: Studies in the Technology of Communication*. Oxford: Blackwell.

Foley 1987   John Miles Foley, ed. *Comparative Research on Oral Traditions: A Memorial for Milman Parry*. Columbus, OH: Slavica.

Foley 1988   _____ . *The Theory of Oral Composition: History and Methodology*. Bloomington: Indiana University Press.

Henige 1988   David Henige. "Oral, but Oral What? The Nomenclatures of Orality and Their Implications." *Oral Tradition*, 3:229-38.

Hobsbawm and   Eric Hobsbawm and Terence Ranger, eds. *The Invention of Tradition*. Cambridge: Cambridge University Press.
    Ranger 1987

Honko 1988   Lauri Honko, ed. *Tradition and Cultural Identity*. Turku: Nordic Institute of Folklore.

Küchler 1987   Susanne Küchler. "Malangan: Art and Memory in a Melanesian Society." *Man*, n.s. 22:238-55.

Lord 1960   Albert Bates Lord. *The Singer of Tales*. Cambridge, MA: Harvard University Press.

Lord 1987   _____. "The Nature of Oral Poetry." In Foley
                               1987:313-39.

Rappaport 1988   Joanne Rappaport. "History and Everyday Life in the
                               Columbian Andes." *Man*, n.s. 23:718-39.

Scribner 1981   R. W. Scribner. *For the Sake of Simple Folk: Popular
                               Propaganda for the German Reformation.*
                               Cambridge: Cambridge University Press.

Sillitoe 1988   Paul Sillitoe. "From Head-dresses to Head-messages:
                               The Art of Self-decoration in the Highlands of Papua
                               New Guinea." *Man*, n.s. 23:298-318.

II

"MY SUMMIT WHERE I SIT": FORM AND CONTENT IN MAORI WOMEN'S LOVE SONGS

Margaret Orbell

It is still widely assumed, despite the writings of Ruth Finnegan (esp. 1977:73-87) and others, that the composition of oral poetry necessarily involves improvisation. But most traditional Maori songs, for example, were prior-composed, and their texts were fixed, in that a song might be memorized and sung in the same form over a period of many years (though on other occasions the words would be adapted to fit new circumstances, and the process of oral transmission might also bring about some changes).

A second assumption has concerned the occurrence in oral poetry of set themes and expressions. Influenced mainly by Albert B. Lord's classic work *The Singer of Tales* (1960), scholars have regarded the presence of these traditional components as a consequence of the method of recomposition-in-performance. In the South Slavic tradition of heroic song which survived into the 1930s, and which Lord describes, a bard would learn from another singer the outline of a narrative song and then go on to perform it himself, finding his words as he went along by drawing upon his knowledge of a common stock of set expressions or formulas, verbal "building blocks." In this way he was able to maintain a constant flow of narration and fit his words to the meter. Since the themes employed—the groups of ideas—were similarly part of a common stock of poetic building blocks, he was also able, in response to the reactions of his audience, to lengthen or shorten a particular performance by adding or subtracting minor themes. In this poetic tradition, and other similar ones, no two performances were identical, and the method of composition clearly required a common stock of set themes and expressions which could be used in this way.

But there exist other traditions, such as that of the Maori, in which songs were not improvised yet were constructed largely from set themes and expressions. The oral-formulaic theory in its present form cannot therefore *fully* explain the presence in oral poetry of set components, and a further explanation must be sought. I suggest that poets in all oral traditions make a greater use of traditional themes and expressions than do poets in traditions in which writing is employed; that this phenomenon is a consequence of a greater stability in the thought-patterns of people living in oral communities, together with the effect on poetic language of a repeated melody; and that it necessarily involves the close association of ideas and language.

The extensive use of set components in oral tradition, in both poetry and prose, is of course well recognized. As well as the studies of scholars interested in the oral-formulaic theory, there are the many works devoted to the analysis of the set themes present in oral prose narratives (for example, Thompson 1955-58). The question of the close association of thought and expression in oral poetry has attracted attention at least since 1930, when part of Milman Parry's definition of the formula as it exists in the Homeric poems was that it was regularly employed "to express a given essential idea" (1971:272). And Walter J. Ong has brilliantly elucidated the role in oral societies of formulaic language as a mnemonic aid: "Fixed, often rhythmically balanced, expressions... can be found occasionally in print... but in oral cultures they are not occasional. They are incessant. They form the substance of thought itself.... The more sophisticated orally patterned thought is, the more it is likely to be marked by set expressions skillfully used" (1982:35).

To this important point one can add that in oral societies a number of other factors—among them the small size of the community, the generally slow rate of technological and social change, the face-to-face contact which oral communication involves—also made for a high degree of patterning of thought and expression (and a consequent subtlety and sophistication within the conventions employed). In orally composed *poetry*, further patterning is provided through the use of a melody as a structuring device. With this feature comes a still greater degree of fixity and sophistication of language—though the character of the language produced in this way will certainly be, as John Miles Foley (1985:68-69) has cautioned, tradition-dependent and genre-dependent: in differing traditions and genres it will take different forms.

The Maori Texts

Traditional Maori songs, as we have noted, were mostly prior-composed, there was a very considerable degree of fixity in the texts, and poets made extensive use of set themes and expressions.[1] The songs recorded in the middle years of the

---

[1] For an introduction to the musical structure, performance characteristics, and functions of Maori song types, see McLean and Orbell 1975:15-22; their language is discussed in the same work (23-30), with some reference to the use of set expressions. For another short introduction see Orbell 1985a.

Unlike the other writers in this volume, I have no firsthand experience of the oral tradition I write about. I have had mentors and informants, and some encounters with old people who still sang *waiata* (in transitional style); but this experience, while of great general interest and value

nineteenth century are of indubitably oral origin, having been dictated or written down from memory by Maoris in the years immediately following their acquisition of literacy and conversion to Christianity; encouraged by interested Europeans, they sought to preserve their songs and prose narratives in this new, powerful medium, and the Europeans insured the survival of the manuscripts they produced.[2] They wrote down so much—uncounted thousands of songs, many of them recorded on several occasions—that there is abundant material available for comparative studies: the set themes and expressions in their poetry can be traced from song to song, allowing the literary historian to recognize them as traditional components and study their use. As well, there are a great many early European works which discuss traditional Maori society, thought, and language; although the eyewitness accounts of individual performances of songs are not as detailed as those an anthropologist or folklorist might have provided (had such persons then existed), here too there is an enormous amount of incidental information. Together these two bodies of writings, Maori and European, make it possible to arrive at an understanding of the relationship between the songs and the society that produced them.

Maori poetic genres were mostly rhetorical; there was no narration, except occasionally in a highly compressed and allusive passage. A few major concerns,

---

to me, has had little direct bearing upon my studies of the earliest Maori texts, and the mid-nineteenth-century records of Maori life and thought which allow one to place these texts in their social contexts. The paradox is that to study genuinely and wholly oral poetry in Polynesia, one must go back to the very earliest nineteenth-century *written* records. Since this time the different genres in different parts of Polynesia have undergone rapid and continuing change, and no one has composed *waiata aroha* in the traditional style since, probably, about 1900. Some people still sing them, in very different contexts from the original ones and sometimes with only a partial understanding of their original significance; but the actual creation of songs belonging to this genre stopped some 90 years ago, and obviously Maori life and thought are vastly different now. In fact it takes a very considerable effort not to allow oneself to be distracted by the present, and to realize just how different the past was. My own work is thus that of a literary historian.

[2] Most of the Maori became Christian in the period between 1830 and 1845, when in most respects their culture and society were still largely intact. The missionaries, being chiefly Protestant, placed great importance upon their converts' ability to read the Bible, and the Maori rapidly acquired this magic-seeming skill. Immediately afterwards, in the years from about 1849 to 1855, a large number of manuscript compilations of songs and prose narratives were written or dictated by Maori authorities; thus the George Grey collection in the Auckland Public Library, mainly formed during this time, consists of nearly 10,000 pages, mostly of poetry. A great many more manuscripts were produced during the remaining years of the century. Because of such cooperation between the indigenous people and the invading colonists, this body of oral tradition was, therefore, recorded at a time when the society had only recently begun to change substantially, and many memories went back to the pre-Christian era. Material collected under such circumstances is less influenced by changes associated with the effects of literacy than are the early writings which have survived in countries where the people recorded their traditions unaided a considerable time after the introduction of literacy.

Some of the manuscripts preserved in New Zealand libraries are entirely unpublished, while others have been published in part but require re-editing and retranslation. There are also many texts of songs and narratives in Maori-language periodicals dating from the second half of the last century. When songs were published in early collections, they sometimes appeared in Maori only. More recent collections, with annotated texts and translations, include those by Ngata (1959), Ngata and Te Hurinui (1961, 1970), McLean and Orbell (1975) and Orbell (1978).

or ideas, were incessantly repeated in these songs, for they reflected basic preoccupations in Maori society and culture. Each of these concerns found expression in a number of set themes, as well, occasionally, as in new themes devised by the poets, and each of these set themes was partially conveyed in set expressions. I consider that in many situations the Maori thought and experienced life in terms of these concerns, themes, and associated expressions, and that to the extent that this is so, we can say that in their poetry thought and expression were inseparable.

It is difficult to demonstrate a relationship between thought and expression, since we have direct access only to the words employed. One particular subgenre, the *waiata aroha* (women's love song), is examined here. A broad approach is initially adopted: after a brief account of the society which produced these songs, the *waiata aroha* is viewed in the context of the other poetic genres, and is shown to give expression to major preoccupations in Maori life and thought. There is then a concentration upon some points of detail: selecting a group of common themes in *waiata aroha*, ones in which the poet in various ways "sets the scene" by placing herself in a landscape, I attempt to show that these passages occur so often because they reflected pervasive patterns of thought and behavior, and that because they were so common, so basic, they were frequently associated with clusters of set expressions. The main purpose is to demonstrate through the use of these examples the persistence in these songs of set themes and expressions, and to relate them to Maori experience. There is also an attempt to convey something of the sophisticated poetic art employed, the freedom with which set expressions are used and new ideas and expressions introduced—though a full consideration of this technique would require separate discussion. The paper concludes with a brief discussion of the attitudes and devices which made for constant innovation in the songs, and the balance between set components and invention that resulted.[3]

Maori Society and Poetic Genres

First, then, let us consider the society and the circumstances in which this subgenre evolved. In the late eighteenth century, when Europeans began arriving, there were perhaps some 125,000 Maori in New Zealand. They gathered wild food plants and shellfish, fished, hunted birds, and in favored localities grew some crops, mainly sweet potatoes. Their tribal system was loosely organized and very flexible, partly because it was not possible, in the hilly terrain and with the available technology and resources, for a single ruler to seize control of a large area. There was much feuding, with constantly shifting patterns of alliance between related and rather small tribes, which for many purposes acted

---

[3] Material relating to *waiata aroha* comes mainly from Orbell 1977. The brevity of these songs (from 2 lines to about 24, with 8 to 14 lines common) makes it possible to compare a large number of texts. The translations in this paper are my own.

independently of each other. Within a tribe, the chief was dependent upon the approval of the leading men, warriors whom he had to persuade rather than order to a course of action; if they were not happy, it was quite common for them to transfer their allegiance to another tribe with which they had connections. The Maori were a confrontational people, much given to impassioned oratory, and a mastery of rhetoric was an essential accomplishment for chiefs in particular. At tribal councils the only speakers were men of some consequence, but in some circumstances women were able to express their views forcefully and publicly on matters that concerned them.[4]

In oratory and in songs the Maori complained about their circumstances more than they celebrated them, frequently addressing the persons held responsible for their difficulties. Often they were ironically self-deprecatory: thus visitors being welcomed with a lavish display of hospitality might hear the food-bearers sing songs claiming that there was no food in the village, that they would all starve. Nearly all genres were highly rhetorical. On musical grounds, they may be grouped into two general categories. Those which were "recited" rather than "sung" had rapid tempos, were through-composed rather than possessing a repeated melody, and were generally accompanied by dancing or other actions. These recited songs were essentially expressions of group sentiment, though the first person singular is often used, and they were generally addressed to a number of listeners; often they were performed when one social group confronted another, and an element of challenge was involved. Sung songs, on the other hand, had slow, intricate, repeated melodies, were not accompanied by much in the way of gestures, and were primarily expressive of an individual's concerns. The most important kind of sung song was the highly elaborate *waiata*.[5]

All *waiata* took the form of rhetorical complaints. There were two main subgenres. *Waiata tangi* (weeping *waiata*) were composed equally by men and women and were usually laments for the dead, though they might lament the loss of land or crops, illness, or some other loss. They were sung by individuals and by groups of people at funerals, and afterwards when it was appropriate to remember and mourn the person who had died; frequently as well they were later sung, sometimes in adapted form, to mourn other deaths. The second of these subgenres, *waiata aroha* (*waiata* of love, or longing), were composed

---

[4] There is no full study of the traditional oratory; for contemporary oratory, see Salmond 1975. In most tribal areas women do not now take part in formal, traditional oratory. However, it is clear that formerly, when public speaking occurred in a greater variety of contexts, women did sometimes address their people on personal and even political issues. For instance John White, in a novel (1874) written to convey the great knowledge of Maori life he had acquired, describes many such occasions.

[5] In modern Maori the word *waiata* has become a general term meaning "song," but it was originally the name of a single genre and in this sense, as used here, it cannot be translated. There are several other subgenres apart from the *waiata tangi* and the *waiata aroha*.

The music, words, and transcription of the first lines of a *waiata aroha* follow below. The musical line is bipartite. The translation is by Mervyn McLean (McLean and Orbell 1975:270).

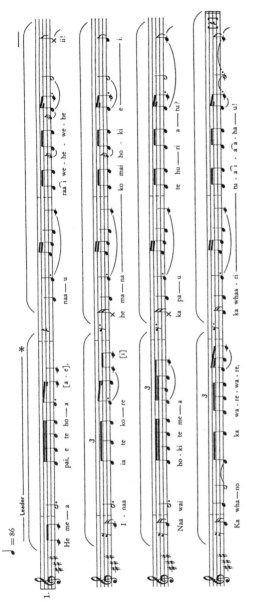

It's a fine thing, husband, that you've left me!
There's no one who wants me now.
Who was it that turned away?
I am forgotten, and put aside.

exclusively by women and usually complained about unrequited love, the refusal of the poet's family to let her marry the man of her choice, or an absent or neglectful husband; occasionally too they lamented the poet's separation from relatives. They were sung in the first place by the poet, whose name and circumstances are sometimes still known, and they might later be sung by others, sometimes in adapted form. These others might be singing the song simply for entertainment, or in memory of the woman or the man she had loved; or they might see themselves as being in a comparable situation to that of the original poet, and adapt the words of her song to fit their own circumstances.

It was not only women who adapted these love laments to make them apply to their own situation. Men did so too, in the course of oratory: for example, a chief who regretted the absence of a man he wanted as a political ally might sing a well-known *waiata aroha*, thereby identifying himself with the poet and the other man with her absent lover. These "secondary" functions of the *waiata aroha* greatly extended the range of circumstances in which the songs were an appropriate means of expression. Only by taking them fully into account can one understand Maori attitudes towards *waiata aroha*, and the hold which these songs had upon their imagination.[6]

Between them, then, the *waiata tangi* and the *waiata aroha* lament and comment upon the experiences of separation through death, and separation in life. There is quite a close correspondence between the two subgenres in the concerns expressed: in each case the poets speak mainly of their distress, and of the separation from a person (occasionally, persons) which has caused it. They are likely to refer to the accompanying circumstances, giving reasons for what has occurred. Frequently there is praise or blame: in *waiata tangi* the poet may praise the person who has died, attack and threaten enemies responsible, reproach the deceased for leaving, or blame himself or herself for not dying as well, while in *waiata aroha* the woman may complain bitterly about gossip and slander, and blame either the man or herself for the events which led to her present situation; sometimes too she asks her listeners not to blame her for her actions. These ideas reflect and give expression to major preoccupations in Maori society and thought. As already noted, it was a society in which persons of consequence were likely to complain publicly when they were in unhappy circumstances, and to name those responsible. There was also a concern with separation which was apparent in many different areas of life and thought.[7]

---

[6] Secondary functions would, however, require separate discussion. They are briefly described in Orbell 1977:II, 29-31. The use of songs in oratory is described by Shortland (1856:186-92) and Grey (quoted in McLean and Orbell 1975:30), and is exemplified in a collection of addresses presented to the governor of the country on his departure (Davis 1855). *Waiata aroha* sung by orators were not always adapted for the purpose. Often the names of persons were left unchanged, being understood as representing the persons whom the orator had in mind.

[7] F. Allan Hanson and Louise Hanson (1983) discuss some of the implications of the concern with separation. One relevant factor in the shaping of this concern must have been the looseness and flexibility of Maori social organization. For example, patterns of residence in marriage were

The composing and singing of an effective *waiata* was always a positive act; as well as serving to relieve the people's feelings, it enabled them to make an appropriate public statement and earn the appreciation and respect due to an eloquent poet. It is noteworthy that while a death could be lamented by both men and women poets, the separation of spouses or lovers was generally lamented in poetry only by women.[8] But while these women spoke of their unhappiness, they were often, in a socially acceptable way, being in fact highly assertive. In many situations the Maori wept as a way of extending an emotional greeting to a person, so a poet speaking of her tears might be making an overture to the man in question—and appropriately so, for women often took an active role in courtship. Sometimes, too, a complaint about unrequited love was really a mock lament, not seriously meant. When the poet was really in difficulties, she was arguing her case and seeking to win her point, or at the very least save face, through the persuasive power of her passionate, clever song.

Setting the Scene: Some Conventions

Waiata aroha are the stylized expression of *aroha*, love and longing. There were socially sanctioned times and places for the expression of *aroha*, and in many of these songs a poet "sets the scene" by speaking of herself, often in the first lines, as being in an appropriate situation of this kind; while the songs were certainly also sung on other occasions, they must often have been sung in the circumstances to which the poets refer. Because these situations were conventional, set expressions were used in speaking of them. For example, unhappy people often wept at sunset or at night,[9] so poets would sometimes begin by referring to the setting sun, or addressing it. In the following song the poet does this, then speaks directly of her sorrow; lastly she addresses the man from whom she is separated (Grey 1853:396):

E tō ra koia ko *te rā*,
E *āhua* iara ko *te whakangaro* ee.
Ka hara-mai *roimata, ka maringi* ee.
He koke ko koe, kia rere mai ee,
Kia tāpapa he maru tangata!

---

ambilocal, with the lower-ranking spouse generally going to live with the higher-ranking one. It seems, too, that many marriages broke up.

8 I know of only two songs by men complaining of the loss of a wife (Orbell 1977:I, 161-62). These are quite different from *waiata aroha*; they were probably recited rather than sung, and the men sound much more aggressive and resentful than the women.

9 See, for example, Orbell 1985a:59. Generally in Maori thought, light and the east were associated with life and success, and darkness and the west with death and defeat (Orbell 1985b:67-68). When the setting sun is addressed, there is sometimes the further implication that the poet wishes to leave the scene of her unhappiness and with the setting sun make her way down to the underworld, and death.

Oh the sun is sinking down there,
How it hastens its departure.
Tears come, and they spill down.
If you were a dart, to fly towards me
So a man's protection would shelter me!

The darts mentioned were light rods, some three feet in length, employed in a game. The words italicized in the first two lines of the Maori text occur often in *waiata aroha*, though usually in two sections making up the first line. Usually, too, the sun is addressed (Orbell 1977:II, 383):

E tō, e te rā, āhua te whakangaro.
Sink down, sun, hasten your departure.

In most *waiata* the melody consists of two musical phrases, the first rather shorter than the second, and the words are fitted to these musical units. Often, as here, two set expressions will occur together, combining to form an entire line; this pattern is especially common in the highly conventional first lines of songs. Or the first section may be set, and the second section take the form of a variation on a predictable idea:

E tō, e te rā, tō atu *ki te rua.*   (Grey 1853:261)
Sink down, sun, sink into the abyss.

E tō, e te rā, rehu ki te rua.   (Williams 1971:334)
Sink down, sun, go hazily into the abyss.

E tō, e te rā, ki' whaka*rehu*a iho.   (Williams 1971:334)
Sink down, sun, be made to go down hazily.

E tō, e te rā, e wawe te *rehu* atu.   (Grey 1853:103)
Sink down, sun, quickly go hazily down.

There is much variation, also, in the length and structure of the musical lines. Not all are bipartite; some are indivisible, and some tripartite. Some *waiata* have longer musical lines than others, and some have lines of varying length. All this makes for variability in the length of set expressions and their position in the line.

Many other natural phenomena were referred to as a way of setting the scene. The moon or stars, for example, may indicate the direction in which the distant beloved is living; or the woman may ask them to take her far away with them; or she may wish they were her lover. Sometimes the moon serves as a focus for emotion with no reason given. A night with a full moon was often the occasion for singing and dancing, so *waiata aroha* must frequently have been sung then. When an unknown woman fell in love with Te Tomo, who was living near the hot springs at Tauwhare, she set the scene in her song by speaking of a moonlit night and by implication contrasting the general merriment with her own unhappiness. She then blamed the hill which—she claimed—obstructed her view of the steam from Tauwhare's hot springs, and she spoke of her emotions (personified as *Roto*, Within). Lastly she addressed Te Tomo, telling him to return to his wife and warning that the wife would otherwise become angry (that is, there would be great waves in the streams at Omoho, although it is far from the sea: as we might say, his wife would "make waves"). In this case the shaping of the language indicates that there was a tripartite musical line rather than the more common bipartite one (Orbell 1977:II, 379):

> E titi koia e te atarau, tīaho i runga ra.
> Hinapōuri ka ahu mai ai au, ka ruru ki te whare,
> Te *roimata* ka hua *maringi* nei kei aku kamo.
> *Mokai* pae nāna i *ārai, tē kite atu* au
> Puia tū mai ki Tauwhare, he wawata na Roto
> *Kei raro* iti iho ko Te Tomo, *e aroha nei au!*
> E hoki koe ki tō wahine, kei ako mai ki te hae,
> Kei tū noa mai ngā tai o Ōmoho kei roto.

> Moonlight, shine down brightly from above.
> Darkness comes upon me, and I shelter in my house
> With the tears gathering and spilling from my eyelids.
> Hateful ridge that bars the way so I cannot see
> The steam rising at Tauwhare, yearned for by Within.
> Te Tomo is just below there, the one I long for—
> Go back to your wife, or she will learn to hate me
> And inland at Omoho the waves will rise right up!

In accordance with poetic convention, the address to Te Tomo follows directly upon the mention of his name. This poet may not have been so very unhappy; she may have had an affair with Te Tomo but been unwilling to accept the lower status accorded a second wife. Her song, which she may well have sung originally on a moonlit night, was a forceful and witty way of saying that the two of them must part.

A scene of this kind at the beginning of a song is generally followed by a line or two speaking of the poet's distress, then a passage giving the reason for this distress (usually, her man has left her); after this there may be a concluding passage in which the poem moves towards a final statement. The reference in the above song to tears (*roimata*) spilling down (*maringi*) may be compared to a similar line, in a similar position, in the first of the songs quoted above. The set word *mōkai*, employed in the fourth line, tends to cluster with the other words italicized in that line. In another *waiata aroha*, a woman longs for a daughter living far away (Orbell 1977:I, 521):

> Tērā Matariki pikitia i te ripa.
> Whea nei, ē, Mere, ka tauwehe i taku kiri?
> *Mōkai* Tararua, nāna i *ārai* mai ai,
> *Tēkitea atu* ai taku piringa poho.
> Nāku te tahakura i whakamoho i te ahiahi.
> Kei tai ki reira, kei mihi mai ki te iwi!

There are the Pleiades, risen over the horizon.
Where now is Mere, who is parted from my body?
Hateful Tararua that bars the way
So I cannot see the one who clung to my breast.
I met her in dreams, deceived in the evening.
Arrived there, send greetings to your people!

The heliacal rising of the Pleiades was a time conventionally associated with the expression of grief for those who had died, or were separated from the mourner. In the third and fourth lines the woman answers her own, rhetorical question; in blaming the Tararua mountains, she is also indicating the direction in which her daughter is living. There are then references to two kinds of union which (it was felt) could be established over the distance: the poet speaks of their ambiguous meetings in dreams, and she asks her daughter to send greetings from the remote region where she is living.

An appeal to send greetings is a set theme which often provides closure. In an early transitional song, the woman speaks of shaking her lover's hand in the English fashion, using English words (Orbell 1977:II, 505):

'Rā te marama ka mahuta i te pae—
Nā runga mai koe, *ko au hei raro nei*
Tiro noa atu ai ki waho ki te moana,
He purenga poti mai nāu, e Tapora,
E ahu ana ia te tai ki Ngāmotu.
Ko au te eke atu, te tēra o waho!
Mōkai Taupiri, nāna *i ārai* mai,
Tēkite atu au te wā ki a Pēhi!
Toro mai tō ringa, harirū tāua.
"Wara wara, taikiha!"

There's the moon coming up over the horizon.
You'll move on above, and I'll be below here
Gazing right out to sea,
For you're pulling on your boat, Tapsell,
Coming through the waves at Ngamotu—
I'll go on board, by the outside sail!
Hateful Taupiri that bars the way
So I cannot see the place where Pehi lives.
Stretch out your hand and we'll "how do you do."
"Very well, I thank you!"

It is common for a poet to speak of a neighboring chief and claim that he will take her far from the scene of her unhappiness; in this song, an early European trader fills this role. Then a mountain is blamed: in the seventh and eighth lines there is again the cluster of set expressions *mōkai... i ārai... tēkite atu*, along with the names of the obstructing mountain and the lover who lives beyond it. If the woman were in fact by the harbor at Ngamotu, as she represents herself as being, Mount Taupiri would have been much too far away to be visible; but since it is a highly prestigious and sacred mountain, it was an appropriate one to name as a way of indicating the direction in which her man was living. If the first line of this song is compared with the first line of the preceding one, it will be seen that in the second sections of these lines two different expressions, of the same length, are used to express a single idea.

Another conventional occasion for the expression of love and longing was described by Edward Shortland, an early European settler (1856:192-93). He speaks of

> an idea frequently to be met with in the poetry of this people—the imaginary connexion between two places established through means of the wind blowing from one to the other.... So prevalent is the influence of this poetic fancy... and so powerfully are their sympathies excited by the simple circumstance of the wind blowing from the country where an absent beloved person is staying, that a wife or lover may frequently be seen, on such occasions, seated with her face fully exposed to the breeze, while she gives vent to her affection in the peculiar wailing chant of the country.

This was no "fancy" but a universal belief. Since the wind and wind-blown clouds could be thought to come from an absent lover, a poet often refers to (or addresses) one or the other in the first lines of a *waiata aroha*; usually she then speaks of the man in question. As well, a wind blowing towards a loved one, rather than away from him, could be thought to take the poet's love with it. Again this was not merely a poetic fancy; there was also, for example, a belief that if a man's wife had run away and he wanted her back, he could consult a religious expert who, when the wind was right, would recite a spell that would be taken to her by the wind and arouse such longing that she would immediately set out to return to him (Orbell 1985b:67-68). In the song that follows, the clouds' journey serves to introduce a reference to the woman's contrasting situation. The set expression *ko au hei/ki raro nei*, "I will be/am below here," which occurs in the second line of the last song quoted above, is found as well in the second line below (Grey 1853:384):

E rere e te ao, ko koe hei karere.
Ko au ki raro nei, koro ai ki te tere.
Te mōkai puku nei, māna rawa e hoatu!
Tēkite hoki au i Awatere rāia.
Ko te wā tonu ia e kore au e kite ii.

Fly on, clouds, you will be messengers.
I am below here, wanting so much to travel.
Hateful belly, so anxious to follow after!
I cannot see Awatere over there.
Oh it is a place that I will never see.

The belly here is the seat of emotion; it is the source of the longing she is experiencing.   Poets often blamed their emotions in this way, frequently beginning with the set expression *te mōkai*, or simply *mōkai*, which we have already seen used in passages where the poet blames an obstructing mountain:

> *Mōkai* ngākau, rangi ra i a au!   (Grey 1853:233)
> Hateful heart that burns me!

> *Mōkai* whakawhenua i taupurua iho!   (Orbell 1977:II, 39)
> Hateful restraint that confines me here!

It is not surprising in such a mountainous country that hills have so often provided reference points for poets, a way of locating absent persons and introducing references to them.   Lookout places on hilltops, *taumata*, were important for emotional as well as practical reasons.   Where possible, people making their way along a ridge would stop to rest in a place where there was a good view of the lands below.   People who were abandoning their tribal territory might climb a hill to gaze upon it for the last time; persons mourning their dead sometimes sat weeping upon hilltops (Elder 1932:196); and women who were greeting a wind from their beloved would often sit on a hilltop, for this allowed a view of landmarks associated with him, a form of visual contact which was significant in itself.   We have seen that the poets often complain about mountains which "bar the way" to their beloved, and that such complaints are a means of indicating the direction in which he is living.   Another way of doing this is to represent oneself as being able to see a mountain, or other landmark, near which the man has his home.   When a poet speaks of this situation, the expression *(kia) mārama (au) te titiro*, "and clearly see," frequently occurs.   Often, though not always, it is followed by *kei raro*, "below is," then *e aroha nei au*, "the one I long for," with proper names and other expressions inserted between them.

A woman named Hariata was in love with Iwi, who lived at the village of Manga-hinahina.   Looking down from the high point of Te Karaka, Hariata could see, or nearly see, his home.   A song was composed for her by "a friendly poetess, Kowhio."[10]

> Ākuanei au ka piki ki Te Karaka rāia
> '*A mārama au te titiro* ki Manga-hinahina ra—
> *Kei raro* iho na ko taku atua *e aroha nei au*.
> Taku hinganga iho ki raro ra, ko turi te tokorua.
> Te roa noa hoki o te pō, tuarua, e Iwi.
> Oho rawa ake nei ki te ao, hopu kau, kāhore ei.

---

10 Guthrie-Smith 1953:75-76.   Although information of this kind is seldom available, it seems likely that persons needing to express themselves in song did quite often receive assistance from specialists.   For a woman who was helped to compose a *pātere*, a recited reply to insults, by the learned men of her tribe, see McLean and Orbell 1975:147.

Soon I will climb up there to Te Karaka
And clearly see Manga-hinahina.
My spirit is just below, the one I long for.
I fall down, and my two [legs] are bent.
Oh in the long night you came to me twice, Iwi,
But when I started up in the world, I felt about in vain.

Hariata begins by envisaging herself as sitting on Te Karaka hill and gazing across to Manga-hinahina. She then refers to the cause of the trouble: Manga-hinahina is the home of her "spirit," the person who affects her more than someone of ordinary flesh and blood could. She complains of the distress he is causing her (bent legs were traditionally associated with grief), then speaks of their ambiguous meetings at night: in the dream-underworld Iwi visited her a number of times ("twice" has this meaning here), but in the morning she was alone again. This last theme gives the poet an opportunity to introduce the name of her beloved, then address him. Although she ends by speaking of separation, in reality her song may have been successful in attracting a response from him.

The theme in which a woman envisages herself as gazing across from a hilltop can also occur in the body of a song, as when an unknown poet wanted to leave her husband for another man. She had first to persuade her kinsmen, especially her brothers. After asking them not to be angry with her (an appeal of this kind is a set theme), she spoke of her longing, then made her public announcement: instead of her present husband she wanted Ngawhare. (*Taku iti*, literally "my littleness," is a set expression, an ironically self-deprecatory reference to herself—"little me.") Finally, the poet speaks of her distress: she is pining away, and the implication is that her relatives have to do something about it (Orbell 1977:II, 320)

E Hura mā ē, Karaone mā nei,
Kaua ngā riri e whakatoa mai ee!
Nohea te aroha e wawae ake nei?
No Roto rawa koe ī! Ka mutu te manako
Ki te tāne ra, ē, i ako ai ki te mahi ee.
Ko Roto e hao ana kia noho taku iti
Ngā puke tū mai, ē, o Te Kura kei raro,
Mārama te titiro ki Waihou ra ee—
Kei raro Ngāwhare, e aroha nei au.
Kāti nei ko te reo ē. Ka hara-mai tēnei,
Ka whakapahoho au, ka takoto kei te whare ia.

Hura, Karaone, and you with them,
Don't bring your anger to bear upon me!
This longing making its way upwards, where is it from?
Oh you come from Right Within! I no longer want
The husband who taught me those things.
Within is eager that my littleness should sit
On the Te Kura hills over there in the north
And clearly see Waihou in the distance—
Ngawhare is below, the one I long for.

That's all I'll say. It's come to this,
I am weak, I lie in the house.

There is a Waihou river, and probably in this case it, rather than a mountain, was
the landmark associated with the absent lover.

Sometimes in such passages the idea is introduced with the set expression *taku
taumata (tonu)*, "my summit is (always)." This phrase can set the scene in the
first line, but more often occurs in the body of the song (Orbell 1977:II, 527):

> *Taku taumata tonu* ngā hiwi teitei kei Tauaki ee,
> *Mārama te titiro*, pae ka riakina kai Rāwhiti ee.
> *Kai raro* a Tawhiti, te awhi tipu a tō wahine ee!

> My summit is always the high ridges of Tauaki
> So I can clearly see the hills lifted up in the east.
> Tawhiti is below—the true love of your wife!

While a passage introduced by *taku taumata (tonu)* can develop in various ways,
the expression *(kia) mārama (au) te titiro*, "so I can clearly see," seems always to
follow at some point (Orbell 1977:II, 428):

> *Taku taumata tonu* ko Te Tuhinga rāia,
> *Kia mārama au me titiro* ki tawhiti
> Ki te tae roto kohu na rā waenga mai,
> Whakapaunga mihinga, e Kahu, ki a koe.

> My summit is always Te Tuhinga over there
> So I can clearly see into the distance,
> And the patches of mist coming straight towards me—
> Where I send all my greetings to you, Kahu.

A small variation in the phrasing of the second line of this passage, the unusual
substitution of the particle *me* for *te*, emphasizes the poet's sense of purpose in
sitting upon her hilltop.

Because this cluster of set expressions was so well known, an ingenious poet
could take liberties with it, at first defeating her listeners' expectations. Since
people who were the subject of gossip were commonly said to be lifted up on the
edge of lips, this woman complains about gossip by naming *te kupu kōrero*,
"spoken words," as her summit. But she goes on to assert herself (Orbell
1977:II, 402):

> *Taku taumata tonu* e noho ai au
> Kei te kupu kōrero, patu ai ora nei,
> Kia tau ki raro ra. Kia eke atu au,
> *Mārama te titiro* te puke ki Te Kurī
> Whakatarawai ana ia!

> My summit where I always sit
> Is on spoken words, which attack my life

So that I sink down. Let me mount up,
And clearly see Te Kuri hill
A speck on the horizon!

The poet at first represents herself as overcome by gossip, but then declares that despite these attacks she will climb to the top of a hill from which she can see, in the far distance, a famous landmark (near which, it is understood by her listeners, her lover is living). This statement is a positive act, a public assertion of her continuing love for the man from whom she is parted. Much of its forcefulness and effectiveness comes from the way in which she at first denies then finally satisfies the expectations aroused by the first words; having introduced an unexpected idea, she then, in the last sentence, completes the theme in a conventional way, employing in so doing the set expression (*kia*) *mārama (au) te titiro*, which normally follows at some point after *taku taumata (tonu)*. She has therefore expanded the usual pattern rather than broken it.

This witty play upon convention does not stand alone, however, for another woman, complaining of her longing, similarly creates a personification: her summits are those of Exhausted Thoughts—that is, all her thoughts and emotions are fully directed towards the person in whose direction she is gazing (Orbell 1977:II, 369):

Ka waia te kanohi i te tirohanga atu
Ngā taumata koe o Whakapau Mahara.
He manu koā nge au, e taea te rere atu—
E taea te hokahoka he parirau mōku?

My eyes water from gazing out
From you summits of Exhausted Thoughts.
Am I a bird, able to fly away?
Can I fasten wings to myself?

This is wordplay of a rather different kind, and the expression *taku taumata (tonu)* is not employed. But it is clear that there were complex ideas and images relating to lookout places, and that each of these poets has made use of this conventional imagery in her own way.

Conclusion

What can be said about the interplay in these songs of set components and innovation? We have seen that the set themes we have examined occur in the songs with such regularity because the patterns of thought and behavior to which they refer were equally common in reality. As well, the singing of these very popular songs must have reinforced and shaped social attitudes and individual behavior; art and life must have been interrelated in complex ways. Or perhaps we should say rather that there was no clear distinction between art and life—between poetic and social convention—since song was an essential, ever-present means of communication. As a product of Maori society, the *waiata aroha* closely reflected certain of its main concerns and also, with other poetic genres, served to maintain them.

So there was a close relationship between social, emotional, and poetic behavior; and it has been argued further that people thought in terms of the songs' set themes and expressions. At the same time, however, there was constant innovation in the content and language of the songs. Although the full extent of their complexity and range of expression is not apparent here (the emphasis has necessarily been upon closely related themes, similarities of phrasing, and songs which are short and readily intelligible), it can be seen that while set expressions were very persistent, there was much flexibility in their use. Within the conventions of the *waiata aroha* there was endless scope for invention (that is, originality) in the approach adopted, the interpretation of themes, the language and imagery. Elaborated and variant versions of conventional expressions and images were highly regarded, along with fine phrases invented by the poets. Why and how, then, did this complexity develop?

The complexity and sophistication are there because they were needed. Given the shortness of these songs, their basically predictable concerns, and the purpose of persuading the listeners and engaging their interest (also the element of competition between poets which no doubt existed), the poets had to display ingenuity, to vary and extend the existing patterns in surprising and pleasing ways, if their performances were to be effective.

Thinking as they did in terms of these inherited conventions, the poets could extend existing patterns without impediment, creating subtle and intricate songs and sometimes themselves adding to the common stock of traditional components. Since they did not have to improvise, their use of these elements was not always bound by metrical constraints. They could manipulate traditional expressions freely, combining them with new material, thinking up variations, and sometimes reinterpreting them in complex wordplay. All these approaches were themselves traditional. Often a set expression does occupy a musical phrase, although the varying length and shape of the musical line was another factor that made for flexibility.[11] Many set expressions, however, do not correspond to a musical phrase; some consist simply of a word or two introducing a sentence which is then completed in any appropriate way, and others are short phrases employed in any position. Most of these songs have clever ideas and expressions that are not recorded elsewhere, or that occur in only a few recorded texts.

The traditional elements, as we have seen, made the poetry possible, and they allowed many persons to compose it. Their presence meant also that the poets' audiences could understand and enjoy even highly complex songs, so that they learned and remembered them, sang them often, and passed them on. As well,

---

11 The variability of the length and shape of the line is discussed briefly above. This variability may have arisen in part, at least, as a consequence of the shortness of *waiata* and the fact of their composition prior to performance. The poet-composers could afford metrical as well as lexical variety, and it seems they often sought it.

they helped to make the songs persuasive; the set expressions, in echoing the language of other *waiata aroha,* gave added significance to the present song, just as a repeated proverb brought with it the certainties of the past. And because their general character was so familiar, songs could be readily adopted by other singers who saw themselves as being in situations comparable to those of the poets. It was the subtle balance between set components and invention which gave this poetic tradition its authority and continuing interest.

References

Davis 1855   C. O. B. Davis. *Maori Mementos: A Series of Addresses by the Native People to Sir George Grey.* Auckland: Williamson and Wilson.

Elder 1932   J. R. Elder. *The Letters and Journals of Samuel Marsden.* Dunedin: Otago University Council.

Finnegan 1977   R. Finnegan. *Oral Poetry: Its Nature, Significance and Social Context.* Cambridge: Cambridge University Press.

Foley 1985   J. M. Foley. *Oral-Formulaic Theory and Research: An Introduction and Annotated Bibliography.* New York: Garland.

Grey 1853   G. Grey. *Ko nga Moteatea, me nga Hakirara o nga Maori.* Wellington: Stokes.

Guthrie-Smith 1953   H. Guthrie-Smith. *Tutira: The Story of a New Zealand Sheep Station.* 3rd ed. Wellington: Reed.

Hanson and
  Hanson 1983   F. A. Hanson and L. Hanson. *Counterpoint in Maori Culture.* London: Routledge and Kegan Paul.

Lord 1960   A. B. Lord. *The Singer of Tales.* Cambridge, MA: Harvard University Press. Rpt. New York: Atheneum, 1968 et seq.

McGregor 1893   J. McGregor. *Popular Maori Songs.* Auckland: Field.

McLean and
  Orbell 1975   M. McLean and M. Orbell. *Traditional Songs of the Maori.* Wellington: Reed.

Ngata 1959   A. T. Ngata. *Nga Moteatea.* Part I. Wellington: Polynesian Society.

Ngata and
 Te Hurinui 1961   _____ and P. Te Hurinui. *Nga Moteatea.* Part II. Wellington: Polynesian Society.

Ngata and
 Te Hurinui 1970   _____. *Nga Moteatea.* Part III. Wellington: Polynesian Society.

Ong 1982   W. J. Ong. *Orality and Literacy: The Technologizing of the Word.* London and New York: Methuen.

Orbell 1977   M. Orbell. *Themes and Images in Maori Love Poetry.* 2 vols. Unpublished Ph.D. dissertation, University of Auckland.

Orbell 1978   _____. *Maori Poetry: An Introductory Anthology.* Auckland: Heinemann.

Orbell 1985a   _____. "The Maori Tradition." In *The Penguin Book of New Zealand Verse.* Ed. by I. Wedde and H. McQueen. Auckland: Penguin. pp. 53-61.

Orbell 1985b   _____. *The Natural World of the Maori.* Auckland: Bateman and London: Thames and Hudson.

Parry 1971   M. Parry. *The Making of Homeric Verse: The Collected Papers of Milman Parry.* Ed. by A. Parry. Oxford: Oxford University Press.

Salmond 1975   A. Salmond. *Hui: A Study of Maori Ceremonial Gatherings.* Wellington: Reed.

Shortland 1856   E. Shortland. *Traditions and Superstitions of the New Zealanders.* 2nd. ed. London: Longman, Brown, Green, and Longman.

Thompson 1955-58   S. Thompson. *Motif-Index of Folk Literature.* 6 vols. Bloomington: Indiana University Press.

White 1874   J. White. *Te Rou; or, the Maori at Home.* London: Sampson Low, Marston, Low, and Searle.

Williams 1971   H. W. Williams. *A Dictionary of the Maori Language.* 7th ed. Wellington: Government Printer.

III

WRY COMMENT FROM THE OUTBACK: SONGS OF PROTEST FROM THE NIUA ISLANDS, TONGA

Wendy Pond

I ask leave from the poets and orators of Tonga, whose inherited metaphors I am about to describe in the plain language of English. My work is the product of many years of joint endeavor with Tupou Posesi Fanua.[1]

The Kingdom of Tonga consists of a group of scattered islands in western Polynesia. In the far north of this group are three isolated islands, Niuafoʻou, Niuatoputapu, and Tafahi, known collectively as the Niua Islands. In the late 1960s, while conducting ethnographic research there, I began to understand how the colonized people of these islands made use of songs to speak ruefully about the hardships of their lives and to assert their independence of thought in the face of political and economic rule from the south. In formal Tongan discourse it is unseemly to speak directly of one's subject or intention, and so poets embellish their poems in order to distract the audience's attention in such a way that their meaning is discerned only by those for whom it is intended. This paper examines three songs, one from each of the Niua Islands, in which poets practice this art. In these elaborate songs there are two levels of meaning, one intended for outsiders and one for the poet's own people. Complex irony, skillful metaphors, and witty play upon convention allow the poets to present their messages with appropriate indirection. To appreciate the content and roles of these songs, one must understand something of the historical background.

---

[1] Tupou Posesi Fanua has lived through the reigns of King George Tupou II and Queen Sālote Tupou III and on into the reign of King Tāufaʻāhau Tupou IV. She is an authority on Tongan tradition and in 1959 was asked by Sālote to work for the Tonga Traditions Committee at the Palace Records Office.

The Colonization From the South

When Captain James Cook visited Tonga in the 1770s (Beaglehole 1967, 1969), it was a great maritime metropolis ruled by the god-kings, the *Kau* Tu'i Tonga, from their seat of power on the island of Tongatapu. The *Kau* Tu'i Tonga had established governors on nearby 'Eua and to the north on Ha'apai, Vava'u, Niuafo'ou, Niuatoputapu, and 'Uvea, and their political influence extended as far as the more distant islands of Lau, Futuna, and Samoa (Bott 1982:95, Gifford 1924:32-35). On the three Niua islands of Niuatoputapu, Niuafo'ou, and Tafahi, the political situation at this time and subsequently was briefly as follows. On Niuatoputapu the powerful lineage of the Mā'atu chiefs had been established as governors in the seventeenth century (Bott 1982:106) and ruled there until 1934, when the Tongan monarch allowed the title to remain vacant.[2] The Niuatoputapu poets brooded over their loss of chiefly leadership in dance-poems, *ta'anga lakalaka*, composed for visiting royalty. In 1959 Filianga complained that

Si'ete ongo'i tu'unga fale	We feel we are an empty house site.
Hungaluopea he 'one'one.	The beach line is strewn with debris.

(Filianga 1979)

On Niuafo'ou, the Fotofili lineage was established as governors in the seventeenth century (Bott 1982:96, 112-13), and Fotofili is still today the highest aristocratic title on the island. The history of the founding of this title was recalled for the Niuafo'ou people by Queen Sālote in a dance poem, *ta'anga lakalaka*, which she composed for her visit in 1927:

Tō e folofola mei mu'a:	The royal command given from the past ahead:
Fakahā ki Fonuamotu tokua	"Advise Fonuamotu," so it is said,
Ke 'ave ha taha 'o nofo fonua	"Send out a resident
'O tauhi 'a e motu ko Niua.	To govern Niua."[3]

(Tupou III 1927)

The people of Tafahi, on the other hand, do not have a tradition of aristocratic chiefs, so this is not a subject for poetry. Instead the poets warn of the hardships of their terrain and the rigors of their unsheltered coastline:

Ka ai ha sola 'oua e ha'u	No outsider should try to come,
He ko e ava ni 'oku toutau	For the waves in the pass are rough

---

[2] In 1979 Tupou IV appointed his second son, Alaivahamama'o, to the title of Mā'atu, thereby according a Tu'i Kanokupolu chief the status of this Tu'i Tonga title.

[3] In Tongan thought, the past lies ahead rather than behind. But as well as meaning "past" and "ahead," the word *mu'a/Mu'a* is the name of the seat of the Tu'i Tonga in Tongatapu, the source of the highest aristocratic authority.

| Ka hao'uli fisi'i peau, | And the boat is steered through the surf, |
| I sakē io! | *I sakē io!* |

(Tavake 1983)

Eventually in Tonga there was a move to constitutional government. After Cook's departure the power of the Tu'i Tonga had been challenged by another powerful lineage, the Ha'a Ngata (Bott 1982:113), and after some thirty years of warfare King George Tupou I assumed power. Subsequently, in 1862, he passed a code emancipating the Tongan people from the power of their chiefs, and then in 1875 he adopted a constitution. Today, while the old Tu'i Tonga governors of Niuatoputapu and Niuafo'ou remain as the highest aristocratic titles of these islands, government is carried out through government representatives, district and village officers, magistrates, police, agricultural officers, and other civil appointments.

The aristocratic and entrepreneurial families of Tongatapu have regarded the Niua people as country bumpkins and their social behavior as perverse: in public places they wore gaudily embroidered waist-mats which Tongatapu people would have reserved for weddings and celebrations. Their musical speech was believed to be old-fashioned Tongan, and Niua people walking along the road would be greeted jeeringly with lines from their stick dance, the *Vaka eke* (*Sōkē*)—but at national festivals this dance brings shouts of enthusiasm, and it has spread through schools as far afield as Auckland, New Zealand. Through their poets and dance choreographers, the people of the Niuas reclaim their reputation. With this background we can now consider the songs of protest from these three islands.

Niuatoputapu

An eroded volcanic island, Niuatoputapu is a land of ancient monuments and chiefly story. The island's nickname in oratory, Niua-teke-vaka, Niua-which-repels-boats, originates from an era in which the governing Mā'atu chiefs were strong enough to cease sending tribute to the Tu'i Tonga and assert political autonomy.

In 1969 King Tāufa'āhau Tupou IV paid a visit to open Niuatoputapu's first Agricultural Show. Preparations and dance rehearsals began three months beforehand. Royal visits entail traditional presentations of kava, pigs, yams, taro, and fine mats. Large pigs and large kava plants are hauled onto the presentation ground on a sledge pulled by villagers chanting a *tau'a'alo*—literally a rowing song, but here used as a hauling song. In the last week of rehearsals, an old chief, Loketi Lapuka, came to the hall late one night and taught the Hihifo people a *tau'a'alo* that had the appearance of a traditional hauling chant. But when we translated it after Lapuka's death, Tupou Posesi recognized that there are two levels of meaning in this complex and sardonic poem.

Tauʻaʻalo	*Hauling Chant*
Fie tau pea fokotuʻu	Want to fight? Then stand up,
ʻAlu ʻo tau ʻi Futuna tuʻu	Go and fight in Futuna. Stand up,
Kae tuku ʻa Niua ni ke toka	And leave Niua in peace.
Fai ai pē tau ʻa e moa	Fight on like roosters,
Muihelu ē ʻalu ʻo vakai vaka	Watch for a boat from the summit
	lookout
Kae pailate Maka-foa-vaka	Piloted [past] Boat-breaker Rock.
Funga Mafa ē ke ke fanafana	From the summit of Mafa—whisper,
Vaihola ē tuʻu ʻo kalanga	Vaihola, stand up and shout,
Tala ki Tonga ke tapu e vaha	Tell Tonga the seas are barred,
He ko au ē Tupa-teke-vaka	For it is I, Tupa-who-repels-boats—
He kuo u taʻuta taʻe taʻovala	But here I sit without a waist-mat!
ʻEi ē ē! ʻEi ē ē!	Heave ho! Heave ho!
	(Lapuka 1982)

Lapuka's chant was performed as the sledge of produce was hauled onto the open ground after the orator's speech of presentation to the assembly of chiefs. In this context of metaphor and deference, the chant appeared to recall and celebrate the heroic eighteenth-century history of Niuatoputapu. At that time, the island's governing Māʻatu chiefs had become so powerful that they were able to maintain independence from Tongan rule; right up until the late 1830s, these chiefs had fought against the peoples of Futuna and ʻUvea. So in his chant Lapuka speaks of fighting in Futuna and of people watching for enemy canoes from the lookouts at Mafa and Vaihola on the central ridge. He then speaks of a famous incident during this period of independence when the Niua chief Tupa prevented the Tuʻi Tonga party from landing. Lapuka identifies himself (and therefore his people) with Tupa, celebrating his island's history in a manner which is in accordance with poetic convention.

Finally, the poet speaks of himself (and his people) as being without a waist-mat because this garment is worn to honor the presence of chiefs. He is thus complaining that he finds himself in a land without leadership, living helplessly in the illusion of past power. This complaint is without ambiguity and comes as a strong conclusion to the song. It is again quite in accord with convention: Lapuka is appealing to the king to appoint a successor to the ʻatu title. But there is another level of meaning. Lapuka is also complaining about the generation of younger, educated people who are leaving the island and abandoning their responsibilities of leadership. On this level, in the first lines he is upbraiding the young men who succeed in education, become teachers, ministers, and civil servants, and abandon their homeland to seek work and status in Tongatapu. In this context, the third line can be understood as meaning "Leaving Niua the loser."[4] In the fourth line, the word *moa* can refer either to roosters or to hens. Most obviously, this passage exhorts the warriors to fight like roosters, but it can also be taken as an ironic and disparaging reference to citizens who are squabbling like hens. On this second level the poet is making a social comment: without leaders of status and competence, the family heads will not work together. He sees hope in the king's visit to the Agricultural Show, and he urges people to pass the message on by word of mouth, calling from signal stations along the ridge at Mafa and Vaihola. In the sixth line the placename Maka-foa-vaka means literally Boat-breaker Rock; however, since metaphorical use is often made of placenames, this line can be interpreted as referring to a people who, lacking leadership, have been piloted onto the rocks.

The placenames Mafa and Vaihola represent also the people of the island; this is why the poet addresses them directly. The name Vaihola, literally "Fleeing Waters," is not a real placename but a metaphor for a spring called Utufeikitu'a. At this spring, water is always drawn (*utu*) with one's back turned (*ki tu'a*), since the water would otherwise vanish (*hola*). The placenames identify the *tau'a'alo* with Niuatoputapu and serve as metaphors of the poet's social criticism.

Niuafo'ou

The second song is from the island of Niuafo'ou, an active volcano with crater lakes and no harbors. After an eruption in 1946, the inhabitants were evacuated by government decree; many of them established new villages on the island of 'Eua. But after 1959 some 600 people returned to Niuafo'ou. They were prepared to face the prospect of an eruption for the sake of living in their ancestral land and for their love of an independent way of life. This sentiment was expressed by one of the people returning, the chief stevedore, Siaosi Telefoni Ongoloka: "My four main ancestors are resting here in Niuafo'ou and they are not transferable.... This is my island and here I intend to stay" (Rogers 1986:127).

In 1967 on Niuafo'ou, groups of young men singing unaccompanied topical songs, *hiva kakala*, would perform at kava parties in the evenings, the singing arising spontaneously at intervals in the kava drinking. Garth Rogers recorded a collection of songs of this kind which had been composed by the wireless operator, Kitione Mamata of Ha'apai (Rogers 1986:105-22). These songs are a witty and wry comment on the hardships the people were experiencing in this outpost in the 1960s, left out of development aid projects and disregarded by the government and by their own aristocratic chiefs in Tongatapu. In one of these songs, "Loading and Unloading Procedures," Mamata describes how the sacks of copra were loaded from the end of a lava outflow at Futu with no protection from the surge of the sea: they were carried down to the beach and out along the rocks

---

[4] This is possible because the word *toka* has several meanings, including "fall in combat," "be at peace (of land)," and "be motionless."

by a team of men supervised by the chief stevedore, then taken out on a lighter to the copra ship.

In the 1960s copra was the island's main source of money. The copra cutters had to pay a portion of their returns to the chiefs who were their landlords, but some of these chiefs had not returned after the eruption and thus did not, as was traditional, repay tribute with leadership. The government, likewise, had not reciprocated the payment of taxes by providing aid for development. This situation is cryptically referred to ("present adjustments") in the last stanza of Mamata's song. His use of the lighthearted *hiva kakala*, a lyric song genre, serves to deflect the audience's attention from his political analysis.

Kitione Mamata outside his wireless hut in Sapa'ata Village, Niuafo'ou, in 1967.
Photo by Garth Rogers

In speaking in the first person, Mamata follows a poetic convention by which the composer speaks on behalf of the people to their chiefs. Although Mamata was an outsider as well as a civil servant who could have placed himself in an elevated social status, he spoke as a social commentator for his friends, allying himself with the copra cutters. Conventionally, in oratory as in the grand dance performances of *ta'anga lakalaka* (a genre performed by the people before their chiefs), a speaker begins his discourse by paying deference to the titleholders and asking that their minds not be disturbed by his unseemly words. The composers of *hiva kakala*, speaking to their peers (and often to lovers), do not need to observe this convention, and in this song Mamata's perfunctory use of the convention is a witticism. His song is embellished with English loan-words, a style favored among contemporary song writers: for example, *Natula*, Nature; *palanisi*, balance; and *houa*, hour.

Founga Fakahifo mo e Fakaheka	*Loading and Unloading Procedures*
Tapu mo ha'a kāvei fonua	Deference to all concerned!
Hūfanga he Aofaki 'o Natula	I take refuge in the Almighty.
Kau fai ha ki'i talanoa hua	If I've got a nerve telling
Tuku ange 'o ka fakafiematamu'a.	This jocular story, ignore it.
Ne u fehu'i ki he sitivatoa	I questioned the stevedore
Founga fakahifo pea mo e fakaheka,	Re loading and unloading procedures.
"Ka loka pea hou leva 'a e taulanga	"Friend, if the anchorage is rough,
'E fēfē 'alā si'etau mataka?"	What's to be done about the copra?"

TAU	CHORUS
"Ko e me'a pē 'e taha 'e lava	"There's only one thing to be done,
Feinga ke toloi'i taimi 'o e vaka."	Try to postpone the vessel's departure."
Takatu'u mai, fai ki he vave taha	Look smart, act on the double,
Kia ho'o niu, lele 'o tu'u 'i he 'utu fakaheka	Shoulder your sack, trot to the loading rock
Teu ki he laku ki vaka, tali mo ha peau 'e laka	Get ready to sling aboard, wait for the double-banger,
Tu'u fakave'etaha, pea palanisi mo ho'o laka.	Take a one-footed stance, stay on balance as you step.
'O ka ke ka vaivai he fie tangata	If you don't feel quite up to being a man,
Ko hono mo'oni ko e ta'e fie tuitala	Streuth, don't believe what you're told
'A e sola tuku mu'a fie taki mamata	By an upstart foreigner acting as guide.
He 'e toe houa pea te ke toe tehanga.	You'll be dead-beat within the hour.

TAU	CHORUS
Si'oto tufakanga pē ke u tō kakava	It's my innate talent to sweat,
Kae 'ahai nai ia 'a si'ono ha'aha'a?	But for whose benefit is it?
Nga'ahoa e mo'ui ni he 'Otu Anga'ofa	I lead a two-sided life in the Friendly Isles.
Ne taha'i senituli si'oto fakakoloa	For centuries I was well endowed—
Fe'amokaki he lelei, he ngo'i si'ota kuonga	Now, a shortfall on wealth under present adjustments.
Hopoate, tukufakaholo ki he lauikuonga.	We're hereditary slaves for the foreseeable future. (Mamata 1986:106-7)

"It's my innate talent to sweat."   Niuafo'ou people loading copra.
Photo by Wendy Pond

Social and poetic conventions require that poets should praise the aristocracy; criticism is normally conveyed in a context of humble deference and hidden in metaphor. Mamata's song is unusually direct, although in the last stanza his criticism is carefully worded so that it refers to the government more than to the chiefs. Nevertheless, in the political circumstances of the 1960s, songs such as this were especially courageous and outspoken. At the time, the staff of the radio station run by the Tongan government would travel through the kingdom recording people's songs for broadcasting, but Mamata's songs were not chosen to be broadcast. At the present time, in the 1980s, a change is coming: commoners publish independent newspapers, challenge aristocratic chiefs to be fair-minded, and write satirical works of fiction.[5] Mamata's songs sympathetically reflect the independent character of the Niuafo'ou people, and in this way they express the spirit of the emancipation granted in the last century by King George Tupou I.

Tafahi

The third song comes from Tafahi, seven miles distant from Niuatoputapu. Because it is a relatively high island, it seems to sit on Niuatoputapu's doorstep, but the crossing, accomplished in a small boat with an outboard engine, can be hazardous in the unpredictable gusts which sweep down the mountainsides. On clear days, Tafahi people working in their gardens can see the summit of Savai'i in western Sāmoa. Niuafo'ou is closer, but not visible because of its low profile. Tafahi is a Tongan government estate. The people live on the mountain slopes in a single village consisting of about a hundred households. They do not have an aristocratic chief in the Tongan tradition. The head man, Vaka, holds an inherited family title which gives him the right of leadership, but it is his own personal qualities of leadership and hard work that earn him respect from the people of Tafahi. The island's poetry and placenames reflect an ironic sense of humor unrestrained by aristocratic dignity.

At a kava party in Tafahi village one evening in 1970 I recorded the group Tavake Oma 'o Piu 'o Tafahi (Tropic Bird from the Summit of Tafahi) singing a plaintive and romantic song, *hiva kakala*, which had been composed by Huhane Vīvī, possibly in the 1930s. To an outsider, a stranger from Tongatapu or anyone not familiar with Tafahi placenames, the song appears to be the composition of a passionate but jilted lover. To one who knows the contours of the land, it is an ironic play on the placenames of Tafahi expressing the poet's fondness for an arduous and difficult landscape. Vīvī was a titled man from Niuatoputapu; his family was associated with Father Jouny, the first Catholic priest in the region, and it is likely that Vīvī visited Tafahi to introduce the Catholic faith there. Despite the fact that he was a chief, he identified himself with the Tafahi people in their lives of hardship. His song was sung as a farewell before his return to Niuatoputapu. In the transcription and translation below, each stanza is followed by a commentary.

---

[5] Pesi Fonua has founded an independent news magazine, *Matangi Tonga*. Akalisi Pōhiva has taken the Tongan government to court. Dr. Epeli Hau'ofa has written *Tales of the Tikongs* (1983) and *Kisses in the Nederend* (1987).

Piu 'o Tafahi	*Summit of Tafahi*
Tapu mo e Piu 'o Tafahi	Summit of Tafahi, I beg your leave
Kau fai si'a fakafeta'i	To express my thanks
Ki si'i Fine-tou-palangi	To the dear Dough-white Lass.
Niu-momoko ko e vale'anga	Frigid-coconut has utterly enchanted
hoku loto.	me.

Like Mamata, whose *hiva kakala* is discussed above, Vīvī makes witty use of customary expressions of deference to the chiefs. In this case he does so by ironically yet affectionately paying his respects to his mountain peak. Dough-white Lass is a bald area on the face of the mountain and Frigid-coconut is the crater at the summit; coconut trees grow there, but do not bear nuts because of the high altitude. Listeners from outside the island, not knowing these are placenames, would assume they are women.

Lupe tau fonua lupe he folau	Dove alighting, dove migrating.
'Aleifua tau'anga folau	Port 'Aleifua,
Mou nofo ā ka u foki au	Farewell! I must return,
Ka u foki au ki Malolo-'ae-hau.	I must return to the Victor's-demise.

Pigeon-snaring was a favorite sport of chiefs, and in Tongan poetry the pigeon is a metaphor for the woman one seeks to ensnare. On Tafahi the native pigeons fly over the canopy of the forest at midmorning, moving to their feeding grounds, then return in the middle of the afternoon; they also migrate between Tafahi and Sāmoa. 'Aleifua is a boulder marking the difficult landing-place for boats. The island is rimmed with a shelf of reef on which the waves break and through which there is no passage to the shore; at high tide, boats are launched through the surf, and at low tide they are hauled on rollers across the shelf and into the surge of the open sea. Victor's-demise is a placename in Vaipoa village on the island of Niuatoputapu. This was the composer's home village, to which he was returning. An outsider might assume that this placename refers obliquely to a man's disappointment in love. In this case, however, the literal interpretation is the correct one.

Hala-'a-fefine, Hala-'a-tangata	Women's-way, Men's-way,
Si'i Tauloto mo e Fakafafa	Beloved Shoulder-burden and Back-burden,
Ka te ka folau te u vale ho anga	If I leave I'll go mad about you.
Ko e lusa'anga hoku 'anga'anga.	You are the ruination of my being.

With these placenames Vīvī is describing the rigors of the Tafahi terrain (though again, in this genre such names evoke courtship). Women's-way and Men's-way are two paths over a volcanic extrusion which interrupts passage along the eastern shoreline. Beloved Shoulder-burden and Back-burden are two volcanic necks which rise out of the sand at this point; they are the burden the mythical Māui carried on a shoulder-stick and deposited there, and the burden he carried in his arms. Vīvī used these placenames to evoke the Tafahi lifestyle on mountain slopes too steep for horses, where all burdens have to be borne by humans: the Tafahi landscape has been the ruination of his body.

"Aleifua, Port of Departure"
Tafahi people hauling a boat across the reef in 1971.
Photo by Thomas Riddle

TAU	CHORUS
Te u hanu launoa kia foʻi falahola	I'll make my complaints to the pandanus tree.
Te u lata ʻi ho hala kakala	I'm at home in your sweet-scented paths.
Siʻi Hāʻanga-laʻe ko e valeʻanga	Beloved Spot-where-foreheads-appear,
ʻA e folau ʻa e kau tangata	Men newly arrived lose their senses here.

Kapakau-tatangi mo e Vai-hanga-ki-langi	Bush-bird's-wing and the Pool-which-gazes-at-Heaven
Ko e hu'i'anga 'o e vai kahi	Dilutant for purgative medicine—
Ha'u ā 'o inu ai ka ke 'ilo hono sai	Do come and drink so you experience the benefit,
Kuo pau pē te ke mo'ui ai.	You are sure to be cured by it.

(Vīvī 1983)

The poet speaks of the species of pandanus tree which occurs in a standard image employed in praise of a person; I do not know who is referred to here. In the line which follows, the sweet-scented paths are those of Tafahi; once again, this phrase could be taken to refer to lovers' meetings. From the landing-place at 'Aleifua, the path follows the coast and then climbs steeply up to the village on the north face. So steep is this ascent that the first sight villagers have of travelers arriving is their foreheads appearing over the edge of the cliff; the top of the path is therefore given this name. Again, listeners unfamiliar with the terrain might understand this line as referring to a lovers' trysting place.

At the foot of the mountain the path passes a very small waterhole called Pool-which-gazes-at-Heaven, where rainwater collects and stagnates. In times of drought, before the island had concrete water tanks, fresh water was collected from such pools, but Vīvī is being ironic, for an insider would know that this pool is too small for practical use. The significance of the reference to purgative medicine is uncertain. It could be taken to indicate rejection by a woman, but almost certainly he is speaking in some way of the difficult terrain.

It is customary for a composer to mention the placenames which are special sources of inspiration and beauty. In aristocratic dance poetry, *ta'anga lakalaka*, placenames are metaphors of chiefly status and genealogical connection. Here, instead, the poet describes the everyday hazards of the Tafahi landscape: the coconuts which do not bear nuts at Frigid-coconut (Niu-momoko), the barren mountainside at Dough-white Lass (Fine-tou-palangi), and the steep ascent to the village (Hā'anga-la'e). He speaks also of the arduousness of the lifestyle and the necessity for men and women to carry heavy loads up and down the mountainside and to launch their boats across the coral shelf. To the outsider, his song expresses unrequited love. To Tafahi people, it is a rueful and apt comment on their landscape, not a claim to greatness and reputation as is made in aristocratic poems but a leg-pull at the expense of outsiders. This witty and entertaining song is composed in a tongue-in-cheek spirit. In Tongan it would be described as *faka'oli, fakalaunoa*, or *fakalaupisi*. In the last lines, the composer expresses his conviction that the Tafahi lifestyle will bring wellbeing to all who try it. To both audiences the song conveys a people's love of life in their own land:

Te u lata 'i ho hala kakala.
I'm at home in your sweet-scented paths.

Concluding Remarks

In Tonga, any song can convey multiple levels of meaning. All of the three songs discussed here are complaints on behalf of the common people. In all of them there is a public message intended for outsiders and a private message intended for the poet's own people. The first song, by Lapuka of Niuatoputapu, belongs to the old genre known as *tau'a'alo* (literally a paddling song, but here a hauling chant). It was composed for performance before the king and his chiefs on a high ceremonial occasion; the public message is for the king and his party, the hidden message for the people of Niuatoputapu. It is quite acceptable for a poet to convey an oblique, metaphorical, and deferentially phrased complaint to his superiors, and Lapuka is being orthodox in so doing. His hidden message reproving his own people was also socially acceptable. Like all three of these poets, he brings his song to a strong conclusion.

Both of the other songs are *hiva kakala*, light-hearted topical songs sung for entertainment and usually concerned with love, but here conveying different messages. Mamata's *hiva kakala* describes in unusually direct language the trials of the men loading copra on Niuafo'ou, then ends by complaining (rather more discreetly, however) about government neglect and chiefs who were absentee landlords. While this particular *hiva kakala* makes no mention of love, its genre remains important. The song is sung at speed, with gaiety and evident enjoyment, and its jocularity serves to soften the impact of the poet's words, rendering his protest somewhat less dangerous. Vīvī's *hiva kakala*, on the other hand, appears to be a love song but is in fact, for knowledgeable listeners, an affectionate evocation of the landscape of Tafahi and the difficulties of living there. In that it is ostensibly a love song, it is a witty leg-pull.

These people are poor and have no political power. Songs give them a voice, a way of commenting upon their lives and their masters with robust humor and finely judged subtlety. Messages, often of protest, are conveyed to outsiders, yet much of the meaning is reserved for the people to whom the poets are closest. Thus, textual analysis alone does not reveal the full import of these songs; that can only be revealed by the social contexts of the poem's composition and empathy with the poet's perspective.

References

Beaglehole 1967

J. C. Beaglehole, ed. *The Journals of Captain James Cook on his Voyages of Discovery*, vol. 3. *The Voyage of the Resolution and Discovery, 1776-1780*. 2 parts. Cambridge: Hakluyt Society.

Beaglehole 1969

_____. *The Journals of Captain James Cook on his Voyages of Discovery*, vol. 2. *The Voyage of the Resolution and Adventure, 1772-1775*. Cambridge: Hakluyt Society.

Bott 1982

Elizabeth Bott and Tavi [Maupiti]. *Tongan Society at the Time of Captain Cook's Visits: Discussions with Her Majesty Queen Sālote Tupou*. Wellington: The Polynesian Society.

Filianga 1979

Sioeli Filianga. "Matafi 'a e Tonga 'i Fale." *Faikava*, 4:1-3, 10-15.

Gifford 1924

E. W. Gifford. *Tongan Myths and Tales*. Honolulu: B. P. Bishop Museum, Bulletin 8.

Gifford 1929

_____. *Tongan Society*. Honolulu: B. P. Bishop Museum, Bulletin 61.

Hau'ofa 1983

Epeli Hau'ofa. *Tales of the Tikongs*. Auckland: Longman Paul.

Hau'ofa 1987

_____. *Kisses in the Nederend*. Auckland: Penguin.

Lapuka 1982

Loketi Lapuka. "Tau'a'alo." *Faikava*, 8:1-2, 31-33.

Mamata 1986

Kitione Mamata. "Founga Fakahifo mo e Fakaheka." In Rogers 1986:106-7, 114-15.

Rogers 1986

Garth Rogers, ed. *The Fire Has Jumped: Eyewitness Accounts of the Eruption and Evacuation of Niuafo'ou, Tonga*. Suva: Institute of Pacific Studies at the University of the South Pacific.

Tavake 1983

Tevita Tavake. "Eke 'a Tafahi." *Faikava*, 9:12-16, 31-37.

Tupou III 1927

Sālote Pilolevu Tupou III. "Malau 'o Vailahi." Unpublished ms.

Vīvī 1983

Huhane Vīvī. "Piu 'o Tafahi." *Faikava*, 10:44-46.

Appendix: Main Sources of Tongan Poetry

Ko e Makasini (a Kolisi), a magazine edited by Rev. Moulton of Tupou College from 1874 to 1899. Some issues are held at the Alexander Turnbull Library in Wellington, the Mitchell Library in Sydney, and the National Library of Australia in Canberra.

Faikava, A Tongan Literary Journal, nos. 1-10, 1978-83. Edited by Futa Helu and Epeli Hau'ofa. Available from *Faikava*, c/o University of the South Pacific, Institute of Rural Development, P.O. Private Bag, Nuku'alofa, Tonga.

Collocott, E. E. V. *Tales and Poems of Tonga*. Honolulu: B. P. Bishop Museum, Bulletin 46, 1928.

Gifford, E. V. *Tongan Myths and Tales*. Honolulu: B. P. Bishop Museum, Bulletin 8, 1924.

The Palace Records Office in Nuku'alofa, Tonga, has song texts among unfiled papers. Song texts, with translations, occur throughout the works of Adrienne Kaeppler. The Tongan hymns composed by the Rev. Moulton are greatly loved and are found in the Methodist hymn book, *Ko e Tohi Himi 'ae Siasi Uesiliana*. A review of dance categories and historical sources is provided in Richard Moyle, *Tongan Music* (Auckland: Auckland University Press, 1987). The only university teaching critical appreciation of Tongan poetry is 'Atenisi Institute (Prof. 'I Futa Helu) in Nuku'alofa, Tonga.

IV

SEX AND SLANDER IN TIKOPIA SONG: PUBLIC ANTAGONISM AND PRIVATE INTRIGUE

Raymond Firth

Tikopia, a small Polynesian island community in the Solomon Islands, has had a great tradition of orally communicated song. This song tradition has had several marked features. It was very largely a choral tradition. Individual singing occurred in the chants of some traditional tales, in a few ritual chants, in laments of emotional release as in farewells or abandonment of mourning, and in practice sessions when a new song was being learned. But such occasions were relatively uncommon; the great mass of Tikopia singing was done in chorus. Correspondingly, there was no virtuoso singing, by a soloist performing for an audience. Nor was any great importance attached to the quality of a voice; memory for songs and vocal power were the criteria of a *purotu*, an expert.

Traditionally, no songs were performed simply as musical occasions. Every song, and the poem which was its base, was part of a more general action field. Dance songs, funeral dirges, songs of praise, ritual songs—each was performed as an accompaniment to some social action, usually with bodily movement, such as dancing, wailing and other physical expression of grief for the dead, and presentation of food or other positive acts. Some modern Tikopia have adopted a convention of purely recreational singing, as in schools or at evening parties, often with ukulele accompaniment. But the traditional forms still persist side by side with these modern developments. Traditional Tikopia song also has had no instrumental accompaniment except percussion; there were no stringed or wind instruments. The most usual accompaniment to dance was handclap or more generally the beat of a sounding board, struck with two sticks or a coral stone. Rarely, laments of a ritual kind were accompanied by a swishing rattle of dried palm-leaf ribs or a stamping tube of bamboo with palm fiber tied over its mouth.

Another marked feature of this oral tradition was that it was a *moving* tradition. An idea sometimes current is that tradition is "immemorial," unchanging, handed down with no modification from one generation to another. But this Tikopia song tradition was dynamic in two ways. It had depth in that many of the songs chanted were known by the name of the composer, often a man or woman who had lived several generations before. But as these songs came to be repeated in the course of time, the text often altered, as memory lapsed and changes of wording entered the singing. Secondly, the songs that came to be preserved were only a fraction of those composed. Every generation, indeed every new dance festival, added fresh songs, often discarded immediately after recital. Only the "catchy" songs, or those of special historical or sentimental interest, remained in the repertoire. So it may be said that while the *form* of this oral tradition remained intact, the *content* was continually changing—a point which can have wider theoretical implications for concepts of social stability and social change.

Traditional Tikopia song has had two major divisions: *mako*—dance songs—and *fuatanga*—laments. (A category of *pese*, or unspecified songs, formerly applied to a few ritual and narrative chants, but now covers a range of modern "pop" productions, indigenous and imported, as well as Christian hymns.) Dance songs and laments are usually short, following a conventional division into two or three stanzas (*kupu*), each of which is composed of several "lines" marked off by caesura. The first stanza is termed *tafito*, or base of the song; the second stanza is *kupu i roto*—middle stanza, if there be a third, or simply *kupu* if there be only two; a third stanza is *safe*.[1]

The themes of both dance songs and laments vary widely. Those of dance songs, with which I am dealing here, range from events of everyday life through celebration of technical operations such as fishing or turmeric extraction to boasting of achievement in a dart match, welcome to a visitor from another island, praise of a friend, or complaint against theft.[2] Dance songs in Tikopia are highly differentiated. Each song is classed according to the type of dance for which it is composed. There are some twenty dance types in all, using different rhythms, choreography, and ancillaries such as wands or clubs. By far the largest category of dance songs, however, belong to the dance type known as *matāvaka* (see photograph 1) if accompanied by sounding board or *ngore* if accompanied by handclap.

---

[1] So in each of the examples cited later, the first verse is normally called *tafito* (base), the second is *kupu* (stanza), the third (when it occurs) is *safe* or sometimes just *kupu* also. The songs in the present paper have all been taken from my notebooks of 1928-29, and can therefore be regarded as "traditional." Sixty years or so later, most of those taunting songs will have been forgotten, but as far as I know, the custom of composing them for dances still persists. Elsewhere in my records I have relatively modern examples. Detailed analysis of Tikopia songs, including the structure of Tikopia music, is given in Firth and McLean 1990. This work also discusses the nature of Tikopia poetic language, including the common transformation of vowel *a* into *o*, with which there is no space to deal in the present paper.

[2] For an example of such songs, see Firth 1930, 1936 (1957), 1939 (1965), 1940 (1967a), 1967b, and 1981.

Young men singing a taunting song in a *matāvaka* dance.
They toss their heads to and fro as they advance with sliding steps.
Photo by Raymond Firth

Within this general dance type, of fairly simple rhythmic form, traditionally the
Tikopia have recognized a special class of dance songs, marked not so much by
their theme as by their style. These are songs of protest, taunting, or insult.
They are termed *mako tauangutu*, which may be interpreted literally as "dance
songs in a war of the lips"—sometimes quite an apt description, as will be seen.
It is interesting that the Tikopia have made a convention of what elsewhere is
usually only an occasional or sporadic practice—the satire or lampoon in song.
Tikopia protest songs are a recognized means of public expression of private
outrage. If offended, a man or woman may compose a song, teach it to a group
of friends, and then introduce it onto a dance ground some evening as a rousing
chorus. Such songs may be composed if a person has had coconuts or areca nuts
stolen from an orchard, if a promise has been broken or a personal slight offered.
The offender is hardly ever named, but the Tikopia theory is that he or she will
feel ashamed at the criticism so publicly if indirectly hurled. Actually, such
effect is dubious. What the taunting song does do is to relieve the feelings of the
composer and, in the more extreme cases, to lessen the possibility of violence and
so help to maintain public order.

An important sector of these taunting songs deals with relations between the
sexes. The Tikopia have recognized the passions that sway men and women,
particularly young men and young women, and have built this recognition into an
overt set of rules. Marriage is the dividing line. Before marriage, men and
women have been virtually free in their personal relations, subject to incest
prohibitions and to the norms of their peer group. After marriage, they should
ideally remain faithful, and nearly all women and most men appear to have done
so. Stringent rules of polite speech and behavior, especially in sexual matters,

also applied to married people, as to relations with any people to whom one was closely connected by marriage. In contrast to the sobriety of married people in public discourse, the conversation of the young unmarried has been full of sexual talk and innuendo; this has come to expression markedly in their dance songs. Many dance songs of *matāvaka* type have had innocuous themes. But many have been of a sexual, even scabrous nature, as response to fancied insult or a product of erotic imagination.

Sex in Song

The Tikopia have not been romantic about sexual relations (Firth 1936:511-18). A custom of individual sweethearting has obtained, the passion of desire is admitted, but love in the sense of intense affection for someone of the opposite sex is hinted at rather than expressed. A few songs have uttered the longing of one person for another, but even this may be a matter for jeering rather than sympathy from others in the peer group. Early in this century a young man was sent abroad for an offense, and his sweetheart mourned for him bitterly. The companions of the young man composed a song which derided the young woman for her tears:

> *Tangi pakū ko nau taka*
> *Tangi semu ki o nga tamāroa*
>
> *Sorosoroi nga roimata*
> *Tangi kai kere ki nga tamāroa.*
>
> Wailing with sobs is the maiden
> Weeping entreatingly for the young men
>
> The tears keep on trickling down
> Crying in a frenzy (eating earth) for the young men.

The song repeats a conventional jibe of young men against girls—that they are tearing their hearts out for men. As in many of these songs, the successive images are not very consistent, nor do they refer to different phases in the event—the girl wails, but also weeps quietly; and she is slandered by being accused of wailing for bachelors in the plural. Whatever may be the facts of a case, a common charge in these songs is to accuse a person of seeking the other sex indiscriminately.

Note also that no names are mentioned. Nearly all such songs are leveled anonymously. This is partly to avoid the scandal of a personal public reference, which would involve family ties, possible links with kin of rank, and embarrassment when in due course the named parties might marry. In confidence I was given a couple of songs which freely cited personal names of men and girls. But my informant was very reluctant to tell me the texts. He said the girls mentioned were now married, so was it good to make the songs known? I reassured him as to my discretion, and his scruples were overcome by his companions. But I was told that these two songs, by young men of different districts in opposition, had been learned for dancing, but that the elders had forbidden their performance because the women would have been ashamed. Dance songs involving proper names did seem to have been extremely rare (cf. Firth 1936:308). Again, many such dance songs conveying sexual insults were no more than generic charges—part of the banter between the sexes with no personal reference. Even where a composer might have a particular individual in mind, as an adamant object of desire or a rejected lover, the allusion was indirect; his or her friends would know at whom the song was aimed, but when the song was chanted in public most people would be ignorant of the particulars. So slander was legitimized and could flourish.

By slander here is meant public pronouncement of unfounded or unproven allegation of defect. A large number of these taunting songs relied upon the impossibility of public proof of accusation. Moreover, by an extensive use of figurative language, there was often enough disguise of the slander to claim innocence if challenged. For example, one use of slanderous songs was to allow young men to score off one another in their competition for girls. Virginity in girls was greatly prized as a public ideal, and young men of ambition prided themselves in having been the first to obtain a girl's favors. To marry a virgin was something to boast about (cf. Firth 1936:518-23, 559). A taunting song then might accuse a man of having taken to wife a woman who was no longer a virgin, but had been the mistress of another man.

Here is one composed by my old friend Kavakiua, later Pa Vangatau, a prolific song-maker, sneering at another man whose bride had already lost her maidenhead:

> *Te rarongo monongi*
> *Ko ai e ko nai fotio*
> *Kua poi vakivaki pouri mai e!*
>
> *Ngongoro ko te tupurongo*
> *Te tāra o te unga mero*
> *Ku riokino.*

> The lower leaves of the aromatic shrub
> Who is he then who plucked them
> And has gone rejoicing in darkness oh!
>
> Snorting (with laughter) are the generations
> The garment-changing of the red hermit crab
> Has been rejected.

The imagery here is complex. In the first stanza the aromatic shrub is a metaphor for a woman. For decoration, the leaf tips of the shrub are plucked, the soiled lower leaves being rejected. The implication is that the woman's present lover has taken other men's leavings, though he plumes himself that he is her first man. The second stanza refers to the scorn in which such a recipient of cast-off

favors is allegedly held by young and old (the "generations"). The last two lines
have an involved sexual reference. The hermit crab is a common metaphor for a
flaccid penis, and redness suggests tumescence. The composer explained to me
the background to this song. He had slept with the girl for a time, then
abandoned her, alleging that he had objected to her large, pendulous breasts.
Then along came another man—whom the composer named to me—and carried
the girl off as his wife. The composer said that she was the only girl this other
man could get, but there may well have been an element of jealousy in this
charge. He also said that this man tended to avoid him, knowing that he had had
first access to his wife. I had no idea how accurate this story might have been,
but thought it plausible.   What the song revealed was the composer's
unsentimental use of a personal episode of emotional quality as a basis for an
aesthetic exercise.
    Another old song has some similarity of theme and imagery:

> Pe ko ai ke fokomumua
> I o raro nga manongi
> Ne poi kamokamotio
> I roto te oro
>
> Tenea fetaukario i te taka
> E nga tamāroa
> Te tumutumu o te manongi
> Te kovopui toto
> Pe ko ai noi ifotio?
>
> Who may it be who preceded him
> Among the lower leaves of the aromatic shrub!
> As he went he was slyly winked at
> In the middle of the path
>
> She who was pursued among all the maidens
> By the young bachelors
> The tip of the aromatic shrub
> The blood-red ginger flower
> Who may it be who plucked them?

The song jeers at a man married to a woman for whom he was not the first lover.
The first stanza asks rhetorically who this first lover may have been, and then
describes the husband as being an object of some contempt for having taken such
a sullied wife. The second stanza states that while yet unmarried the girl was
eagerly sought after in competition by the young men, and inquires again who
may have been the man who in the end was able to take her virginity. The song
uses a great deal of floral imagery. The leaves of the aromatic shrub and the
ginger flower are the symbols of virginity. The ginger flower symbolism is
somewhat complex. A spray of this plant (*Hedychium flavum*) is commonly
worn as a back ornament for dancing by men. Traditionally, it was also worn
occasionally by a husband as a token of rejoicing at having found his wife a

virgin on their marriage night. So the reference to the plucking of the ginger flower is again an indirect allusion to the taking of the girl's maidenhead.

These two songs have dealt with marital situations, but most sexually slanderous songs relate to the unmarried. The sexes accuse each other in general of unbridled desire, of unchastity, of boasting baselessly about sexual prowess, and of eagerness to marry despite all claims about the delights of celibacy. The songs are vigorously frank, full of sexual imagery, in a style of high exaggeration calculated to tease and irritate the other sex. Yet a marked characteristic of these taunting songs is that they avoid explicit mention of the physical aspects of sex—genitalia or coition. Although long familiarity has made the highly allusive language of the songs pretty plain in meaning to all listeners, the songs remain within the bounds of *taranga laui*, proper speech. (A sub-category of songs using gross sexual terms, *taranga pariki*, improper speech, is mentioned later.) So the songs can be chanted in public where elders or people constrained by the obligation of marriage need have no embarrassment.

Varieties of Sexual Imagery

A variety of floral imagery conveys sexual reference, especially to women. Here is a traditional song, the authorship of which was unknown even in 1929, but which was probably composed by a woman:

> *Te foi tiore*
> *Fu i te toko*
> *Ko ai ka poi ono ki oi*
> *Au fatu roi ki ei*
>
> *Te nofo mamao*
> *Sē rafi ki oi e!*
> *Totoro ki te manongi*
> *O te toko.*
>
> The gardenia flower
> Hidden in the maiden
> Who will go and look at it
> Then come and make up a tale about it?
>
> He who is living afar
> Why not draw near to her oh!
> Come crawling to the sweetheart
> Of the unmarried.

This is a song against men. The theme is that while young women preserve their virginity, young men come crawling after them without success and lie about their supposed conquests. In the first stanza the girl's maidenhead, still unbroken, is likened to a beautiful aromatic flower, hidden in her body, and a man's claim to have cast eyes upon it is derided. The second stanza is ostensibly an invitation to the man to approach the girl, but it is made with a suggestion of scorn, that he is too timid to carry out his desire. The term *totoro* bears multiple imagery. It is a continuative extension of the verb *toro*, to creep or crawl. In general, when applied to human beings it indicates some degree of inferiority, in some contexts an attitude of apology. But it has also been a mode of approach of would-be lovers to sleeping girls whom they wished to seduce, and as such was a matter treated with some disdain by the girls. So the implication of the song is that men are rather contemptible creatures given to unrealized passion.

Songs composed by men take a different line. They use imagery of opened buds and soiled leaves to display their charge that the young women are no longer virgins. They also use metaphors from ordinary technology to denigrate the status of young women. One such song from the male side is quite blunt, while remaining within the canons of "proper speech":

> *Rongo ko Tikopia*
> *Rongo fafine taka e mingimingi*
>
> *Na ka peke ake i raro*
> *Na ka peke ake te kuoni fokoAnuta.*
>
> Let Tikopia hear
> News that the unmarried girl is very tiny
>
> Now she'll shrink up below
> Now she'll shrink up, the Anuta bag-net.

The slur here refers to a girl's sexual parts. The word glossed as "tiny" refers to something very thin or narrow, the implication here being that the woman has a very small orifice, shrunken from much intercourse. The second stanza repeats the slander, using the metaphor of a hand-operated bag-net for deep-sea fishing. The Anutan form of the net may be smaller than the local Tikopia form, but the insult lies also in the general analogy of a woman's organ to a bag-like receptacle. The song was probably not directed against any particular girl; it expresses a common male denigration of a woman's sexual equipment.

Another common metaphor in male songs is that of a woman as canoe. This allows of many elaborations of sexual imagery, about the condition of the vessel, boarding it, stretching out on the deck, steering it, and so on. A frequent accusation in song is that the vessel is in poor condition, that is, that the girl has lost her virginity. A song of this type is:

> *Oño atu ki te vaka*
> *Ku samusu*
> *Tou fakanapara*
> *Kua kā pe se ofi*

Tu moi, tu moi kove
Ke tau oro masike
Mosike moi kove
Ke tau oro i tou
Fia fai rongorongo.

Look at the canoe
Got into a bad state
Your slot (in the holding chock)
Has become burning like fire

Stand up to me, stand up to me, you
That we two go and rise
Rise up to me you
That we two may go in your
Desire to make a reputation.

The first stanza of the song puts forward two common propositions advanced by young men against young women—that they have lost their maidenheads, and that they are hot for sexual intercourse. To do this, two separate metaphors are employed. The first is simply a broad assertion that the girl's canoe is imperfect, in need of repair. The adjective here is unusual. Tikopia composers have been fond of using foreign words to embellish their songs, and I was told that *samusu* was a Fijian word meaning "bad." Then the metaphor changes. A canoe at rest on shore is kept stable by its keel sitting in slots cut in timbers holding it off the ground. This slot is an obvious synonym for a woman's vulva, and a further metaphorical twist, familiar also to Western poetry, uses the image of "burning" with sexual desire. The second stanza is a challenge: let the woman stand up and face an inquiry into her reputation. She wishes to appear as of unblemished virtue, but the truth will be otherwise if she be put to the proof!

Akin to the symbol of the unopened bud of the gardenia or frangipani, is the smooth, white, small gasteropod shell of a species of *Polinices*. Traditionally, this was often worn in the nose septum by young people, especially as a token of virginity by girls. A constant charge in the songs of young men has been that this is a lying token. An old song refers to this in the context of the *pea*, a privilege ceremonial (now abandoned) for girls of rank who were presumably still maidens (Firth 1967b:62-68):

Fokotu tiu ki te pea
Ke tou savaina
Ke tou makoa
Kumikumi rei a tatou ke tua
Ko tatou ku lesia.

Te matarafi mai te vaka
O nau toko
Ke fau manga ko te oa
Masāra kesekese ki tua.

Set up the nose shell for the *pea*
That we may gesture at it
That we may dance at it
And squeeze straight our backs
For we have been deceived.

The wedge from the canoe
Of the unmarried woman
To secure with cross-lashing the topstrake
Release it and put it aside to the rear.

Vigorous dance by men using hand and arm gestures.
Photo by Raymond Firth

The basic meaning of this song is that if the girl puts up her nose shell as a token of virginity for the *pea* ceremony, then the young men will deride her. This song, as is so often the case, has two main metaphorical images. The first stanza is the image of the dance which was a prominent feature of the *pea*. The stereotype of such a dance is of young men moving along rhythmically, swinging their arms vigorously and occasionally making series of formal display gestures with fists and open hands, bending and straightening their backs in male pride as the dance proceeds.

Here, it is implied, these male gestures are made in scorn against the false claims of the principal girl. The men straighten their backs as an affirmation of the truth of their allegation that she is no longer chaste. The second stanza is a variant on the canoe metaphor. Wooden wedges are important in holding firm the cord lashings of a sea-going canoe (no nails or rivets being used), so if a wedge is removed the upper timbers of the canoe become loose. The girl's maidenhead is likened to such a wedge; it is alleged that it has been taken away and her virtue thereby rendered unsafe. In the original, this is a powerful song, and I was told that when it was first sung by the young men the girls felt it to be such a telling diatribe that they could find no effective answer to it!

But the girls have had their own taunting songs against the young men, with plenty of bite. One poetic image propagated by the young women has been that of young men swaggering around in their masculine pride, eager to get girls and boasting of their sexual conquests, but often quite falsely, while the girls laugh at them. Here is one such song of ridicule:

> *Tangata ka karo mai*
> *Fakamafatifati ko ona rima*
> *Ana fainga ki se manongi mōna*
>
> *Sā ra atu ou*
> *Tupotu i tou pou*
> *E nofo tiotio i te au toko i Rangi*
>
> *Tongoto kua tara morotofi*
> *Ne fenoke rava ki tou suru uri*
> *Rava ki tou koliko.*

> The man will stride here hastily
> Jerking his arms to and fro
> In his actions to get himself a sweetheart
>
> When I appear
> With your back against your post
> You sit peering out at the set of maidens from Heaven
>
> The man has donned his orange girdle
> You have come clad in your dark kilt
> Clad in your calico.

This is quite a descriptive picture of a young man "dressed to kill," but, alas, not impressing the girls. The first stanza shows him bustling along in search of a mistress, in a somewhat ludicrous way. In the second stanza he is represented as sitting in his house, with his back against a post in Tikopia male style, peering out under the thatch eaves at passers-by. He is attracted by the bevy of girls, but is afraid to appear when they do come close. There is a suggestion in the song that they have materialized "from Heaven" in a mysterious way for him. Finally, even though he puts on his best clothes, the implication is that the girls reject him.

Another girls' song laughs at the false boasts of men:

> *Tangata fia fai rongorongo*
> *Ne muna tou surusuru*
> *Ne fafati i te vao manongi*

> *Sē ne rafirafi ke fenoke*
> *Ku morio ifo*
> *I te fio foi rongorongo.*

> A man seeking a reputation
> Said that his back ornament
> Was broken off in the aromatic shrubbery

> But he never got near to approaching us
> He's been carried away
> In his wish for renown.

The accusation here is plain. A man pretends that his symbol of sexual conquest, his leafy back ornament, was plucked from the aromatic shrubs; in other words, the implication is that he had culled the virginity of a young woman. But he merely wanted to make a name for himself—he never came near the girls, and was lying, and his reputation goes for nothing.

Some songs are vividly descriptive of the physical effects of passion. One composed by young women evokes a picture of a young man moved by frustrated desire—and rather an absurd sight:

> *Ou manava āke*
> *Ke moe ma fofine*

> *Ou kaponga te tongoto*
> *Na ku manavanava*
> *Fifiti ake ku rarapa*
> *Kua ukauka tou ua.*

> There's a feeling rising in your belly
> That you want to sleep with women

> Your male throat pulse
> Has begun to throb there
> (Your veins) have swollen up and stood out
> Till your neck has become a mass of cords.

The alleged uncontrollable sexual lust of young men is thus held up to ridicule. (Any notion of response by young women is carefully kept out of consideration by the female composers!)

Many of these taunting songs have been quite ephemeral, and completely forgotten. But some have endured as stock dance songs, ready to be sung as standard responses in the continual challenge of the sexes. One such, by an Ariki Kafika, father of the chief Sivoia whom I knew, was composed in the late nineteenth century; it was still in vogue as a dance song in 1929, when it was chanted during the religious rites of Uta:

Tou fiofio maino
Tou fiofio taurekareka
Te kovi o Raro
Teka i Nukuātea

Ne poi muno i te raki e!
Ne kau rotoa
Ne kau pukea
Moku taina ke iroa

Totosi e totosi
Ki te oro
Ke tofokino
I oku fare i Murifenua.

Your desire to be like the moon
Your desire to be beautiful
You ugly one of Tikopia
Fallen in the rubbish place

You went and tattled in Faea oh!
That I desired you
That I embraced you
And my brother whom you know

You've been dragged, dragged down
Into the path
To be trampled upon
In my house in Murifenua.

I heard this song chanted at the Uta dance. The grandson of the composer, who
gave me the text, said that only the first two stanzas had been sung because the
crowd did not know the third stanza. He told me the name of the woman against
whom the song had been directed. It was said that she had claimed falsely that
the composer had planned with his brother to carry her off as his wife—in
accordance with Tikopia custom, but possibly here a ploy on her part to try to
force his hand. Angry at what he declared to be a lie, the composer replied to her
story in this song, accusing her of vanity and loose morals. The song is full of
idiomatic allusions. *Raro* is an Anutan name for Tikopia; it means "Below" and
refers to the position of Tikopia southwest of Anuta. Its use here is an instance
of Tikopia composers' liking for foreign words. *Nukuātea* is literally a "place
outside," where things are thrown away. But specifically, as used here, it refers
to a place of excretion in Faea, and implies that the woman is no more than a bit
of excrement. The second stanza details the composer's complaint against the
woman. In the third stanza he gives vent to his anger by imagining her being
degraded in public, particularly in his own territory—Murifenua being an orchard
and house of his in Faea.

Formal Exchange of Insults in Song

For much dancing the young folk of both sexes join together, roaring out in chorus some popular chant, irrespective of its theme. But on some occasions the young men and young women separate, and sing and dance alternately in groups against each other. Here is a striking phenomenon, the formal exchange of musical insults. One side or the other will begin to sing a taunting song. This is listened to very carefully by the other side, in silence. They then reply, either with an apposite old song, or with a new song freshly composed on the spot. As one of my informants said, "If you make a song, and I listen to it, my song will be ready as soon as yours is finished; it will not be delayed." That this facility of composition was true I could confirm from attendance at various dances. The improvised songs usually follow fairly well-worn musical and linguistic paths. By long training, a great store of conventional metaphors was available to would-be composers, and their quick sense of analogy made them very alert at composition on the spur of the moment. Usually, one or two leaders supplied the main inspiration, and some of the reply songs showed a quick wit. The formality of this traditional system of song and counter-song is shown by the use of the term *tongoi* for it, indicating an exchange comparable to a formal exchange of food. Sometimes the exchange of taunting songs has been simply restricted to a pair of songs, but often it has gone on in a series, each sex finding a reply to the taunt of the other.

Here is a sample of four songs chanted as part of a larger exchange. The young men begin:

> *Fofine tena kua nofo*
> *Sopo ra ki tou voko*
> *Motokā poi taritari*
> *Tāngata, tere i te roto fenua*
>
> *Taukirokiro tāngata ki ai ra*
> *Taukirokiro tamāroa ki ai ra*
> *Tou vaka te lelu*
> *Na kua poi fakorikoriko*
> *I a tofo o tomōroa.*

> Woman who has been sitting there
> Jump up then onto your vehicle
> The motorcar which goes carrying
> Men, rushing along through the countryside
>
> Men gaze at it from afar there
> Young men gaze at it from afar
> Your vehicle with its running load
> Which has gone revolving
> At the side of the young men.

This song jeers at young women by likening them to a motorcar which carries men; the sexual metaphor is obvious. But, it is alleged, the young men look warily at the vehicle from afar and refuse to enter, though it rolls invitingly near. In other words, they are chary of a relationship with promiscuous young women. The imagery is reinforced by the term *lelu*, which at first sight is obscure. The word means "running," but in a special sense, of kicking with the legs, as in a game in which someone is dragged along while he kicks out in a running movement. The imagery, not very precise, is intended to suggest the ridiculous sight of a woman, in her lust for young men, running alongside them, although rejected by them; the notion of her legs vigorously agitated has a sexual reminiscence.

The reply of the girls, composed on the spot, did not take up the theme directly, but reversed the idea of a sexual approach, so that it is the young man and not the girl who is rejected:

> *Ka fakapiripiritia moi*
> *Riele te tama*
> *Au ku fokomotukutuku*
>
> *Tou vaka ku poi pouri*
> *Ku ngoro ku vini i te taka*
> *Ngongoro ki oi.*
>
> He'll keep on drawing nearer to me
> Hurrah! the lad rejoices
> But when he comes he takes fright
>
> Your canoe has gone in the dark
> It has been snorted at and whistled at among the girls
> Who keep on snorting at it.

The first stanza accuses the young men of sexual cowardice. When a lad approaches a girl he is overtaken by shyness and retires. The second stanza pursues this theme, with the metaphor of the young man as a canoe. He and his companions go in the darkness in the shadow of the trees, skulking there and mocked by the girls after having been discouraged in their fumbling approaches.

The answer of the young men immediately to this song was a renewed attack on the reputation of the young women:

> *Ie! Te vaka rakarakafio*
> *Ie! Te vaka rakarakafio*
> *Au i te ara sē maleku*
> *Ngaope mai*
>
> *Tou tiu futikaki*
> *Ke tu ki rungo*
> *Ku ngoroa e tamāroa*
> *Fakato tuku ki raro.*

> Ho! the canoe that's been hurried around
> Ho! the canoe that's been hurried around
> Comes in the path, not invisible
> Dangling toward us
>
> Your noseshell that persistently
> You set up above
> Has been laughed at by the young men
> Let it drop and lay it down.

This song picks up the "canoe" term from the previous song, the notion of the vessel having been "hurried around" implying that it has been much used, that is, that the woman has had many relations with men. The image then changes, to a more immediate one of a woman with dangling breasts advancing in the path, again suggesting that sexually she is well experienced. The image then changes again, to the common symbol of chastity worn, whether merited or not, by many young women. The assertion here in effect is that its use as an ornament is unwarranted, that it provokes the scorn of young men and should be abandoned.

To this song the young women replied with spirit, exulting in their virginity (*sic*) and stigmatizing the young men as a lot of rubbish:

> *Ma te atua te tama*
> *Ki a nga ātua peia*
> *Te Vai Rokupenu*
>
> *Kau vakivaki toku ra teki*
> *Kau sava rima rua toku foi tiu.*
>
> But the lad is a goblin
> To the spirits thrown
> In the Pool of Tossed-out Rubbish
>
> I rejoice in my flower-bud twig stuck (in my hair)
> I gesture with both arms (in the dance) in favor of my noseshell.

The composer of this song was the daughter of the local mission teacher, an assertive young woman, unmarried, and already with a reputation of some freedom with men. But she and her companions stoutly maintained their purity. The first stanza accuses the young men of being nothing more than spirits—in other words, not true men—fit only to be consigned to the traditional rubbish pool of the afterworld. The second stanza returns to the theme of the symbols of chastity, alleging that flower-bud and noseshell are rightfully worn, and that the girls will demonstrate this in the formal open-armed gestures of pride in dancing (incidentally, such gestures have been traditionally a male prerogative, so whether the girls actually did make them or not, they were challenging the men in a verbal display of female aggression.)

In such interchange of songs between the sexes the slander is sometimes quite gross, or very pointed. A song composed by some young men against the young women is very blunt:

Oie! Te oi e pā
Te fafine ku tunua ki te afi

E au o mako mate mai
Ko tafito i ū malulu.

Oh! Oh! a moan explodes
As a girl is roasted by the fire

Now she comes here and dances furiously
But most obvious are her soft breasts.

This is a direct accusation that the girl has had an abortion—one method said to
have been the application of hot stones to the belly, a very painful process. The
second stanza describes the sequel. The girl comes and dances vigorously ("to the
death") as if nothing has happened, but her soft dangling breasts—traditionally
men and girls were bare to the waist—betray that she is no longer a maiden.

The girls' reply to this was ingenious. They took up the theme of soft breasts
and developed it in a witty retort:

Fererei oke o t utu
A rākei o te taka
Tu mai fakamanīnia
I ke fatu ki a ū e!

Kokove te nea
Ne ora i take vosia!

They grow and stand up
As ornaments of maidenhood
Standing as objects of envy
And yet you slander breasts indeed!

You were the one
Who lived (as a babe therefrom) at a former time!

To this neat reply, mingling boasting and reproach, I do not think the young men
found any answer.

For the most part, these taunting songs avoided any mention of the specific
coarse terms for either genitalia or the sex act that are often heard in ordinary life.
In addition to the images already set out, a man's song may refer to the
Hernandia berry of a woman, pink, often holed by children to whistle through.
A woman's song may complain that she has been deceived by a tiny bird's beak,
that of the swiftlet (*Collocalia* sp.), instead of receiving the stout male member
she expected. These and many other such picturesque metaphors were appropriate
to any public dance occasion. But a special category of taunting songs was
provided by *feuku*, in which inhibitions were cast aside and the crudest sexual
words were used.

Generally, these bawdy sexual songs, composed by men and women alike,
served the dances of young people when the night was far advanced and the elders

had retired. Then restraint could be abandoned, and the young men and girls
reveled in the exchange of highly titillating and blunt sexual words. Yet these
songs also had traditional validation of another order; they could be sung at an
advanced stage of the religious dancing of Uta. Although even there the *feuku*
should be sung only in the presence of unmarried people, both sexes took part in
the chanting and dancing, and they were given the sanction of an established
ritual context. Indeed, some Tikopia elders justified them to me on the grounds
that they served to educate young people in sexual matters—which I thought a
very dubious argument! The poetic value of such songs is usually not very high,
so I give only two examples here.

The first is a song composed by a man of rank in Ravenga, in boasting strain:

> *Tu ko te ure toa i Ravenga*
> *Tokatokai ki te ngaru*
> *Sē ne fetiri*
>
> *Au mai ko te rongo*
> *Ka mai te roki*
> *Ku sorosoroio*
> *Ko te lala ku konio*
> *Ko te lala rei ku konio.*
>
> The ironwood penis stands up in Ravenga
> Thrusts and peers into the waves
> But does not disappear
>
> When the news is brought
> They will come from the west
> They've been scraping along
> The cunts that have been fucked
> The cunts indeed that have been fucked.

The claim here is that the composer's massive organ has been so attractive to
women that they have streamed in from the other district (of Faea in the west) for
copulation. The term for penis, *ure*, is still rather more formal than the ordinary
coarse term *laso*, but the terms for female genitalia and sexual intercourse, *lala*
and *koni*, are the ordinary vulgar words. So the song was classed by my Tikopia
informants as a *feuku*.

A *feuku* composed by young women against young men was of stronger
challenging texture:

> *Sakiri ki vere reu*
> *Te vere tau uo te tangata*
> *Toku foi mimi*

Toku mimi fu ke sakiria
E takatakai te kokona
O te vere reu.

Seek for the ripe *Barringtonia* fruit
The *Barringtonia* hung round the necks of men
My personal vulva

My hidden vulva that you seek
The pungency is pervasive
Of the ripe *Barringtonia* fruit.

This was rather a shocking song, even to Tikopia men. The young man who gave me the text of the song broke out ruefully into cursing when he had done so. "Set of she-devils eat filth!" he said. The reason was that the ripe *Barringtonia* fruit, of a purple color, has a very strong, not particularly pleasant smell. It is used as a decoration by either sex in dancing, held at the breast or around the waist in a garland. But to associate it with a woman's vulva, and suggest that it be hung round a man's neck, was an image that did not please the men. The song is an index of the women's toughness, that they could make such an identification publicly, and of the tartness of some of their song-challenges to the men.

But on occasion even Tikopia women could be silenced. An elaborate song (with an involved text unnecessary to give here) composed by a young man depicted a girl in the spirit world. There she was scrutinized by the guardians, not so much of morality as of status, and rejected for her loss of virginity. In accord with traditional lore, the song portrayed her as being thrown into a rubbish pool of the afterworld. "Ashamed are your folk; your virgin bud droops down" ran the song, meaning that her flower symbol of maidenhead had wilted. It was said that to this song the girls found no reply in the song exchanges. But, I was told, colleagues in the spirit world came to their rescue. A dead sister of the composer, seemingly moved by the embarrassment of her living former companions, composed a song in reply. Then, it was said, she communicated it to her brother among the spirits, and he in turn issued it through the mouth of his human spirit medium. This man, in trance, then sang the song on behalf of the girls. It scarified the young men. A young bachelor was depicted as standing among the rubbish in the afterworld, his own symbol of sexual prowess with virgins having been falsified, and so he was laughed at by all the spirits. This song thus evened things up in the musical sphere.

In actual fact, of course, the real composer of the song was the human medium himself, evidently stirred by the charge leveled against the young women. In his ordinary life he was a prolific song composer, but he often went into trance, in which his subliminal self also was capable of song composition and delivery. The Tikopia seemed to see nothing inconsistent in what was putatively a girl's song being the product, in effect, of a male composer, since their theory of spirit behavior gave a cogent explanation of this phenomenon.

A notable feature of these exchanges of musical insults has been their formalism. This is demonstrated by what may seem to outsiders to be an odd custom. When a dance festival using taunting songs has been planned on some scale, with folk from more than one district involved, a curious interchange may take place. The young men of the visiting side join the young women of the hosts in singing their songs, while the young women of the visitors likewise assist the local young men in their chants. This arrangement helps to give the occasion an institutional stamp of an impersonal aesthetic order, and to lessen the friction that might otherwise occur if two bodies of men and women were opposed to each other in simple sexual confrontation.

I conclude by emphasizing two general features of these song exchanges of young people. The first is the complex implications of this open eroticism. Some Tikopia argued that it was instructional—but this left me unconvinced. What did seem clearer was that it helped to channel sexual impulses into a relatively acceptable form, allowing public expression of frustrations and resentments with less danger to private relations. It is true that sometimes lovers and their mistresses fell out in private over some particularly outrageous musical slander against men or women. But the public insult in song could always be claimed as merely a general joke, without personal reference. There appears to have always been a lot of sexual talk among the unmarried. But the institutionalization of erotic language in song in standardized, traditional form before marriage may, from a speculative viewpoint, have contributed to the subsequent relative tranquility that many marriages seem to have enjoyed.

The second notable feature of these song exchanges is the freedom which they allow to young women. In general, Tikopia society has been male-oriented, with few official roles given to women, and in ordinary public life unmarried women have played an almost insignificant part. But the equality of the sexes in the unmarried state has been remarkable, especially in the sphere of dance-song composition (cf. Firth 1981). The tone of many of the songs composed by unmarried young women is an indication of the independence of thought and firmness of action shown by many Tikopia women in the conduct of ordinary affairs in later life.

References

Firth 1930   Raymond Firth. "A Dart Match in Tikopia." *Oceania*, 1:64-96.

Firth 1936 (1957)   _____. *We, the Tikopia: A Sociological Study of Kinship in Primitive Polynesia*. London: Allen and Unwin.

Firth 1939 (1965)   _____. *Primitive Polynesian Economy*.   London: Routledge and Kegan Paul.

Firth 1940 (1967a)   _____. *The Work of the Gods in Tikopia*.   London: Lund Humphries (Athlone Press).

Firth 1967b   _____. *Tikopia Ritual and Belief.* London: Allen and Unwin.

Firth 1981   _____.   "Sex Roles and Sex Symbols in Tikopia Society." *Kroeber Anthropological Society Papers*, 57 and 58 (for 1978):1-19.

Firth and McLean 1990   _____, with Mervyn McLean. *Tikopia Songs: Poetic and Musical Art of a Polynesian People of the Solomon Islands*. Cambridge: Cambridge University Press.

V

WEPT THOUGHTS: THE VOICING OF KALULI MEMORIES

Steven Feld

The study of lament forms, including ritual wailing, sung-texted weeping, keen, mourning songs, dirge, and elegy, is complexly located in discourses of the humanities and social sciences. Because lament varieties are reported throughout the world, questions as to the universality or cultural specificity of their structures and meanings are important and implicitly comparative. Folklorists, philologists, ethnomusicologists, literary scholars, and anthropologists have drawn our attention to a great variety of lament forms. Some researchers have taken a more micro-analytic view of the poetics of lament texts, others a more macro-analytic view of the role that laments play in mourning customs (see Ajuwon 1981 and Honko 1980 for an overview). Some have concentrated on the differences between laments and other verbal and musical genres. But the key factor that situates all of these studies of laments firmly in the area of research on oral traditions is the dynamic interplay of individual expression and collective forms and sentiments. Vladimir Propp put this quite forcefully in his essay on "Folklore and Reality" (1984:16-38). There he draws attention to the fact that while formulae and motifs (like the poetic rhetorical question to the deceased) are common in laments, the genre is more clearly defined by improvisation, by lack of close variants, and by a certain lack of close similarity despite common motifs. "Each lament contains unique motifs," Propp writes, "for example a kind of biography" (32). This biographical dimension, and its linkages to what Propp termed a "subjective evaluation of reality" (33), speaks to the complex interplay of generic norms and individual creativity in lament, and additionally emphasizes how the analysis of lament texts must necessarily be situated in their socio-historical contexts.

Before pursuing these issues in a specific case study, it is worth stepping back to review the broad programmatic location of an explicitly interdisciplinary study of lament forms. One easy place to start is with the *boundaries of speech and song*. As a classic region of text/tune interplay, we can ask what linguistic and musical creativities interact in the form and performance of these expressions?

How are they related to or differentiated from other speech and song styles? What sonic features of the crying voice and what sonic and semantic features of verbal articulation intersect in these forms? The concern with understanding the boundaries of speech and song is closely linked to a second global issue for lament research, namely, *composition-in-performance*. As a classic region of emergent structures in oral performance, we can ask what interplay of improvisation with formulaic, memorized, and precomposed verbal and musical elements characterizes these forms? Is there anything specific to or highlighted in these genres that distinguish their manner of composition-in-performance?

In addition to these two fundamental structural issues, the linkage between lament and sadness points to the significance of *emotion*: how are these stylized expressions linked to the ethology of anger, grief, and despair? How do unique ethnopsychologies shape the role these expressions play in the social construction of emotionality, and in the collective responsibility for its display and interpretation? Fourth, and closely linked in many studies to the question of emotions, is the issue of *gender and genre*. How gender-specific are these various lament genres? If these expressions are largely women's work, what cross-culturally gender-specific statements do they make about suffering, bearing witness to distress, and the association of women and emotionality? Finally, and to link laments to their most forceful social context, there is the issue of *rituals and metaphors of transition and renewal*. As these expressions are always embedded in larger social events marking separation or aggregation, how are they central to the evocation and symbolization of transition? How do they figure into the social construction of memory, nostalgia, and sentimentality?

In this paper I discuss the sung-texted weeping tradition of the Kaluli (Bosavi) people, a small-scale society in a relatively isolated rain-forest region of Papua New Guinea. My discussion will both describe some particular ethnographic, linguistic, musical, and textual characteristics of a form of women's ritual wailing that Kaluli call *sa-yalab*, a term that can be glossed as "sung-texted weeping" (or more literally, "inside weeping" or "inner-texted weeping"), and relate that description to some recent discussion of the five issues cited above.

The Kaluli People

The Kaluli (Bosavi) people number about twelve hundred and live in the tropical rain forest of the Great Papuan Plateau in the Southern Highlands Province of Papua New Guinea (detailed ethnographic descriptions are E. Schieffelin 1976, Feld 1982, B. Schieffelin 1990). On several hundred square miles of rich land at an altitude of about two thousand feet they hunt, fish, and tend land-intensive swidden gardens that yield sweet potatoes, taro, pandanus, pumpkin, bananas, and many other fruits and vegetables. Their staple food, sago, is processed from wild palms that grow in shallow swamps and creeks branching off from larger river arteries that flow downward from Mt. Bosavi, the collapsed cone of a volcano reaching eight thousand feet. Kaluli live in about twenty distinct longhouse communities; in each, most people still reside in a single communal house comprising fifteen families, or about sixty to eighty people. In recent years, under influence from Papuan evangelical pastors and government officers, there has been a trend toward smaller houses occupied by single families, or at most two or three families.

This is a classless society that has only begun to feel the impact of occupational specialization, stratification, and socially rewarded differentiation since the intensification of outside contact in the last twenty-five years. Overtly, the tone of everyday Kaluli life is strongly egalitarian in social and political spheres. People hunt, gather, garden, and work to produce what they need, taking care of themselves and their families and friends through extensive cooperation in food-sharing and labor assistance, all organized informally through networks of obligation and reciprocity. While gender differences are quite overtly marked, there was traditionally little structural stratification produced by accumulation of goods, rewards, or prestige. Although that is changing rapidly, there is still, evidenced by our recent ethnographic experiences, a general lack of deference to persons, roles, categories, or groups based on power, position, or material ownership. Obvious recent exceptions include pastors, Aid Post Orderlies, and government and mission workers; gender differentials are clearly becoming more pronounced as well.

My use of the term "egalitarian" is not meant to be static and typological. Existing and emerging differentiation, subtle or overt, is a significant historical facet of Kaluli life. While a full discussion of this issue is not offered here, I am concerned to use the word egalitarian cautiously, lest it be assumed that the kind of poetics I will describe is somehow assumed to be a pristine reflection of a perfectly "primitive," communal, oral society. At the same time, it is important to relate Kaluli egalitarianism to gender differences and a local view of personal autonomy and creativity; these issues turn out to be crucial for understanding the poetic and performative context of *sa-yalab*.

Kaluli *sa-yalab*

Sa-yalab is one of five named patterns of Kaluli crying, situated on several continua in relationship to the other four (see Feld 1990:88-99). The five terms are all prefixed specifications of the same onomatopoeic verb for "cry" or "weep"; all five are considered expressive varieties of weeping, and all co-occur in situations of loss or abandonment or separation. Of these five, three tend to be short, loud, uncontrolled, and associated with men. Two others are more typically reflective, sustained, controlled, and associated with women. *Sa-yalab* is one of these two latter variants, and is considered the most refined, performed, reflective, and aesthetic form of weeping. The keys to this form are elaborated though improvised texts and a highly patterned and stable melodic contour using four descending tones: the first two a major second apart, the next a minor third below, and the last a major second below (as in the descending tones D-C-A-G).

This sonic pattern is said by Kaluli to derive from the call of a fruitdove (birds whose calls contain the intervals of the descending major second and minor third), and this relationship is the subject of a myth that underscores the cultural character of Kaluli associations among sadness, birds, and human expressive sound.

Kaluli weeping types are experienced in two context sets, one including ceremonies and seances and another including funerals and occasions marking personal loss. Ceremonies and seances are preplanned events that involve the staging of composed poetic songs called *gisalo*. These songs move listeners to tears and the resultant weeping is patterned, but involves little if any text. The tendency in the cried response is toward loud falsetto wails, using the three or four tones of the prescribed melodic contour mentioned previously. These kinds of weeping are largely performed by men, although women are also heard to do them. Funerals and occasions of loss, on the other hand, provide the stage for the two musically and textually elaborated female weeping variants. While men are heard to wail at these events, they tend to do so in the three less elaborated forms that also mark their responses to ceremonial songs. Women also wail this way at funerals, but the principal mourners are distinguished by the manner in which they sit together around the body of the deceased, and perform *sa-yalab*, singing while shedding tears.

Polyphony, Heterophony, *Dulugu Ganalan*

While *sa-yalab* can be characterized as basically monophonic, personal, and soloistic, in point of fact it is far more often the case that two, three, or four women wail simultaneously, sometimes beginning like a chain reaction, with one woman moved by the initial wails of another, and additional voices adding on, then some dropping out. I was so impressed by a solo *sa-yalab* performance that I made that the centerpiece of my chapter on women's wailing in *Sound and Sentiment* (Feld 1990:107-29). Yet while that performance was extremely powerful and often commented upon by Kaluli people, my singling it out for a case analysis perhaps obscured the more typical quality of simultaneous multi-part *sa-yalab* performances. How then to describe the relationship of the voices? This question cannot be answered merely by a technical musicological discussion, since the voice relationships index the deeper issue of social relationships, which is to say the interplay of the individual and collective, personal and traditional dimensions of experience.

The term "polyphony" generally refers to music in many parts, particularly when all or several of the parts proceed independently. It is the dialectical independence and interdependence of the parts that is a key feature of polyphony from the perspective of European music history, such that the parts simultaneously have a distinct identity and structural-functional implications for one another and the resultant totality. The term "heterophony," on the other hand, contrastively refers to the superimposition of a modified musical structure on its original, or put more simply, simultaneous variations of a single melody. From the standpoint of western European Art Music, heterophony is a "simpler" phenomenon, and polyphony (particularly with full harmonic elaboration) represents the height of musical evolution and sophistication.

Outside of the European traditions (and some would argue even within many European traditions), it is often hard to apply the terms polyphony and heterophony distinctly with no ambiguity. This is particularly so in the South Pacific, where forms of polyphony and heterophony are common, but often described with European models as a baseline. In the case of Kaluli weeping we might prefer the term heterophony since the multi-part relationship results from simultaneous performance of slightly variant or elaborated versions of the same basic melodic contour and rhythmic divisions. But there is the problem of different texts and differentiated line lengths. Another reason to avoid the term is that it misses a crucial processual dynamic in many multi-part *sa-yalab* (and in all Kaluli multi-voiced singing), namely, that whatever the initial order of voices they are completely free to switch roles at any point and to continually change order, submerging any sense of "leader" and "follower" roles. If on the other hand we choose the cover term polyphony to stress the structural and functional interdependence of the voices, we have the difficulty of reconciling it with the fact that their musical materials (tones, melodic contours, metrics) are not particularly independent. This terminological problem is widespread in Melanesian music, leading some to adopt the term "echo-polyphony" in order to describe styles involving overlapped repetition of similar melodic and textual elements, just split seconds apart.

Kaluli have a term and clear metalinguistic/metamusical concept that covers the stylistic and performative dimensions of this kind of vocalizing (whether in song, talk, wailing, or bird calls). They call it *dulugu ganalan*, "lift-up-over sounding."[1] *Dulugu ganalan* is a spatial-acoustic metaphor, a visual image set in sonic form and a sonic form set in visual imagery. Intuitively, "lift-up-over sounding" conjures up images of continuous layers, sequential but not linear; of non-gapped multiple presences and densities, overlapping without internal breaks. By calling attention to both the spatial ("lift-up-over") and temporal ("sounding") axes of experience, the term and process explicitly presuppose each sound to exist in fields of prior and contiguous sounds.

"Lift-up-over sounding" in fact refers to numerous typical aspects of Kaluli musical forms and processes, from the very technical (overtones) to the very general (relations of any deliberately coordinated or simply co-present sounds). In the context of *sa-yalab*, *dulugu ganalan* is a stylistic term for how staggered entrances and overlaps as well as breathy, creaky-grained vocalizations "lift-up-over" one another and over the background din of other voices crying and speaking in the longhouse, and over the ever-present background of high-frequency forest sounds.

---

[1] The discussion of *dulugu ganalan*, "lift-up-over sounding," that follows is a very brief condensation of the analysis reported in Feld 1988.

Another way to get the feel of "lift-up-over sounding" is by contrast with its antithesis, unison. All "lift-up-over sounding" sounds are dense, heavily blended, layered; even when voices or sound types momentarily coincide, the sense is that the unison is either accidental or fleeting, and indeed, it is entirely by chance. The essence of "lift-up-over sounding" is part relations that are *simultaneously in-synchrony while out-of-phase.* By "in-synchrony" I mean that the overall feeling is of togetherness, of consistently cohesive part coordination in sonic motion and participatory experience. Yet the parts are also "out-of-phase," that is, at distinctly different and shifting points of the same cycle or phrase structure at any moment, with each of the parts continually changing in degree of displacement from a hypothetical unison. This is the independent-interdependent dynamic that is so tricky to describe in a non-ethnocentric fashion.

Moreover, *dulugu ganalan* is essentially leaderless and egalitarian. "Lift-up-over" is an image of non-hierarchical yet synchronous, layered, fluid group action. Wailing together as sounding together focuses the tension between egalitarianism (activity requiring a concerted cooperation) and individualism (the personalized aspect of each wailer's performance and text). The echo-sounding of wailing together reproduces the quality of "joining-in" as a model of sociability, of maximized participation amid personal distinction, of making a collective "we" from multiple "I's." Individual autonomy and collective sociability are thus simultaneously promoted in the process of "lift-up-over sounding."

Intertextuality

It is difficult these days to use the word "intertextuality" without raising the name of Mikhail Bakhtin, and with it the literary debates his work has stimulated surrounding the issues of dialogism and intertextuality (for a good exposition, see Todorov 1984:60-74). Even though I am quite sympathetic to the force of Bakhtin's positions, I do not use "intertextual" here in the broad theoretical sense that makes claims for the relations of all utterances in juxtaposition, nor in the specific sense that distinguishes the prose of the novel from other forms of artistic verbal discourse. Rather I use "intertextual" descriptively to mean a discourse relationship where the spatio-temporal character of multiple voice utterances is indexical to a process of emergence as a cohesive text. It is the jointly produced, collaborative quality of Kaluli multiply-voiced texts, implicating a particular kind of leaderless, egalitarian, and participatory relationship, that interests me here, because Kaluli intertextuality as a discourse relationship is also the key to the social relationships shared by its producers, and to the emergent understandings and feelings evoked for their audience. It is the cumulatively "layered" and interactive dynamic of the jointly produced text that situates the problematic of Kaluli intertextuality parallel to the problematic of polyphony/heterophony, and resolves it in the local concept and aesthetic of *dulugu ganalan*, "lift-up-over sounding."

The process of performing *sa-yalab* wailing as *dulugu ganalan* involves two or more women simultaneously voicing personal memories, thereby situating their immediate emotions, their relationships to each other, the deceased, and those listening, and their social biographies in a layered collaborative text-voicing. Two kinds of intertextuality are clear in Kaluli *sa-yalab* performances; the first variety is performance-internal, and the second variety is cross-performance. In performance-internal intertexts multiple voices wail at the same time, and their texts interact by "lifting-up-over" one another, continually staggering, alternating, and interlocking such that in addition to the purely sonic layering of the four-tone descending melodic contour, the linguistic messages interact to build jointly produced themes.

For example, the opening of a *sa-yalab* for Bibiali at Asondo in November 1976 (Feld 1985:A3) has Hane wailing "cross-cousin, you and I were together at Kowani [a sago-place], cross-cousin; cross-cousin, having seen *falu* sago at Kowani, I will remember you, cross-cousin." These lines are overlapped by two other voices, Famu, wailing "father, we were together at Kowani, father; father, you have no brother at Kowani, father [meaning, you have no relations left there, just sago palms]; father, being hungry, you left and came here [no more sago at Kowani, metaphorically linked to no more family there]"; and Gania, wailing, "*nasu*[2] [bridewealth relation], Fagenabo is not your brother [implying that his classificatory brother, Fagenabo, never came to stay with him at his place, Tabili], *nasu*; *nasu*, where so far away have you gone, *nasu*?" Then these lines are overlapped again by Famu, wailing "father, have you gone to your place by the bank of Sago creek?" In a matter of seconds, then, the themes of food, family, relationship, and place are chained from one voice to the next and back again. This process deeply interlinks textual themes as well as the specifically situated biographies and memories of three women who are cousin, daughter, and bridewealth relation to the deceased. While each voice is personal and unique, each is also closely tuned-in to the others, developing, extending, commenting upon, or echoing the previous text.

This interpersonal, intertextual, and intermusical relationship continues. After the voices of Hane and Gania drop out, Famu continues in "lift-up-over" fashion with Fofo, who is also related as *nasu* (giver-receiver of bridewealth) to Bibiali. Fofo wails, "*nasu*, if you had a son, that son would be remembering you every day" [angry lines in a hypothetical subjunctive implying that Bibiali's son did not care much about him, creating the kind of vulnerability that courts death]. Her voice is overlapped by Famu, wailing "father, your son is like a *falu* sago palm at Obesana" [meaning, you have no son, he is dead wood]. She continues, "father, you have no son, father; father, if you had a son he would be thinking of you every day, father." During these lines Fofo's text cites placenames linking

---

2 *Nasu* is a reciprocal relationship term for a giver or receiver of bridewealth. The *nasu* relationship, like two other reciprocal relationships available to Kaluli—namesake (*daiyo*) and one who shares a certain kind of food (*wi aledo*)—carries special affect. Unlike kin relations, these sorts of relationships mark special categories of mutual caring and sentimentality for Kaluli, categories that have been voluntarily created and reproduced.

her to Bibiali; then she returns to the joint theme: "*nasu*, you were Halisa's [Fofo's daughter's] father, *nasu*; *nasu* from now on you will only talk secretly to your daughter." Fofo's distancing from textual references to Bibiali's real son [Beli] parallels Famu's distancing of the same theme: "father, when you get hungry, you will go to Gunambo's place, far away." In tandem, then, both voices build an image situating Bibiali, the deceased man, in closest relation to people more distant than the one—his elder son Beli—who would be most expected as a close source of support.

Both voices interact to close out the *sa-yalab* with the same theme. Fofo's wailing has lines like, "you are not my son, you'll say like that" [ending the line with a special imperative form telling the deceased to speak the words that opened the phrase]; "your son will look on the ground and see the footprints you will put there"; "if you had a son I would be happy with him"; "you and I have no son"; and "my little boy left me, you say like that to me." She ends by repeating the image that Bibiali will now speak secretly to his daughter, and mentions another son (absent from the scene, but on his way at that moment) by name. At the same time, Famu overlaps with lines like, "a young boy is coming back across the flat land now"; "who will give food to your son?" [referring to the aforementioned returning son, coming home from the mission school]; and "you and I were together at Ukini, your son is a *bol* tree at Ukini" [*bol* trees stand alone; the image delivers an angry message about Bibiali's sons' lack of commitment to their father]. In these lines, then, chaining through the central portion of the *sa-yalab* and its closing words, a cohesive theme is jointly produced and evoked: Bibiali's death was a result of the vulnerability that springs from a rupture of family solidarity, particularly poignant as one older son (Beli) had nothing to do with his father, and one younger one (Siyowa, also known as Wosoli) was away five of every seven days at a mission grade school, five hours distant.

While this thematic type of performance-internal intertextuality is quite typical of *sa-yalab* performed in *dulugu ganalan* style, there is also a notable second level of performance-internal intertextuality simultaneously taking place. This is the sequencing of placenames, what Kaluli call *tok*, literally "paths" that deeply signify what people have experienced together and shared in life. For instance, in this same *sa-yalab* Famu cites the placenames of Kowani, Sago se, Seloyasi, Obesana, Gunambolowa ["Gunambo's place," meaning his longhouse community, Sululib, three hours' walk away], Asondo, Ukini, Galagido, and Tabili. Fofo cites only the placenames of Yogalimi, Salo sawel, and Misini. Notice that there is no correspondence between the names as cited; each voice is distinct. But an examination of the overlapped or staggered placement of the names in the text, and then an examination of an actual map of the lands mentioned points to a more complex picture. The places chain together from one wailer to the next in the overall text, and they are also either closely proximate locations or similar kinds of places with similar kinds of meanings to the two distinct biographies. When one wails about a sago place where she was together with Bibiali, the other follows in turn citing her sago-place connection with him.

When one uses a distant placename, so does the other. When one cites the name of a longhouse community, so does the other. Again, it is clear that the two wailing women listen closely to one another, and, as personal and specific as their texts may be, there is also a continuously cumulative and interactive layering; the aesthetic and emotional force is to intensify and make denser the kinds of messages and meanings evoked.

A second variety of intertextuality is cross-performance, namely from one *sa-yalab* event to another, separated by time and/or by participants. The effect is to draw the temporal process of the mourning event and the larger process of multiple participants into a kind of more coherent social space where thoughts and feelings are focused and kept in social circulation. The example cited above, for instance, was followed ten minutes later after a quiet period by another *sa-yalab* with one of the same participants and a number of the same themes. In this next sequence Famu continues to wail to her "father," and she is joined within a minute by Galisimi wailing to her *mamu* [distant relation]; later they are both joined by Dulumia who wails with no text, only kin terms.

In this second *sa-yalab* Famu develops the theme of social disruption and alienation. Her text contains lines like "if we hadn't come here this wouldn't have happened" and "we shouldn't have come here to Asondo." These are alternated with lines such as "you and I were together at...," citing places she had been with Bibiali, and phrases like "won't we be together?"; "have you gone by yourself?"; and "wake up now so we can go to our lands." These lines affirm her connections to Bibiali through the places where they spent time and shared together, and these places are contrasted to Asondo, the site of a new longhouse for the people of Tabili. Asondo was a new community of an atypical sort. Members of Tabili and Feliso built adjoining longhouses linked in the center by a common church. Many of the older members of the community opposed this new form of social organization. Famu's text insinuates that the divisiveness and upset surrounding this unnatural community and move, engineered by a pastor and the zealous young Christians of Tabili and Feliso, led to Bibiali's alienation, his general absence from the community, and his death. This theme is developed from her previous *sa-yalab*, which contained the line "we shouldn't have left our place."

Famu's last lines are "we were together at Ukalin; we were together at Kamaido, come back to stay there; your son is a *bol* tree at Ukini (2x); don't you remember Moase? You planted many things there, Siyowa liked to eat them every day." Here Famu's portion of the *sa-yalab* closes by linking three themes: the first is the theme of significant places (Ukalin, Kamaido) where Famu shared with Bibiali; tied to this is the theme that these places are Bibiali's homes in contrast to Asondo; and tied to this is the anger at Bibiali's son Beli (repeating an image from the previous *sa-yalab*, not reiterated in earlier portions of this one) and concern about his younger son, Siyowa (questioning whether he will have food, and implying that Siyowa cannot reciprocate what Bibiali supplied him, that is, food from the large communal Asondo garden at Moase). These images chain from Famu's previous *sa-yalab*, which contained the line "who will give food to your son?" Famu's closing thus explicitly links this *sa-yalab* text thematically to her previous one around the issues of lands, food, sense of home, alienation, vulnerability, anger at Bibiali's sons, and future provision.

At the same time that Famu wails here, she is overlapped by Galisimi, whose text is slight and contains no placenames. Her main theme is disbelief and shock over Bibiali's death, carried in lines like, "are you tricking me?"; "now that you've tricked me this way you are going off"; "wake up"; "stay alone by yourself"; and "I came to look for you" [referring to the way people went to search for Bibiali when he was missing for several days, only to find him dead at his garden house at Salo waterfall]. While brief, Galisimi's lines have internal intertextual connections to Famu's here. Famu's text, for example, contains overlapping lines on the theme of disbelief like "come back again"; "won't we be together?"; "you never tricked anyone before"; "wake up"; and (several times) "wake up now so we can go off to our lands." On the other hand, Galisimi's lines do not have much intertextual connection to the previous *sa-yalab* phrases of Hane sulo, Gania, Fofo, or Famu.

About one hour and fifteen minutes later Hane wept a long solo *sa-yalab* (transcribed, translated, and annotated in detail in Feld 1990:108-28; recorded on Feld 1985:A4). Each of the themes from these two earlier multi-voiced sequences is represented and developed: disbelief, lack of family solidarity, anger at Bibiali's sons, the surprise and shock about to greet Siyowa coming home from the mission school, and Bibiali's and others' alienation and displeasure over moving Tabili to Asondo for the purposes of a new type of community. Like Famu, Fofo, and Galisimi before her, Hane uses some of the same phrasings and imagery to enunciate, reiterate, and further develop these central personal and social feelings surrounding Bibiali's death.

As with the case of internal-performance intertextuality, thematic materials are embellished by placenames across performances as well. Placename intertextuality contributes importantly to the larger set of *sa-yalab* sequences. Placenames signify how each mourner shared something special with the deceased but how each of those special things is of a highly social type and quality: where people live, where they garden, where they travel, where they work, where they exchange and share, where their future lives, as reflections in the form of birds, will take them. Collaborative invocation of placenames builds a large map (about seventy-five names are cited in the three above-mentioned *sa-yalab*) that positions the deceased, the wailers, and their audience in the geographical and social space that links overlapping personal histories and meanings.

These two kinds of intertextuality—performance-internal and cross-performance—and the two textual levels in each—thematic and placename—are not just matters of evocative names and phrases in juxtaposition; they point to a social process that reveals the power of spontaneous joint production to co-articulate personal and collective biography and memory. This embedding is consistent with a larger Durkheimian claim about ritual wailing generally, advanced recently by Gregory Urban (1988), namely, that through overt expression of emotion ritual wailing points toward the desire for sociability. In the Kaluli case this pointing is intensified specifically by the deep relationship between the form (multi-voiced "lift-up-over sounding") and content (thematic and placename intertextuality) of the texts, and the way they in turn point to the social positioning of all involved.

At the same time, this particular kind of wailing indicates that another of Urban's claims needs to be somewhat embellished; he writes: "wailing is a process of making public the feelings of the person who is wailing. It is intended not to be heard, in the ordinary linguistic sense, but rather to be *overheard*. Ritual wailing purports overtly not to engage an addressee, but to allow anyone within earshot access to something that would otherwise be private" (392). In the Kaluli instance the otherwise privacy of the messages is not the issue; wailers are speaking out to the deceased, other wailers, and the present collectivity. Their mode of expression places them forcefully in the social domain as performers. Their words are in some sense very much meant to be heard rather than overheard in that they function as an invitation to others to collaboratively enunciate felt thoughts about the death at hand and the social position of the deceased, through thematic and placename resources.

Boundaries of Speech and Song

Since lament forms take on various manifestations, some more recited, some more sung, some more cried, some more improvised, some more composed, it is important to describe clearly the exact features that are subsumed by the type labeled "ritual wailing." Urban's recent comparative study of ritual wailing in AmerIndian Brazil isolates three code-feature commonalities of diverse wailing manifestations. These are "(1) the existence of a musical line, marked by a characteristic intonational contour and rhythmical structure; (2) the use of various icons of crying; and (3) the absence of an actual addressee, which renders the ritual wailing an overtly monologic or expressive device, despite the importance that may accrue to its status as public, with the desired presence of someone to 'overhear' it" (386). These code-feature commonalities found in AmerIndian Brazil transpose clearly to the Kaluli situation, although all can be elaborated or refined more specifically in relation to the local case.

The existence of a musical line, with a specified contour, and a series of precise phrase and sub-phrase possibilities for that contour are quite marked in the Kaluli instance. A phrase schematic breaks down easily into four subsections, each of which has a series of eight to twelve typical "rewrite" possibilities for pulse (but not pitch) expansion to accommodate words of various syllable lengths. This generates a basic matrix of phrase types, of which about twenty are highly typical combinations. These phrase types can be further expanded by embedding and conjoining. It is neither the linguistic intonational contour nor rhythmic structure that characterizes the line so much as the relationship among line length, phrase and sub-phrase demarcation, and breath groups. Distinctive characteristics such as those Urban found to correlate with line-time length do not occur in the Kaluli instance due to the line variability that results from embedding and conjoining.

Urban isolates four icons of crying found in ritual wailing, the "cry break," voiced inhalation, creaky voice, and falsetto vowel (389). The cry break, sonically realized as a diaphragm pulse accompanied by friction and labeled by the term "sob," is quickly recognizable in Kaluli *sa-yalab* and, as he argues, is the most transparent index of a crying voice. Continuous sobbing, streaming of tears, and nasal discharge by Kaluli wailers link the cry break to reduction of the vowel space, nasality, vibrato voice, and marked volume reduction at the end of breath and sub-phrase groups. Voiced inhalation, which Urban links to heightened emotional involvement, is also characteristic of Kaluli *sa-yalab*, particularly at phrase and sub-phrase onsets and offsets. This feature contributes to the sense of bounded lines, of short, startled bursts of vocalization. Creaking voice, produced through slower glottal chord vibrations, manifests itself clearly in *sa-yalab*, although its interaction with continuous sobbing and nasality produces a sound rather more "raspy" than the "creaky" types Urban found in his Shavante, Bororo, and Shokleng sample. As in those cases, the creaky/raspy quality does clearly distinguish the wailing voice from the speaking voice, except in the cases of those who are ill, particularly with bronchial disorders, or the aged, whose voices become more creaky as the effects of years of living in smoky longhouses takes its toll on their lungs and throats. Urban points out this association between creaking voice and various abnormal states of the organism. His final icon, falsetto vowels, does not typify Kaluli *sa-yalab* the way the other three do.

Finally, Urban points to the prominent absence of an addressee in ritual wailing, and the importance of the "overheard" quality of wailing. While technically true in the Kaluli case as well, a code feature of *sa-yalab* is marked linguistic structure as a direct speech to the deceased. In this case the deceased is fully an addressee, while those who wail simultaneously and those who are more generally co-present constitute "overhearers." This somewhat complicates the use of the descriptive term "monologic" when applied to this form of wailing. It is certainly monologic or multiply monologic in that there is no returned verbal interaction from the deceased. Yet it is also imaginatively dialogic in its intended linguistic structure and communicative type, and intertextually dialogic when multiple voices participate.

These features help locate *sa-yalab* vis-à-vis boundaries of Kaluli speech and song. Presence of icons of crying gives *sa-yalab* its distinct quality as a voice type, apart from the conversational or singing voice. Yet its linguistic form and intertextual possibilities also give it a conversational quality distinct from song poetics. At the same time its distinctive melodic contour marks it as a kind of non-talked conversation. While there is some awkwardness to the gloss "melodic-texted-sung weeping," that gloss indeed communicates the complex interaction of speech and song characteristics that interact in *sa-yalab*.

Composition-in-Performance

Ruth Finnegan's recent review of the complexities of oral composition practices in the South Pacific (1988:86-109) notes several difficulties with mapping the Parry-Lord oral-formulaic theory onto the extraordinary diversity, flexibility, and variety of compositional techniques known to Oceanic poetries. It is instructive there, as in her earlier, more general discussion of memorization and oral poetry (1977:52-87), to note the issue of variety across and within Pacific societies, genres, and specific items. The Kaluli materials are a further illustration of intra-cultural and cross-generic variety in compositional practice, and it is worth reviewing several key characteristics of oral-formulaic qualities in *sa-yalab* as they compare with those of Kaluli oral song genres.

Finnegan succinctly summarizes four of the key principles of the oral-formulaic theory associated with Parry, Lord, and their followers (for elaboration, see Foley 1988): "(1) The text of oral literature is variable and dependent on the occasion of performance, unlike the fixed text of a written book... (2) The form of composition characteristic of oral literature is composition-in-performance, i.e., not prior composition divorced from the act of performance... (3) Composition and transmission of oral literature is through the process mentioned above and not (as was once thought) through word for word memorization... (4) In oral literature, there is no concept of a 'correct' or 'authentic' version" (Finnegan 1988:88-89).

On the whole these four characteristics apply rather well to Kaluli *sa-yalab*, although they apply rather poorly to Kaluli song. *Sa-yalab* are clearly highly occasion-sensitive and textually variable, with an elaborate continuum of more to less formulaic, repetitive, durative, metaphoric, stylistically dense, and poetic features. Additionally, *sa-yalab* do not seem to involve composition prior to performance, although interviews clearly brought out the fact that Kaluli women are aware of and contemplate (and hence "compose" in some sense) the kind of poetic images, particularly placename sequences, that are employed in the texts. Likewise, memorization seems not to play a part in *sa-yalab* performance, although, again, interviews indicated that Kaluli remember poetic lines and images that they have heard in other *sa-yalab* and thus might commit certain forceful ones to memory and then "reinvent" them at a later time. And finally, it seems quite true that there is no focus on "correct" or "authentic" versions, as each *sa-yalab* is, as a whole, valued as a momentary and reflexive performance, rather than a specific instance of a preformed item, judged relative to a pre-existing standard or image of that preformed item as it is performed.

This profile rests quite in distinction to Kaluli song in general, and the five kinds of Kaluli song in particular. In the cases of some song genres, none of the four characterizations apply; texts can be fixed in advance, divorced from performance, worked up and memorized, and listened to and judged as to whether they are correct and authentic versions of a particular song linked to a specific composer. In the case of one song genre, *gisalo* (the most important Kaluli song genre), there are two performance manifestations: ceremonies and spirit-medium seances. In the former instance none of the four characteristics apply (as noted above); in the latter instance criterion one applies, two and three partially apply, and four does not apply. In the cases of the four other song genres (*heyalo*, *koluba*, *sabio*, and *iwo*), at least two of the four do not apply, although this is further complicated by whether the song is performed in a ceremonial context or in an informal everyday context (for example, during garden or sago work). This kind of variation nicely illustrates Finnegan's point about problematic attempts to simplify oral composition with across-the-board generalities.

This variation also illustrates how the oral-formulaic theory must be considered carefully in relation to genre, and in relation to the social dictates and expectations of the situation. Kaluli value some genres for their more spontaneous, improvised, composed-in-performance, and emergent properties. Others are highly valued precisely for their difference—as performances of carefully pre-crafted melodies and texts, even if they recycle very familiar melodic contours or textual themes. *Sa-yalab* conform well to the parameters of oral-formulaic theory, in good part for reasons of local aesthetics: what makes a *sa-yalab* compelling for Kaluli listeners is the sense that it is truly unique and spontaneous, with in-the-moment and immediate thoughts rendered poetically, a simultaneous voicing of personal and collective memory, an evocation of the pain of separation and the ratification of shared experiences. While Kaluli songs have much of the thematic focus of *sa-yalab* (food, sharing, maps of experience, personal relationships and their ruptures), their evocational stance is the inverse: they are crafted to make others cry. The craft of *sa-yalab* crying, on the other hand, is the spontaneous creation of song. The strong character of this ethnoaesthetic creates a kind of dual *modus operandi* for Kaluli oral poetics, with one variety similar to the features evinced by the oral-formulaic theory, and one greatly dissimilar.

Emotion

Another way to open up some dimensions of how the practices of *sa-yalab* involve a complex interplay of collective and individual sensibilities is to address the socio-psychological role played by the wailing itself, and then to review the issue of singing improvised lines while wailing. This perspective takes us to the issue of just how the physiological production of tears is linked to the feelings encoded and evinced by *sa-yalab* texts in performance. Jerome Neu, a philosopher concerned with the representation of emotion, has recently surveyed the literature on crying and critiqued the commonplaces on the topic that derive from Darwin, James, Freud, and those ethologists and psychologists who reify the mind/body split in their theories. In contrast, he argues that "emotional tears, unlike mechanically induced or reflex tears, are mediated by thought. This is not to say they are the product of conscious deliberation and calculation, but it is to say that they depend on how we perceive the world, on how we think of it, rather than on how the world simply, in fact, is. They express our nature as well as the nature of the world" (1987:35).

Neu's thesis, that we cry because we think, is nicely borne out by Kaluli metalinguistics, ethnography, and ethnopsychology. In Kaluli metalinguistics, the term *sa-yalab* consists of the prefix *sa-* and the verb *yalab* (third-person present form). This is an onomatopoeic verb formed from the sound word *ya-*, signifying the sound of the wailing voice, and *-alab* (from imperative *alama*) meaning "say like that." Several Kaluli verbs are formed this way, with an onomatopoeic stem attached to the verb for "say like that." The prefix *sa-* is semantically quite complex; it can be attached to any verb of soundmaking to denote that it is texted, with an "inside." For example, when the verb for "whistle" is prefixed by *sa-* it means to whistle with words in mind. When the verb for "sing" is prefixed by *sa-* it means to "compose," that is, to add text to the sound. *Sa-* can also be prefixed to sense verbs or verbs of communicative modality; when added to the verb for "hear" it means to "gossip," when prefixed to the verb for "speak" it means to "speak poetically," that is, with "inside" meanings. *Sa-* then carries the sense of "inside," "text," "thought," "meditation," mental activity apart from apparent surface physical substance (for linguistic and social elaboration, see Feld 1990:92-93, 132-38, 165-70, 252). In the case of *sa-yalab*, the *sa-* prefix distinguishes the kind of weeping as a thoughtful, melodic, texted, meditated variety, different from the other kinds of *yalab* mentioned earlier. This metalinguistic construction of the term *sa-yalab* argues for the idea that Kaluli women weep tears of ideas; they cry to think and think to cry. *Sa-yalab* is the height of intellect as affect for Kaluli; it is thoughtful crying, an evocation of memory through the process of melodic-sung-texted weeping.

Psychologists and psychoanalysts have in the past equated weeping with urination, with a cleansing of toxic substance, and with a safe dissipation of aggressive impulses. "Having a good cry" is thus regarded as a cathartic but useful purging of negative substance and feeling. The larger Western commonsense assumption, bolstered by some academic psychology, in which this view of catharsis is situated, is that art and expressive behavior generally act as a safety valve in social life; when emotions "build up" to a "boiling point" they must be released, and the release is accomplished by some outpouring. Expressive behavior like ritual wailing is thus sometimes taken in a strictly functionalist sense to represent a bursting of the social seam, an overflow, a chaotic falling apart whose venting leads to the restitution of normal, orderly, rational, integrated behavior. This view sees the dispersal and elimination of excessive, negative, or destructive feelings as key functions of expressive acts.

I think it much more reasonable to argue the opposite scenario, that the key affective quality of Kaluli ritual wailing is a creative "pulling together" of affect rather than its "falling apart" signaled by dispersal of emotional byproducts. Ritual wailing for Kaluli serves much more to centrally display and focus the aesthetics of emotionality, and to positively value these social articulations as organized, thoughtful expressions of personal and social identities as deeply felt. The kind of musical and textual cohesiveness articulated by "lift-up-over sounding," multi-voiced *sa-yalab* is in many ways the prototypical case of productive sociability for Kaluli. Wailing is not a chaotic indication of personal aggressive impulses but rather the placement of felt thought and memory at center stage, articulated simultaneously with maximized autonomy and sociability. It would be hard to imagine such a spontaneous yet socially orchestrated, productive, and coherent manifestation as anything "mediated by thought." *Sa-yalab* are surely as much about thinking as they are about feeling, as much head-felt as heart-felt, as much intended as impulsive, as much cultural as natural.

Indeed, in many ways the most appropriate gloss for the Kaluli term *sa-yalab*, a gloss that captures the mélange of affect and cognition involved, is the one suggested in the main title of this essay: "wept thoughts."

The Kaluli bias is entirely in the opposite direction of the Western valuation when it comes to situating the meaning of emotionality as encoded in these performances. Playbacks of recordings of women's *sa-yalab* spontaneously elicit highly positive evaluative remarks; there is clear appreciation for the way women articulate for the collectivity the essence of what it means to be in the moment, to be fully saturated in a sensibility that brings thoughts to the mind with tears to the eyes. Traditionally no attempts were ever made to constrain *sa-yalab*; these performances were considered vital and necessary parts of social life. In recent years, however, attempts to discourage *sa-yalab* and to negatively value their performance have emerged. Such attempts emanate entirely from evangelical missionaries and from evangelized Kaluli under their influence. The irony of course is that nothing about *sa-yalab* really violates Christian teaching; what they violate is the particular cultural background of the Australian missionaries, who tend to emphasize strong repression of emotional display in all affairs.

Gender and Genre

Many authors have cited a link between the expression of emotion and the voicing of social and personal tensions and conflicts; this is often related to the question of role distance and the position of lament as a largely (and in many places, exclusively) women's genre (for an overview, see Sherzer 1987:112-14). Catherine Lutz's recent work opens a new window to this issue through an accounting of Western ethnopsychological biases linking gender and emotion. She observes that "emotion occupies an important place in Western gender ideologies; in identifying emotion primarily with irrationality, subjectivity, the chaotic and other negative characteristics, and in subsequently labelling women as the emotional gender, cultural belief reinforces the ideological subjugation of women" (1986:288). Moreover, "the association of the female with the emotions is reinforced by the naturalness that the two purportedly share. The view of men and of cognition as each more cultural and more civilized contrasts with the primeval associations of the concepts of the female, the emotions, and nature, each of which is simpler, more primitive, and more anti-structural than the male, cognition, and culture" (300).

It is interesting in this regard how much the Western ethnopsychological link among women, emotionality, and irrationality is not shared by Kaluli. For them, men are by far the more typically and stereotypically emotional gender, the more unpredictable, potentially irrational, the more moody, prone to burst out in tears at any moment or become flamboyantly seized with tantrums of rage or sadness. Kaluli men seem to have more trouble controlling anger and upset than do Kaluli women, and this fact is clearly recognized. Men's crying—*iligi-yalab*, *gana-yalab*, *gana-gili-yalab*—is less controlled, momentary, hysterical, and often accompanied by physical trembling and angry gestures. Women's crying—*gese-yalab* and *sa-yalab*—is more melodic, texted, controlled, reflective, and sustained. These qualities parallel general emotional display patterns: Kaluli women typically act more steady, reliable, and even-tempered in everyday matters, and the obvious composure under intense stress that is indicated by their *sa-yalab* performances is an expressive extension of that constellation. Kaluli men, on the other hand, are given to marked sudden affect changes, moody grimaces and gestures, aggressive or withdrawn posturing, and bursts from sulkiness to exuberance; in common parlance Kaluli men basically "let it all hang out."

While Kaluli men and women all value *sa-yalab* as a positive social performance and essential expressive ritual, the contrast with male poetic song is instructive. Song is obviously a more highly valued form and is considered more powerfully evocative, especially by Kaluli men. Song is aimed at, and succeeds in, making others cry. Because of its controlled, composed, calculated, premeditated, and highly planned construction to move others to tears in the context of elaborate ceremonies, poetic song is presented by men as the fine high point of their ability to evoke, to initiate, to place themselves in the social spotlight.

While positively valuing women's *sa-yalab*, Kaluli men do certainly regard it as a more spontaneous, natural expression. But that does not mean that they regard it as impulsive, wild, irrational, uncontrolled, or less thoughtful than song—only less refined and manipulative in the outcomes and social ends served. That male forms of weeping are momentary outbursts that are not sustained is read as distinctly uncontrolled by both Kaluli men and women. Kaluli men have explicitly told me that women's *sa-yalab* are distinct from more typically male forms of wailing precisely insofar as the male forms are impulsive, wild, and often require others to restrain or help the convulsing wailer gain some composure. On the other hand, Kaluli men evaluate women's weeping by stressing a direct principle: the more song-like the better. What this means is that as *sa-yalab* become more textually cohesive they become more like song in the way that they induce and demand contemplation from listeners. When the thematic images and placenames build and develop into a cumulative climaxing structure ("making hard," *halaido domaki*), then *sa-yalab*, like composed ceremonial songs, can also move listeners to tears.

What we have here is an expressive economy in which both male and female forms are positively valued, but where the controlled elaborate ceremonial arena gives special emphasis to male forms. Yet the egalitarian dimension comes in through the way in which the evaluative heightening of male song does not proceed through a devaluative lessening of female modes of expression, nor through an ideological move that situates the character of the female expressive form at the irrational, impulsive, uncognized, noncultural border. Kaluli men do not seem particularly threatened or agitated by the importance accorded to *sa-yalab*, but they do tend to point out that what makes *sa-yalab* most forceful to them is the quality of being musically and (particularly) textually close to the craft and feeling of a composed song. Men seem to be saying that *sa-yalab* is intrinsically important and good, but better when it sounds and feels like their way of doing things, in other words, their mode of constructing poetic song.

For their part women tend not to draw this comparison—*sa-yalab* is *sa-yalab* and song is song; they are just "different" (*kole*). When I told Ulahi what men had to say about *sa-yalab*, namely that a song-like construction is what makes them good, she simply responded "men can hear it that way" and would make nothing more of it. I was particularly interested in Ulahi's views on this because she had composed many songs, was an accomplished singer, and was quite articulate and knowledgeable about song form and poetics. But Ulahi and other women with whom I discussed this issue seemed to feel that *sa-yalab* and song were just very different things. They did not relate the positive valuation of *sa-yalab* to song-like textual properties. Rather they related the positive valuation to the way women can singly speak out in *sa-yalab* to articulate feelings that concern the collectivity.

Despite these differences of rationalization, it is clear that the focus of gender specificity in *sa-yalab* is not really in the area of message content. The texts of women's wailing are not about issues or feelings that are unique to women, nor about specifically female anger or distress over death. The message content (generally, shock and disbelief; shared experiences centered around lands, food, and family; insinuations in "turned-over words" as to the underlying cause of the death) is socially general. Gender specificity in *sa-yalab* is marked more singularly at the level of the stylization of spontaneous crying into a melodic-sung-texted form that may be performed in solo or multi-voiced fashion. This stylization into a reflective, sustained, controlled form in the context of intensely charged sentiments speaks to the highly culturalized and cognized presentation of Kaluli female emotionality, whatever Kaluli men might venture about its more natural and improvised character in comparison to compositionally crafted, ceremonial poetic song.

The "Paths" of "Placenames"

Keith Basso has recently urged that "placenames are arguably among the most highly charged and richly evocative of all linguistic symbols. Because of their inseparable connection to specific localities, placenames may be used to summon forth an enormous range of mental and emotional associations—associations of time and space, of history and events, of persons and social activities, of oneself and stages in one's life." He continues: "Poets and songwriters have long understood that economy of expression may enhance the quality and force of aesthetic discourse, and that placenames stand ready to be exploited for this purpose" (1988:103). Basso's ethnographic and linguistic work elaborates these propositions, detailing the "pictured depictions" of Apache conversation as "a reciprocal representation and visualization of the ongoing thought of participating speakers" (109) which must be embellished with "add-on" interpretations. He shows that descriptive precision is essential to Apache narrative; listeners must be able to imagine settings for events, and "the evocative power of placenames is most dramatically displayed when a name is used to substitute for the narrative it anchors, 'standing up alone' ('*o'áá*), as Apaches say, to symbolize the narrative as well as the wisdom it contains" (112-13).

Basso's analysis resonates well with the expressive uses of placenames in Kaluli song, narrative, conversation, or *sa-yalab*. Human relationships, all metaphorically encapsulated through what Kaluli call "paths" (*tok*), are literal "maps" of places (*hen wi*, "placenames") whose naming evokes specific shared life experiences as well as embodiments of identity and value. In *sa-yalab* the most common form of placename citation is the formula: "my + {kinship/relationship term} + you and I + {placename}." These translate as "my {relation}, you and I were together at {place}." Intensified emotional force accrues to such lines by the use of an abbreviated linguistic formula, namely *nani* ("you and I") + placename, with no verb. Dropping the verb from the last position of the word order centers the placename in that focused, final position, somewhat animating it with a verbal quality (Kaluli is a verb-final language). This formula marks a particular directness and affective projection; it signals the sensation of co-being at a place. Such lines are sometimes followed or embellished by a second parallelistic line citing a kind of tree, physical feature, or bird found at the place, or followed and embellished by a rhetorical question or remark about the rupture of what has been or could continue to be experienced at that place. Other common follow-ups include quote directives, for example, "my {X}, you and I were together at the {A} tree at {B}, my {X}; 'always look up to the top branches of the {A} tree,' you say like that to me, my {X}." Here the wailer invokes the place and memory, and follows with the directive for the deceased to say her quoted words back to her. This signals that the deceased should direct her attention to the way he will appear to her (as a bird in the top branches of that tree) in the future. The lines thus link the power of the habitual past association with the rupture and the durative potential future recasting of the relationship, embodied through the same places.

Particularly in the context of their intertextual recitation in *sa-yalab*, placenames and their sequences signal the recognition that life proceeds through actions and events given uniqueness and singularity through locales; locales become an embodiment of the pleasures and difficulties associated with those actions and events. Through placename intertextuality each text is grounded not only in its moment but also in prior, contiguous, imagined, or actual experiences which multiply the referents of the words as well as the qualities of the performance and intensity of feelings in the moment. *Sa-yalab* placenames do more than encode sequences that give texts cohesion; they reveal the cohesion processually and thematically, intensified through performance. Moreover, placenames do not just encode memory; they stimulate social recall and imagination, and they revive and reveal and foreshadow feelings, again intensified by the specifically bounded nature of performance. Voicing memories through placenames in *sa-yalab* performance produces emergent feelings of empathy, connectedness—the sense of sameness through difference. As Kaluli so often said to me listening to a playback of another's *sa-yalab*, "yes, I've felt/understood it that way too."

Speaking of what the Apaches call the "strength" of expressive discourse, Basso concludes that "it is my impression that those utterances that perform the broadest range of mutually compatible actions at once are those that Apaches experience as having the greatest communicative impact. In other words, the expressive force of an Apache utterance seems to be roughly proportionate to the number of separate but complementary functions it accomplishes simultaneously..." (1988:121). This general proposition and the Apache metalinguistic label ("strength") and aesthetic ethnotheory outlined by Basso also resonate deeply with the Kaluli situation. Kaluli speak of the "hardness" or "force" (*halaido*) of utterances, texts, and performances, and of the *halaido domaki*, their "making hard" through dramatic cumulative climaxing structures (Feld 1990:126-29, 138, 142, 153-56; also see Feld and Schieffelin 1982). "Making hard" is an essential aspect of the planned climaxing structure of Kaluli songs, and it is their "hardening," typified by sequences of placenames, that moves listeners to tears. While "making hard" is not an essential distinctive feature of the construction of all *sa-yalab*, it is clearly a feature that makes *sa-yalab* powerfully evocative, and it is among the most highly valued features of the genre, one that distinguishes well-remembered voices and texts from others.

The aesthetic feeling of "hardness" that accrues to placenames in Kaluli *sa-yalab* derives from several forms of poetic intensification, or, in Jakobson's famous formulation (1960), "auto-referentiality," the drawing of attention to a message's form and the consequent pleasure of that recognition. Sequence is the key device that accomplishes this poetic function in large measure.   The progression of places, moving closer to the scene of the death, or farther away from it, moving through the text and through the time of its voicing, submerge the listener in a bounded mini-reality of places and their evocation. When several voices cite a progression of places, and the progression interacts as well as follows separate trajectories, then the poetic possibilities are complexly multiplied.   This is the kind of poetic "hardness" that results from the intertextuality previously discussed.

Finally, the textual environments of placenames evidence a key feature that poetically intensifies their force. This is the use of aspectual markers for the continuous past and durative future. The constructions of "were always," "had always," or "would always" utterances, and their parallelistic shifts to "will always" and "from now on and forever" utterances, provide a powerful means to frame the instantaneous signification of temporality, liminality, and transition, generally mediated through placenames. This force is situated in lines like "we would always garden at {X}, I will always hear your voice in the {A} tree at {X}." Such lines link the experiences and evocative power of places with the recognition that rupture and change are in process, that continuities embody transformations.

Conclusion and Questions

To close I want to underscore that the approach taken here is hopefully a generalizable one not specific to any historical moment or cultural-geographical area. No doubt the next step in a study like this would be to provide an entire text and a detailed musico-poetic analysis and explication. But I would urge that lament forms, and particularly the collective ritual wailing varieties of lament that are found throughout the South Pacific and elsewhere, can profitably be approached first as very thick texts indeed, texts whose form, function, and meaning can be apprehended by confronting the intersection of musical, verbal, folkloric, literary, psychological, gender-related, and sociological constructs indicated by the five topic areas that began this inquiry. Such an intersection points us to questions that get right to the heart of terms like "oral tradition" and force us to provide rigorous ethnographic assessments of their vicissitudes.

On a more specific level, I want to offer a conclusion about ritual wailing that begins by emphasizing, as Urban (1988) has, the importance of the way human societies do not confine or model ritual forms of wailing within or upon the sonic and durative patterns that strictly characterize cries indexing pain, hurt, injury, momentary sadness, or joy. Ritual wailing hosts continua of musical and linguistic elaboration, and these features are organized in culturally specific and performatively evocative ways. Some musical features along these continua of elaboration include: pitch level, degree of pitch stability, melodic contour, metric and rhythmic organization and stability, correspondence of phrase group and breath-point, degree of phrasal and sub-phrasal repetition, and amount of improvisation from base or formulaic schemes. Some linguistic features along these continua include: degree of pure sound vocalizations to use of conventional well-formed words, line length and format, phonological, syntactic, and semantic micro- and macroparallelism, correspondence of line and sub-line units with breath-points and melodic contours, ellipsis, and formulaic phrases to full syntactic constructions.

More often than not, melodic and rhythmic aspects of tune and phonological and syntactic aspects of text interact in the organization of phrases, breath groups, and lines. This interaction stylizes the musical and linguistic properties of the wailing, and further interacts with the stylization of crying icons cited by Urban to mark the wailing as a culturally specific vocalization type, and as a performance genre indexed to a range of specific situations appropriate for its enunciation.

The specific hypothesis I want to add here springs from the fact that when we move from this code level to the study of performances it is clear that many of the world's ritual wailing forms involve multiple voices interlocked in musical and textual dialectics of independent and interdependent voicing, a crucial factor in considering the potential varieties of culturally specific wailing stylizations. These distinct ways of creating a social "we" out of multiple "I's" lead to the conjecture that *humankind's earliest experiences of and experiments with musical polyphony and orally artistic intertextuality might have been intertwined in collectively improvised ritual wailing.* This hypothesis means to suggest that culturally specific styles of wailing can become codified through emergent improvised processes, and further, that this codification may be the dynamic basis for understanding facets of polyphony and intertextuality more formally codified in the verbal and musical compositional practices of the same society.

To question the hypothesis as an implicational universal, we might ask the following. Do all societies whose verbally artistic oral traditions involve multi-voice intertextuality, and/or whose musical practices involve polyphony also have some form of significant intertextual/polyphonic dynamic in their ritual wailing? Are there societies that have a significant intertextual/polyphonic dynamic in their ritual wailing yet no verbally artistic intertextuality or musical polyphony, codified or elaborated otherwise? These questions could form the basis for an interesting comparative project aimed toward locating ritual wailing in the evolution of human expressive culture, and more critically in relation to other varieties of verbal and sung lament.[3]

References

Ajuwon 1981   Bade Ajuwon. "Lament for the Dead as a Universal Folk Tradition." *Fabula*, 22:272-80.

Basso 1988   Keith Basso. "'Speaking with Names': Language and Landscape among the Western Apache." *Cultural Anthropology*, 3, ii:99-130.

Feld 1985   Steven Feld. *The Kaluli of Papua Niugini: Weeping and Song* [disc]. Kassel: Bärenreiter (Musicaphon/Music of Oceania BM 30 SL 2702).

Feld 1988   _____. "Aesthetics as Iconicity of Style, or, 'lift-up-over sounding:' Getting into the Kaluli Groove." *Yearbook for Traditional Music*, 20:74-113.

Feld 1990   _____. *Sound and Sentiment: Birds, Weeping, Poetics and Song in Kaluli Expression.* Philadelphia: University of Pennsylvania Press. 2nd ed.

[3] My research among the Kaluli in 1976-77, 1982, and 1984 was generously supported by the Institute of Papua New Guinea Studies, the National Endowment for the Arts, the National Science Foundation, the American Philosophical Society, and the Wenner-Gren Foundation for Anthropological Research. I am grateful to these institutions, and equally to my collaborators E.L. Schieffelin, B.B. Schieffelin, Jubi, Gigio, Kulu, Ayasilo, Honowo, and Ulahi for their interest and help with this research. For many helpful suggestions on the manuscript I am grateful to Ruth Finnegan.

Feld and
  Schieffelin 1982   _____and Bambi B. Schieffelin. "Hard Words: A
                          Functional Basis for Kaluli Discourse." In *Text and
                          Talk*. Ed. by Deborah Tannen. Washington, D.C.:
                          Georgetown University Press. pp. 351-71.

Finnegan 1977   Ruth Finnegan. *Oral Poetry*. London and New York:
                        Cambridge University Press.

Finnegan 1988   _____. *Literacy and Orality*. Oxford and New York:
                        Basil Blackwell.

Foley 1988   John Miles Foley. *The Theory of Oral Composition:
                        History and Methodology*. Bloomington: Indiana
                        University Press. Rpt. 1992.

Honko 1980   Lauri Honko. "The Lament: Problems of Genre,
                        Structure, and Reproduction." In *Genre, Structure and
                        Reproduction in Oral Literature*. Ed. by Lauri Honko
                        and Vilmos Voigt. Budapest: Akademiai Kiado. pp.
                        21-40.

Jakobson 1960   Roman Jakobson. "Linguistics and Poetics." In *Style
                        in Language*. Ed. by T. A. Sebeok. Cambridge, MA:
                        MIT Press. pp. 350-77.

Lutz 1986   Catherine Lutz. "Emotion, Thought, and
                        Estrangement: Emotion as a Cultural Category."
                        Cultural Anthropology, 1, iii:287-309.

Neu 1987   Jerome Neu. "'A Tear is an Intellectual Thing'."
                        Representations, 19:35-61.

Propp 1984   Vladimir Propp. *Theory and History of Folklore*.
                        Trans. by Ariadna Y. Martin and Richard P. Martin.
                        Minneapolis: University of Minnesota Press.

B. Schieffelin 1990   Bambi B. Schieffelin. *The Give and Take of Kaluli
                        Everyday Life*. New York: Cambridge University
                        Press.

E. Schieffelin 1976   Edward L. Schieffelin. *The Sorrow of the Lonely and
                        the Burning of the Dancers*. New York: St. Martin's
                        Press.

Sherzer 1987   Joel Sherzer. "A Diversity of Voices: Men's and
                        Women's Speech in Ethnographic Perspective." In
                        *Language, Gender and Sex in Comparative
                        Perspective*. Ed. by Susan U. Philips, Susan Steele,
                        and Christine Tanz. Cambridge and New York:
                        Cambridge University Press. pp. 95-120.

Todorov 1984   Tzvetan Todorov. *Mikhail Bakhtin: The Dialogical
                      Principle*. Trans. by Wlad Godzich. Minneapolis:
                      University of Minnesota Press.

Urban 1988   Greg Urban. "Ritual Wailing in AmerIndian Brazil."
                      American Anthropologist, 90:385-400.

VI

PROFILE OF A COMPOSER: IHAIA PUKA, A *PULOTU* OF THE TOKELAU ISLANDS

Allan Thomas and Ineleo Tuia

By the designation *pulotu* Tokelau Islanders acknowledge master-craftsmanship in their contemporary song-poetry tradition. The title is only given to experienced and distinguished composers who have built for themselves a reputation through many works over a considerable period of time. *Pulotu* may be translated as "composer-maker of songs," but "poet" would be equally apt as the words of a song are the first element to be created and are the foundation for the music and dance features. The composer/poet is often also the choreographer who devises dance movements that extend and express the words of the song, and he or she may perform in the work as dance leader or as part of the singing or dancing group.

Songs are composed by unique individuals, who have their own complex relationship with the communities and cultural traditions to which they belong. This article describes a remarkable composer/poet, Ihaia Puka, against the background of the tradition to which he belongs; some of his songs are given, and extracts from interviews. Through this portrait of a single individual we also attempt to describe something of the work of all Tokelau *pulotu*: their roles and status, their genres and the subjects of their songs, and the performance context.

Ethnomusicologists have been slow to acknowledge the composers/originators of the musical material they are studying. There is very little literature on Pacific composers, though plenty of evidence of their work. This study, focused on an outstanding exponent and innovator, moves away from a generalized and static view of the music system. It emphasizes a particular preference and individual contribution within the musical domain.

Ihaia and His Background

The atoll of Nukunonu, the Tokelau community in which Ihaia has lived most of his adult life, is a small-scale, isolated, and intensively regulated traditional society. Its population is about four hundred. The three Tokelau atolls, Nukunonu, Atafu, and Fakaofo, are in touch with one another only by radio telephone and through the monthly visits of the supply ship. Each atoll consists of a group of islets around a lagoon, with the population more or less concentrated in a single village area and the remainder of the land area planted in coconut palm. Within the society much work is undertaken in common, and authority is exercised by *toeaina*, senior men. In the nineteenth century the Tokelau societies experienced major disruption from the visits of slave raiders, epidemics, the setting up of missions, and the activities of traders (Hooper and Huntsman 1973). Although the atolls are isolated, various circumstances in this century have brought the people into contact with other Polynesian islands, and these contacts have enriched the cultural life of Tokelau by providing composers and performers with dance and music adopted, accepted, and altered from several sources. New Zealand Tokelau communities date from the 1960s and are now located in four main centers: Auckland, Porirua, Hutt Valley, and Rotorua-Taupo. Although members of these communities maintain close links with other Tokelauans in New Zealand, and with family members in the islands, they are also integrated into the work, residential, social, and sporting patterns of other New Zealanders. It is chiefly in the fields of traditional music and dance that Tokelau identity is celebrated and renewed in the New Zealand Tokelau communities.

Ihaia is an outstanding and prolific composer, and at eighty-two years of age a commanding personality. With his direct speaking and ready humor he dominates any gathering, whether in Nukunonu where he lived until 1987, or in the Hutt Valley in Wellington, New Zealand, where he now lives. He is recognized as an authority in many areas of traditional lore, and his opinion is sought after and deferred to. But he is also something of a tease, has a sly sense of humor, and hugely enjoys a joke. At gatherings of Tokelau people his speeches are greeted with unusual attention out of deference not only to his age but also to his knowledge and forceful opinions. To this attention is added the tension which comes as the audience waits for the next skillfully aimed and witty barb: sometimes a criticism of dancing, drumming, or composition, sometimes an observation on community events. As a storyteller, he is a fluent raconteur of traditional tales, *kakai*, often emphasizing the more lurid aspects to hold his audience. He talks about his life too with relish, though sometimes straying from the literal truth of events. He can be willful and walk out of a group rehearsal if he thinks that his compositions are not receiving due attention. He can be wickedly funny at others' expense. Above all he is unpredictable and, one senses as the community listens to him, he needs to be carefully watched; a wary as well as respectful attention is accorded him.

Ihaia says of his early life:

I was born in Atafu in 1907 and lived there until I went to Nukunonu in
1931. There was a group traveling to Fakaofo, for a cricket match. We
traveled on the ship Tamalina, a very small boat with hardly room for the
passengers; quite a few of them had to stand up all the way it was so
overcrowded. We stopped for the night at Nukunonu, and the ship left in the
morning, but I stayed behind.

My real mother was Mativa, who had sisters Sui, Tapogi, and Inosia and
brothers Hakai, Hale, Teo, Etoma, and Matagi. The father of that family,
Kalepo, had a brother called Ihaia. It was his wife, Patisepa, who was mother

to me, she was a Kiribati woman. They met in this way. [Great-uncle] Ihaia went to Honolulu as a laborer but decided to train and study as a pastor. He met Patisepa, who was servant to an American couple called Pinamu. That's how they met. He was ordained and returned to Atafu and brought Patisepa with him. She was from Tapitoua in Kiribati.

Patisepa was a great dancer, a beautiful singer, she had a beautiful voice. For Kiribati dance you get a small mat on your knee, then... could she dance! How marvelous it was when she danced, and she was very good in music and had a wonderful voice. She always sang in Kiribati language.

I don't remember Ihaia so well, but I can remember when he was going over the lagoon he would pick me up and put me on the canoe, and give me a coconut. When he came back from a fishing trip he would give me a raw fish or flying fish. When Ihaia died Patisepa married Ielemia. It was through Ielemia that I acquired knowledge of things-Tokelau. In my younger days I didn't bother, but when Ielemia died some of the things he had told me came back to me. But most of them were lost.[1]

Among the "things-Tokelau" to which Ihaia refers are the traditional fisherman's knowledge of moon, tides, and winds and the traditional tales, *kakai*, told for entertainment. He is a consummate performer of these tales, and they are often the inspiration for his *fatele*, "action song compositions."

Judith Huntsman, who recorded traditional tales told by Ihaia in 1968, remarks that "three of the 10 tales which Ihaia told have to do with a protagonist who decimates the inhabitants, ogre or human, of some village or island and takes over the land for himself" (1977:138). This perhaps reflects a fact of Ihaia's adult life which is also apparent from the autobiography above, namely that his status in Nukunonu has been that of an "immigrant" or "landless" person. In the Tokelau Islands, people inherit land from their families, so an immigrant has no land rights. Ihaia had access to his wife's family land in Nukunonu, but his own family land is in Atafu. During his adult years in Nukunonu, Ihaia built a reputation as a more than ordinarily fine fisherman, a skilled canoe maker, an expert in traditional lore, and a keen leader in communal work. These, together with his activities as a composer, are all activities outside the responsibilities and concerns of land-holding. Ihaia mentions this landless status in a *mako*, or "love song":[2]

---

[1] Interview extracts are composites from two taped interviews carried out in January and March 1989 by Tuia and Thomas, with translation by Tuia. The tape cassettes of the original interviews are lodged in the Asia Pacific Archive School of Music, Victoria University of Wellington, and in the New Zealand Music Archive, National Library of New Zealand, Wellington.

[2] As the orthography of the Tokelau language only became standardized in 1986 with the publication of the first dictionary, some irregularities may be expected in the song texts published here. In addition, some Tokelauans write Tokelauan song texts in Samoan. Texts in this article are in Samoan, Tokelauan, and Tuvaluan. Long vowels are not indicated. The translations attempt to convey what is understood by these short songs rather than simply translate the words. Translations are by Tuia, except for the first song quoted and the last three, which are from the UNESCO Territorial Survey of Oceanic Music, 1986 (Thomas 1988) and were translated by Kotelano Kele.

> Toku vaka e toku se alofa e
> Oku vae ka fatifati ki salasalaga kia koe.
> Maua i Motuhaga e fifili oma fou
> Fifili fakatahi ma te pua talotalo.
> Sea sea sea e kita si matua e
> E ke iloa foki i au se fakaalofa.

> My love, I didn't give you true love
> I am worn out looking for you.
> I found you weaving at Motuhaga
> Making leis of pua and talotalo flowers.
> Why why why [do you love me], I am old,
> You know I am a poor man.

Because of his great-aunt's upbringing Ihaia knows the Kiribati language, and he has learned other languages from visitors to Nukunonu. He composes most often in Tokelauan and Tuvaluan, but also in Samoan and Kiribati. While his skill with languages is notable, it is common for Tokelauans to be bilingual or trilingual.[3] Language itself, and difficulties with communication, are a common theme in the atoll society, appearing in the hilarious *faleaitu*, "dramatic skits." In these performances some participants portray foreigners who speak a gibberish that provokes gales of laughter from the onlookers. In such dramatic entertainments the foreign-sounding nonsense, with a few Tokelauan swear-words thrown in for effect, is mostly an imitation of the languages of Korean and Japanese fishermen who have visited the islands.

Tokelauan Song: Change and Continuity

In secular contemporary Tokelauan music there are three main genres: *fatele*, "action song"; *mako*, "love song"; and *pehelagilagi*, "choral song." *Fatele* are the major form of the three, and generally celebrate aspects of Tokelau life and the environment: fishing, history, traditional tales, biblical stories, current events. The *fatele* are distinguished by their epigrammatic brevity; a story or incident is not told, but only indicated by the song text. This brief *fatele* by Ihaia, for example, is drawn from the traditional tale of the *fahua* clam (Huntsman 1980:51-53). In it Hina is calling on her mother, who is transformed into a clam, to come to dance for the chief Tinilau. The drama or emotions of the situation are not elaborated in the short *fatele*, and can only be understood by those who know the background:

---

[3] Linguist Even Hovdaugen gives the opinion of Ihaia's Tokelauan speech that "phonetically he has undoubtedly developed his own style by exaggerating the 'dark' character of Atafu pronunciation and combining it with phonetic aspects of colloquial Samoan.... I think that this is done to create a specific artistic, maybe archaic impression on the audience. But in other respects his language is not archaic at all. I would rather characterize it as modern and colloquial" (personal communication 1.18.89).

> Amutia mua koe e mamoe te fahua e
> Kako kita nei e he mamoe te fahua e.
> Taeao te fakatinoga o ilamutu e
> Taeao te fakatinoga o matua e.
>
> *Fahua* [clam] you are lucky to be sleeping,
> But I can't sleep like the *fahua*.
> Tomorrow the children perform,
> Tomorrow the parents perform.

Similarly, with *fatele* drawn from the Bible, a story may not be made explicit but only brought to mind. The story of Noah is a favorite in *fatele*, with the fact of the "boat" being grounded causing considerable amusement:

> E ia Noa
> Kua nofo i tona vaka
> Kua kasa i te mauga.
> Talofa ia Noa
> Kua kasa i te mauga.
> Ta la la.
>
> Look at Noah
> Stuck on his boat
> Grounded on the mountain.
> Poor Noah,
> Grounded on the mountain.
> Tut tut tut.

The composer exercises his skill first in the selection of an incident that captures the imagination, and then in the economy and precision of his text. It must be remembered too that his short text is appreciated in actual performance rather than through reading. A *fatele* begins with the text sung slowly, unadorned by the dance. As the text is repeated dance movements are added (some of which highlight aspects of the text), the tempo accelerates, and other music and dance intensification creates an exhilarating experience. The repetitions of the text provide opportunities for enjoyment and contemplation of its message and craftsmanship. Typically a group of thirty or more dancers performs a *fatele* in rectangular formation in lines of men or women, with a group of drummers and singers sitting behind them. For a formal performance a *fatele* will have been rehearsed and a uniform costume for the group will have been made. But *fatele* can be sung informally as well, for example during work, at a cricket match, or on a journey. Formally or informally sung, a *fatele* mobilizes a group and unites them in the presentation of a song. The *fatele* is truly the "national" song, frequently heard and with a large repertoire that is continually being increased.

The *mako*, "love song," is quite different. It is a solo song which is mostly sung on solitary pursuits such as fishing or climbing a coconut palm to collect the juice—when the song is said to sweeten the drink. The text is private and romantic, and the only time it is likely to be heard in public is at weddings, when a *mako* teases the groom or compliments the bride. On these occasions the *mako* is led by a solo singer, with a group repeating each line after the leader. The only dancing involved is improvised by the leader.

The *pehelagilagi*, the third major contemporary form, is a song with a much longer text with several sections. The form originated in the Samoan *laulausiva*, "introductory *siva*," and it follows the conventional pattern of Samoan oratory (sections of welcome, thanks to God, reference to the departed, message for the gathering). *Pehelagilagi* are composed in Tokelau to mark special occasions.[4] For the performance of a *pehelagilagi* there is a seated choral group with a standing "conductor" who interprets the text to the audience with improvised gestures. Ihaia does not compose *pehelagilagi*, although there are Tokelau composers who create both them and the shorter *fatele*.

Of these three contemporary forms the *fatele* is by far the most common and the best loved. While it is acknowledged to be of Tuvaluan origin, it has been composed and performed in Tokelau since at least the beginning of the century, long enough for it to have become thoroughly Tokelauan. Ihaia observes: "As time passed Tokelau just carried on until they came to create their own *fatele*, and now the Ellice [=Tuvalu] people are saying the Tokelau *fatele* is more interesting and beautiful than theirs."

Ihaia has also remarked that in *fatele* in the early days the dance gestures, *taga*, could be "as you like," not choreographed and uniform for the whole group.[5] A feature of the performances today of which he is critical is the playing of the *pokihi*, or box drum. He says that the acceleration in the *fatele* that the *pokihi* leads should occur much more gradually. (This feature, as he also notes, marks the Tokelau *fatele* as different from its Tuvaluan counterpart.) In addition, he notes that when the dance moves from the slow to fast tempo the pitch often goes too high, and the people cannot sing it properly. In addition to such performance differences between the Tokelauan and Tuvaluan *fatele*, there are differences in theme and subject. These too have changed over time:

> In my younger days, as far as I can remember most of the *fatele* were from Bible stories. I can't remember any about *kakai* [tales] or traditional dances, all were Bible *fatele*. The composers [in Atafu] were Temusu, Temo, Lua, Tanielu [the Samoan pastor for 28 years], and Tai. Mostly old people.

At the time of Ihaia's arrival in Nukunonu a group of younger people were responsible for *fatele* composition, a fact which may indicate a later adoption of the *fatele* in Nukunonu. These composers were Ihaia's wife Selina, Niu, Lui Kena, and Atonio, all on the Amelika side of the Nukunonu village. There was probably rivalry as well as collaboration within this group, and there are distinct differences of style and emphasis among the composers. For example, Atonio's compositions are often extremely abbreviated:

---

[4] A related choral form, *viki*, is often used for commemorative songs for a person who has died. It lacks the Samoan oratory form of the *pehelagilagi*.

[5] Tuia Aselemo and Ana Tuia confirm this.

E e e te mavaega
A Tavita ma Ionatana.

Oh the farewell
Of David and Jonathan.

Here a contemporary farewell, perhaps to families moving away from the island to live in New Zealand, is likened to the grief expressed in the biblical story. Ihaia's *fatele* on the same theme makes the comparison explicit:

Te faigata ote alofa
Ko tatou ka mavae
Na iloa e Tavita ma Ionatana.

The deep love
Of our parting;
Like David and Jonathan.

Another active composer was Ihaia's wife Selina, who died in 1987. Her *fatele* often emphasize the domestic, as in this example located in Talikilagi, the center of Nukunonu village:

Te matagi agi mai e agi malie e
Te namo kua likiliki e.
E nofo au i Talikilagi toko lotu kua
Pupu ite alofa e.

The wind blowing softly
The lagoon so calm.
There I wait at Talikilagi
My heart full of love.

Composition

Ihaia's composition sometimes involved an element of collaboration. He says of his wife Selina:

I worked with Selina. Sometimes I would get into difficulties and would say "Could you listen and watch this *fatele*?" Or I would make the tune and Selina the words. I am missing her, we worked together a lot in *fatele* making.

Another kind of collaboration is reported of Ihaia; he has been known to sing a *fatele* to someone and tell them to remember it and bring it to a group rehearsal. This is not usual for Tokelau composers, but it is a feature of traditional composing in some nearby areas.[6] It is intriguing that this use of a composer's

---

[6] Composer's assistants are a feature of certain kinds of Kiribati and Fijian composition; see Laxton 1953 and Saumaiwai 1980.

assistant occurs in Kiribati, and that Ihaia had a Kiribati stepmother, but rather than explaining his habit as an "inheritance" from his upbringing it is probably better to observe that Ihaia seems to have a fertile imagination and the ability to compose songs rapidly, but not a retentive memory: he often needs to be prompted or reminded of a *fatele*.

In discussing the compositon of *fatele* Ihaia also explains his own personal contribution:

> When I begin a *fatele*, I don't think or worry about it, it will come naturally. No guessing or uncertainty, I will just pick it up. For the words: a bit here, a bit there, a bit here, a bit there, and . . . got one! The *fatele* can be about fishing or the wind, or from a Samoan *siva*, or a Tuvaluan song. There is nothing difficult about creating a Tokelau *fatele*. Once the words are in my head the tune is also already there. What I am telling you is that when I make a *fatele* it is like a movie: if I do one there is another ready in my head; I present one and there is another—like looking into a book. More words, more ideas keep coming into my mind. It is a gift of God, there is nothing about it which is difficult for me. It is quite simple to create a *fatele*, the more you do it the easier it is.

Here Ihaia is speaking as a prolific and outstanding composer, but he is also aware of others' difficulties and has often criticized or guided other composers' compositions.

There is another kind of *fatufatele* (*fatele* composition) in Tokelau which is not original work by an individual *pulotu* but collaborative work. In this type members of a performing group, or an individual, may put together familiar lines or alter an existing *fatele* to suit an occasion. In the Lower Hutt suburb of Naenae, Ihaia's daughter Meli made a *fatele* of this kind for a wedding in 1982. The song bids farewell to the bridegroom; the second and fifth lines have phrases common in *fatele*:

> Taku manamea Pio,
> E he galo i te loto
> A ta mahaniga
> A ta nofonofoga.
> Pio e he galo i Naenae.
>
> My loving Pio,
> Never in my heart will be forgotten
> Our relationship,
> Our life.
> Pio will never be forgotten in Naenae.

Such *fatele* can have a slightly disjointed feel to them, as lines have been borrowed from other songs and are known elsewhere. However, they are ideal occasional pieces, quickly learned because of their familiarity.

Frequently, too, *fatele* are reworkings of old Tokelau song types (*tafoe, hiva, hahaka, tagi*). Often here the text remains the same or is shortened, but the music and choreography are new. Ihaia recommends this procedure as a way of starting *fatele* composition. Several of his songs are such reworkings, particularly of the *tagi*, short songs sung in the course of telling traditional tales, or *kakai*. Because such songs are heightened moments in the tales, often revealing the denouement of the story, they make ideal *fatele*. While such compositions may not seem to an outsider to be very original, the composer is selecting from an enormous range of old songs and tales. One of the effects of such songs is to popularize these tales and old songs and to remind listeners of their contemporary relevance.

Ihaia's Songs

Ihaia's earliest *fatele* was composed in 1931 during his first year in Nukunonu. It was composed for a specific occasion, a farewell to Samoan builders on the completion of the community's large church building, and consists mainly of the names of those who are about to leave:

> Faamavaega
> Ma Falaniko, Pepe,
> Punefu, Taemoa.
> Tofaina koutou.

> Farewell
> Falaniko, Pepe,
> Punefu, Taemoa.
> Goodbye to all of you.

In contrast to this brief piece are his later works with developed imagery. While many of the *fatele* quoted in this study are derived from old songs and tales, the two examples below draw instead upon the community and the natural world. First, *Tiga te pouli*:

> Tiga te pouli kautatago tiga te agi o te timu-a-toga
> Kako au e fitoi atu ke pa atu kia te koe.
> Agi mai te laki momoka mai ma ua
> Oi aue toku tino kua tatapa i te makalilia.

> However dark the night, however strong the *timu-a-toga* wind
> I will still try to reach you.
> The *laki* wind is coming, the rain is falling
> And my body is shaking with the cold.

This song, composed in 1983, is a strikingly original *fatele* in its use of the names of the two hurricane winds (the second one, the *laki*, is the stronger of these), and in the graphic image of a person searching for his or her lover. *Fatele* are seldom about such individual passions; they are most frequently community expressions of joy and solidarity. The few that communicate such emotions as grief at a parting are presented as belonging to incidents in traditional tales or biblical stories, as in the case of the songs about David and Jonathan quoted above. In speaking of strictly personal matters in *Tiga te pouli*, Ihaia is bringing into the communal dance of the *fatele* the more private world of the *mako*.

This private, hidden world is also referred to cryptically in a *mako* by Ihaia. The poet speaks of a house in which he has met his lover; the identity of the woman and the house remain concealed:

> Ta toku nemu ta i te gasu e
> Te gasu e tautafa pito ki te ala e.
> Na vau o kisi mai e kisi faka loiloi
> Kisi lomilomi kisi faka mavae
> I au e ki, oi au, ke!
>
> Write my name on that house,
> The house at the roadside.
> Give me a playful kiss
> More kisses, kiss goodbye.
> Oh my dear!

In a much more conventional mode is a *fatele* from 1970-71. Composed in collaboration with Dr. and Mrs. Simeona, this is a conventional celebration of the elders and the elected leaders (Faipule, Pulenuku) who provide a model for the community, a position maintained not without strain in the modern world. Although the sentiments are conventional, the *fatele* itself is a forthright statement and it is arresting in performance; the dance movements, the melody, and the words are all powerfully dramatic. This outstanding *fatele* is a eulogy of traditional ways and an expression of support for the community.

> E taku fatele
> Tenei ka uhu o faka—
> Fakamatala toku nuku fagahele.
> Te Faipule, Pulenuku ma Toeaina
> E he galo koe i toku loto.
> E tu ve he ata ioku mua
> I au faifaiga gali katoa.
>
> Look! My *fatele*
> That I am singing you now,
> Explains the beauty of my village.
> My Faipule and Pulenuku and my elders
> I'll never forget you in my heart.
> You are like a reflection in a mirror
> With your beautiful way of life.

Ownership and Anonymity

There are two features of the work of a *pulotu*, or composer, which are distinctively Tokelauan and need to be emphasized: the lack of "ownership" controls over the finished composition, and the composer's "anonymity" at the time of performance. When a *fatele* is performed at a gathering it becomes common property, and anyone who hears it may perform it elsewhere. In doing so these others may make changes to the *fatele* either unintentionally or intentionally, and create a different version of it. The original composer and the performing group have no control over when the work will be performed, or over the versions of it which may be made.[7] If a distorted version has been performed, all the *pulotu* can do is teach a correct version for a subsequent performance. Clearly "ownership" is not a feature of the Tokelau system—unlike in Samoa, for example, where a village commissions and pays for a song (Moyle 1988:14), and in Tonga, where the composer of a major commission is identified with the work and largely controls its performance.[8] Ihaia says:

---

[7] Changes to the dance actions and melody are accepted; it is changes to the text of a *fatele* that can cause concern. Such changes can easily occur when a word is spread over a number of notes of the melody and the syllables are perceived as separate words.

[8] In Tonga, once a composition has been given to a village it remains their dance and whenever they revive it they will attempt to recreate the original, often by asking the original choreographer (*punake*) to prepare the performance (Wendy Pond, personal communication).

> A lot of *fatele* that I have composed have been distorted. I feel unhappy because I directed and taught the *fatele*, but they changed it. At a dance practice I can stand up and say the tune is like this, the action like this. Then they must hold onto it, otherwise I wouldn't want to come back to the dancing practice again.

At the performance of his work the Tokelau *pulotu* is in a significant way "anonymous." His name will never be announced at a performance, either beforehand or in the elder's remarks at the end of an event. Everyone will know who the *pulotu* is, especially if the song is a new one, but it will never be publicly mentioned (whereas in the Cook Islands, for example, a composer may be announced before a dance is performed).

This habit of strict anonymity for the Tokelau *pulotu* is not easily explained. When a new *fatele* is being rehearsed the *pulotu* is center stage; he drives the group, he makes them get the song right, he corrects the dancers. Then at the moment of the performance he "disappears;" as a member of the performing group or the audience, he will not in his demeanor indicate his earlier role. Tokelauans have not explained this feature of their music, but the situation could be likened to other co-operative enterprises (Thomas 1986:92):

> When a group prepares food for a feast, or goes on a fishing expedition, in neither case is it appropriate for the individual to be acknowledged (who caught the most fish, or who cooked a special dish) though of course the participants are aware of the identity of such people. A public acknowledgement of their special contribution would diminish the collective achievement. This was brought home to me at a meal with the dancing group when I inadvertently asked a member of the group if the fish we were eating were those caught by him in a fishing expedition that he had been recounting. My remark caused embarrassment and unease. It was acceptable to talk about individual activities (fishing, shopping, cooking) but not to *individualize* the feast itself which was a group product.

In creating the songs which will be presented by the community, the *pulotu* is a contributor to a group effort. If the similarity with other co-operative enterprises is accepted, it can be seen as appropriate that the *pulotu* will be "anonymous" like other contributors. Indeed, at a celebration there will be a feast as well as music, with speeches, *fatele*, and food all included in the festivity, and members of the hosting group specializing in particular tasks—making the performers' costumes, or gathering gifts for the visitors, or preparing food. None will be identified separately for their contribution.

The balancing of individual contributions against group cohesion is a particular feature of the small-scale Tokelau society. Leadership, apart from the authority exercised by the elders, customarily falls to the best person for the job, and is a temporary prerogative while that occupation lasts. A general social equality is emphasized; *maopopo*, unity of purpose and action, is a key cultural value. Yet although there are no gifts in payment for compositions, and the composer is not acknowledged at the time of performance, in the Tokelaus a talent for composition is recognized in individuals. Like a talent for fishing, weaving, or carving, skill in composition is acknowledged especially in a person's later years, when skill and talent are matched with experience and achievement.

Conclusion

In these small-scale communities *pulotu* are *individually* known, and their works are enhanced by their public personality.[9] This is strikingly so in the case of Ihaia. As we have endeavored to indicate, Ihaia at this stage of his life is a commanding presence, an engaging and humorous speaker, yet inclined to willful behavior. This image of him is most completely revealed in his speeches of admonition at community gatherings and in his recounting of humorous tales. Although this profile has not covered other aspects of his life such as his expertise as a fisherman, his talents as a woodcarver, his family relations, and so on, all these probably have a bearing on his composition. They provide subjects for his compositions and are part of the social context in which the *fatele* are received and understood.

Fatele, as we have outlined, are an extremely abbreviated and allusive song form; they gain their significance and meaning from their text associations and their context at the time of performance. That meaning includes the community's familiarity with the composer himself. The resonances of the *fatele* are thus not only textual and contextual but include also the attitudes and personality of the *pulotu*, who has left his mark on his compositions in a way that the community who know him will identify.[10]

References

Clifford 1978   James Clifford. "Hanging up Looking Glasses at Odd Corners: Ethnobiographical Prospects." In *Studies in Biography*. Cambridge, MA: Harvard University Press. pp. 41-56.

---

[9] We have used the term "individual" mindful of the cautions in Shore (1982:133-49) that European and non-European cultures have different views of the person, and in Clifford (1978) that "life-writers" should make more open-ended ethnic life studies rather than creating biographies in the European mode.

[10] The two authors have contributed complementary views: one as performer on many occasions, sometimes as group leader, and "nephew" of the composer, and the other as ethnomusicologist and researcher. Work on this profile was carried out in the early months of 1989 but has built on previous work, especially Thomas 1988, supported by UNESCO and the New Zealand Lottery Board; Thomas 1986; and a collaboration between Tuia and Thomas (forthcoming; supported by the Internal Research Committee, Victoria University of Wellington, and the Maori and South Pacific Arts Council). The authors would also like to acknowledge the hospitality and assistance of Ihaia's daughter Meli and her husband Avito, and the generous cooperation of Ihaia himself. The photographs are by John Casey, University Photographer, Victoria University of Wellington.

Finnegan 1977   Ruth Finnegan. *Oral Poetry: Its Nature, Significance
                           and Social Context*. Cambridge: Cambridge
                           University Press.

Hooper and Huntsman   Anthony Hooper and Judith Huntsman.   "A
    1973   Demographic History of the Tokelau Islands." *Journal
                           of the Polynesian Society*, 82:366-411.

Huntsman 1977   Judith Huntsman. *Ten Tokelau Tales*. Auckland:
                           Working Paper 47, Department of Anthropology,
                           University of Auckland.

Huntsman 1980   _____. *Tokelau Tales*. Auckland: Working Paper 58,
                           Department of Anthropology, University of Auckland.

Kaeppler 1988   Adrienne L. Kaeppler. "The Production and
                           Reproduction of Social and Cultural Values in the
                           Compositions of Queen Salote of Tonga."
                           Unpublished paper presented at the first meeting of the
                           Oceanic Study Group of the International Council for
                           Traditional Music. Deakin University, September 3-5.

Laxton 1953   P. B. Laxton. "A Gilbertese Song." *Journal of the
                           Polynesian Society*, 62:342-47.

Moyle 1988   Richard Moyle. *Traditional Samoan Music*.
                           Auckland: Auckland University Press.

Saumaiwai 1980   Chris Saumaiwai. "Melanesia 2: Fiji." In *The New
                           Grove Dictionary of Music and Musicians*. Ed. by
                           Stanley Sadie. London: Macmillan. pp. 82-85.

Shore 1982   Bradd Shore. *Sala'ilua, A Samoan Mystery*. New
                           York: Columbia University Press.

Thomas 1986   Allan Thomas. "The Fatele of Tokelau: Approaches to
                           the Study of a Dance in its Social Context." M.A.
                           thesis, Department of Anthropology, Victoria
                           University of Wellington.

Thomas 1988   _____. *Report on Survey of Music in Tokelau Western
                           Polynesia*. Auckland: Working Paper 79, Department
                           of Anthropology, University of Auckland.

Tokelau Dictionary   Anon. *Tokelau Dictionary*. Apia, Western Samoa:
    1987   Office of Tokelau Affairs.

VII

FICTION, FACT, AND IMAGINATION: A TOKELAU NARRATIVE

Judith Huntsman

Some years ago I read and later published (1981a) a short paper proposing that Polynesian oral narratives be viewed as creative art rather than sacrosanct "tradition," and that this change in perspective called for a very different approach to the study of narratives. Instead of seeking the authentic "tradition," scholars would listen to and record many renderings of the same narrative (or similar narratives) and talk about them with their tellers and audiences. I concluded (221): "If we listen to the same 'tale' again and again, finding it always different, and appreciate these variations, we will be celebrating creativity." This proposal arose from my own studies of Tokelau narratives but was largely motivated by my disquiet with the veneration of "tradition" by Polynesianists and Polynesians at the expense of creativity (cf. Wendt 1983).

What follows is one outcome of following my own prescription.[1] By way of several versions of a rather intriguing narrative, I explore the distinction between "fact" and "fiction" in Tokelau narrative. Although the primary question has to do with the status of the "narrated event," it entails consideration of the "narrative texts" and "narrative events" (see Bauman 1986), and also consultation with the tellers.

Fact and Fiction

Tokelau raconteurs normally preface a narrative by declaring either "I shall relate the *kakai* of..." or "I shall relate the *tala* of...," and end it by at least announcing either "The *kakai* is finished" or "The *tala* is finished." As well as

---

1 That prescription of course was not my unique concoction; it drew upon recent work on performance (Bauman 1977), context (Ben-Amos 1972), and creativity (Finnegan 1970), as well as a rather neglected essay by Paul Radin (1915).

framing the narrative, these statements tell and remind the audience what kind of narrative it is, and how it is to be appreciated or judged.

A *kakai*, here glossed "tale," is a fictitious narrative told to entertain. An accomplished raconteur enhances a tale's entertainment value by choice of words and phrases, by pacing, pause, mimicry and intonation, and so forth. An audience judges a particular rendering of a tale primarily in terms of performance, and rarely is a performer faulted for embellishing well-known episodes and even adding bits to the tale. Of course most of the audience knows the tale, so the rendering should fulfill their expectations. Chants, songs, and key phrases spoken by protagonists should be repeated exactly as they are known, even though their meaning may be somewhat opaque. A performance may be criticized if the raconteur deletes an episode—a *potu kakai* ("part of the tale") has been forgotten—or leaves out a linking transition between episodes so that the tale does not *hohoko* ("hang together"). In short, raconteurs of *kakai* have a good deal of latitude to elaborate or play with their text to entertain their audiences, but their performances are marred if they fail to include what their listeners expect. They may add, but they should not forget.

A *tala*, here glossed "account," tells of something that reputedly did happen at some time from *i te kaloā* ("in the beginning") to *i te ahonei* ("in the present day, recently"). I am concerned here with *tala* ascribed to a generalized past that should faithfully recount past happenings.[2] These are what are variously labeled myths, legends, historical narratives, oral traditions, and so forth by scholars; Tokelauans call them *tala anamua* ("accounts of the past"), which have been transmitted from their pre-Christian forebears, from one generation to the next, as true and accurate. *Tala* are told less widely and less frequently than *kakai*, and, although they may indeed be entertaining, their purpose is to inform. What they impart is knowledge, or intimations of knowledge, and they are judged in terms of their content. The issue is whether the raconteur has recounted the narrative accurately; the listeners' judgments are of course based on what they know as the correct account. If something is left out, it is usually regarded as a memory lapse, which may be either remedied by a tactful comment or simply disregarded by listeners who know better. However, any recognized addition or change is viewed with suspicion, for it is assumed that the *tala* has been tampered with for some reason, and, even if there is no apparent motive, one is suspected. Consequently, raconteurs are apt to be cautious about relating *tala*, both in how they tell them and to whom they tell them. They may delete bits they know are controversial, for it is better to appear forgetful than to seem devious—unless one wants to provoke controversy.

---

2 Narrators are granted a good deal of freedom of exaggeration in their *tala* of recent events, which are sometimes acted out at public gatherings. The responses of their audiences, some of whom have witnessed the events, encourage this elaboration. What really happened may become the mere kernel for a hilarious farce, which is constrained only by the fact that it may compromise real relationships. Some of these acted-out *tala* become set pieces. Hypothetically, recent *tala* should in time become "accounts of the past" and an analysis of this transition would be an intriguing study. (See Huntsman and Hooper 1975:415ff for examples.)

I have used the most neutral English lexemes—"tale" and "account"—to gloss the Tokelau terms *kakai* and *tala*, respectively, for it makes little sense to try to assign them to some more specific foreign category or genre (cf. Burridge 1969:197-98). Tokelauan has no term which subsumes them both; I use "narrative" as a neutral non-differentiating term. The Tokelau lexical distinction is in no way unusual in Polynesian languages; in Tikopia there are *kkai* and *tara*, in Tongan *fananga* and *tala*, in Samoan *fagōgō* and *tala*, in Futuna *fananga* and *fakamatala*, all of which roughly correspond to Tokelau *kakai* and *tala*. What the salient contrastive attributes of each are may vary from place to place, and whether a particular narrative is one or the other may be debatable in some instances. The important point is that a distinction is made and the relevant inquiry is "what is the difference" (rather than what foreign genre is each most like). Tokelauans are very clear about the matter: *kakai* should be *mālie* ("entertaining") and *tala* should be *hako* ("right, straight"), not *hehē* ("wrong") or *piko* ("crooked"). Since raconteurs always preface their narratives by identifying them as *kakai* or *tala*, any collection of Tokelau narratives may be confidently divided into their two genres.

Indeed, I did just that when recording in the field and soon thereafter decided to first attend to the *kakai*.[3] Sometime later, when I was well acquainted with the tales, I happened to play a tape labeled *tala* and immediately recognized the narrative as a version of a *kakai*. It was not a case of mislabeling; the raconteur introduced it as a *tala*. Furthermore, it is the only instance I know of where versions have been presented as both,[4] so there is no reason to question the Tokelau distinction between *tala* and *kakai*. Rather I take this instance as an opportunity to explore specifically what marks a narrative as a *tala* rather than a *kakai* and to raise questions about the relationship between them, questions which impinge upon the old debate about the degeneration and creation of folk narratives. But before beginning I should provide some context.

---

[3] Most of the narratives were tape-recorded between 1968 and 1971. The performance contexts were structured to the extent that it was arranged during the day that I would be present at some named place in the evening with a tape recorder and so would one or more raconteurs. Venues varied and so did the size and composition of the audience. The situations were "natural" but the performances were not wholly spontaneous, and the sessions often attracted additional audiences and other raconteurs. Listeners were urged by others to tell "their *kakai*" and all narratives offered were recorded. Narrators frequently proposed a *kakai*, asking if I had already recorded it. I always urged them to tell it even when I honestly admitted that I had previously recorded it, and they usually did. Several *kakai* were even recorded from the same raconteur on different occasions. The corpus includes about 150 texts, and, excluding repeats, about 80 items. The texts were transcribed by native speakers and then checked back against the tapes by me. I take responsibility for the translations, although I consulted with English-speaking Tokelauans. They, however, could rarely explain meanings which escaped me, so for these I consulted the raconteurs, none of whom spoke English. I have come across no cognates of the Taetagaloa narrative in published collections, though I have not made an exhaustive search. Since most well-known Tokelau *kakai* have cognates elsewhere in Polynesia, this is notable.

[4] Whether a particular text is a version of another or a quite different narrative is debatable in some instances, but not, I think, here.

Tokelau consists of three atolls—Atafu, Nukunonu, and Fakaofo—located north of the Samoan archipelago, east of the Tuvalu atolls, south of the Phoenix atolls, and west of the northern Cook atolls. Some facts about Tokelau pertinent to this paper are: (1) it is tiny in size and population (the total land area is about 12.2 sq. km. and the largest population ever recorded was 1900); (2) the three atolls are well out of sight and not within easy voyaging distance of one another; (3) Tokelauans speak a distinctive Polynesian language and have a common ancestral and cultural heritage; (4) yet, the separate atoll populations are largely endogamous and assert their social distinctiveness; (5) in the 1860s Tokelauans became Christians, in particular Atafuans became London Missionary Society Protestants and the people of Nukunonu Society of Mary Catholics; and (6) on each atoll there is one clearly bounded, densely organized, and tightly controlled village community.[5]

Narratives of Taetagaloa/Tae-a-tagaloa

I first recorded a *kakai* about Taetagaloa[6] as Kave told it one evening in Nukunonu. He introduced it as "The Tale of Kui and Fakataka," but I recognized it as a version of "The Story of Tae-a-tagaloa" published by Gordon Macgregor (1937:85-86) that had been told to him, through an interpreter, by Mika at Atafu in 1932. Mika died in 1935 having, it is said, reached his 100th year, and it was from his daughter, Lili, and his grandson, Ioane, on separate occasions that I recorded at Atafu "The Tale of Tae-a-tagaloa," which they both said they had learned from Mika. I have no reason to doubt their assertion that they learned the narrative from Mika. Others of his children and grandchildren have been raconteurs of some reputation telling many of the same narratives, although each renders them somewhat differently. But this was sometime after Palehau had told me his "Account of Taetagaloa" at Nukunonu. He emphasized that it was a *tala* and I failed to realize that it was a version of Kave's *kakai*.[7]

---

5 For further ethnographic and historical information about Tokelau see Hooper 1985; Huntsman 1971, 1981b; Hooper and Huntsman 1973; and Huntsman and Hooper 1975, 1976, 1985.

6 The focal character of the narrative is named either Taetagaloa or Tae-a-tagaloa. If the latter, Tagaloa, the ubiquitous Sky God/father of Polynesia, has a role, and the Tae-a-tagaloa, literally "Tagaloa's shit," is bestowed by him. Henceforth I shall refer to the narrative as that of Taetagaloa.

7 For simplicity I refer to the Tokelau raconteurs by a single name. Their full names are Alosio Kave Ineleo, Manuele Palehau Leone, Lili Fakaalofa, Mika Tinilau, and Ioane Toma.

Aloisio Kave Ineleo, 1968

Here I provide the Tokelau texts and English translations of three versions of the narrative of Taetagaloa. The first two are from Nukunonu—Kave's *kakai* and Palehau's *tala*—and serve as the main texts for the discussion that follows. The last is Lili's rendition, which stands for all three Atafu versions and which I chose because it is most like her father's, of which there is no Tokelau text. The reason for its inclusion will become apparent in due course.

An exhaustive analysis and interpretation of the texts is not undertaken here, although a few explanatory notes are appended to each and an overview of the narrative is provided to facilitate the discussion that follows. That discussion addresses two issues: (1) what makes Palehau's narrative a *tala*, and (2) what is the relationship between the two narratives told contemporaneously at Nukunonu, one as a *tala* and the other as a *kakai*. The story is about an importuning loner who exhibits extraordinary abilities, first as a craftsman, then as a fisherman, and finally as a man endowed with supernatural knowledge and power.

The Narratives

Narrative 1 (by Kave)

KO TE KAKAI O KUI MA FAKATAKA

E i ei te tahi ulugaalī nae nonofo i te tahi fenua, ko Kui ma Fakataka. Nonofo nonofo te ulugaalī kua manava kīkī ia Fakataka. Oi olo ai lā kua fia olo ki te tahi fenua—olo ai. Fano fano lava te vaka, agi ai te matagi, kua hou te moana, goto ai te vaka. Oti ai ia Kui ka kua kaukau ia Fakataka. Kakau kakau ia Fakataka, ake ki te tahi fenua. Fano ai oi nofo i te papa i nā tāfeta i te papa, oi fānau ai tana tama, he tamaiti tāne. Oi fakaigoa ai kia Taetagaloa. Kua fanau lā te pepe kae lele mai te tuli oi tū mai i te papa. Oi fakaigoa ai lā e te fafine iē tahi itūtino o te tamaiti kua kamata i te igoa o te tuli: tuliulu, tulilima, tulivae.

Olo ai ki gāuta i te fenua. Tauhi tauhi te tamaiti kua matua, kua mafai ona fano oi tāfao. Fanatu nei i te aho nei kua hōhō atu, kua mamao heleka atu ma to lā fale, oi hau ki to lā fale. Fai fai lava kua matua lele te tamaiti oi fano kua tāfao mamao atu ma te mea e nonofo ai. Fanatu e fai mai te gāluega a te tahi tamana ma tona ataliki. Ko Likāvaka te igoa o te tamana—he tufuga, ka ko tona ataliki ko Kuikava. Fanatu loa lava ia Taetagaloa oi tū mai i te ika o te vaka kae lea—kae fai vē tana kupu: "Ko te vaka e piko." Meākē ko Likāvaka kua ita ki te kupu a te tamaiti. Lea atu ia Likāvaka: "Ko ai lava koe kua hau ai koe ke lea mai ko te vaka e piko?" Lea atu ia Taetagaloa: "Hau oi tū atu i kinei oi kikila ko te vaka e piko." Oi fanatu ai ia Likāvaka oi tū mai i te mea nae lea mai ai ia Taetagaloa i te ika o te vaka. Kikila atu e hako ia Taetagaloa, ko te vaka e piko. Toe hehele ai nā tūta o te vaka kae toe fakahako nā lākau. Kua fakahako lā nā lākau. Kua muamua ona toe hauni nā lago, tuku tonu ai nā lākau ki ei, kae fanatu lava ia Kuikava te ataliki o Likāvaka oiū ki luga i te tahi lago. Kae oho atu lava tona tamana ia Likāvaka oi tā tona ataliki ia Kuikava i te toki. Oi oti ai lā ia Kuikava. Fanatu loa lava ia Taetagaloa oi toe fakaola te ataliki o Likāvaka ia Kuikava. Kae toe tuku tonu e ia nā lago ma fehoahoani kia Likāvaka i te faiga o te vaka. Fai fai te vaka—uma.

Ka ko te fenua foki tenā ko te fenua o atu, ka ko te mea e hēai lele ni atu ma na vaka e maua. Kua uma te vaka, kua laga ai e fanatu ka fano ki moana. Fano ai lā ia Taetagaloa kua fano oi kave te vaka o Likāvaka. Fano ai te vaka ālo, fano fano te vaka fetaui ma te inafo. Lea atu te fāoa: "Taetagaloa, tātou fano ki te inafo tēia." Kae lea atu ia Taetagaloa: "Hēai, ko te inafo e kavaifo e ni lakia." Kalaga ai ia Likāvaka: "Ko atu nā, ko atu kukū, ko atu manuheku, ko atu e hēki tiu i te faga o Lākulu." Fano ai te vaka kua tiaki te inafo tēnā kae fano. Fano fano te vaka toe fanaifo foki te inafo. Lea atu te fāoa: "Taetagaloa, tātou fano ki te inafo tēnā." Kae kikila atu foki ia Taetagaloa ko te inafo e kavaifo foki e ni lakia. Kae lea atu foki ia Likāvaka: "Ko atu nā, ko atu kukū, ko atu manuheku, ko atu e hēki tiu i te faga o Lākulu." Fano te vaka e hēki ino ki te taumanu. Fano fano te vaka kae lea atu te fāoa, "Te inafo tēnei e fanaifo!" Kikila atu ia Taetagaloa ko te inafo e kavaifo e nā lefulefu ma te akiaki. Lea atu lava ia Taetagaloa: "Ko atu nā, ko atu manogi, ko atu kakala, ko atu kua tiu i te faga o Lākulu." Fanaifo ai lā te inafo ko hēki pā atu te vaka o Taetagaloa ki te fakamanu ka kua hī ia atu e takafakauli. Hī hī hī ia atu e Taetagaloa, goto te vaka. Hau ki gāuta. Hau ai kua tufa nā atu ki te nuku kua fai te fakahoa.

Nonofo nonofo i te tahi aho meākē nei ko Likāvaka kua fia fano oi folau ki Hāmoa. Fano ai lā te vaka kua fano ki Hāmoa. Kae i ei foki te tagata e vē he hāuai e nofo i Hāmoa ko Likāvaka foki tona igoa. E hē mafai he vaka ke hao ki gāuta. E fanatu lava he vaka ki ei oi tuhi ifo te lima o Likāvaka oi oti te fāoa. Ka ko Taetagaloa foki e i ei ona hāhā, e poto foki i nā mea fakahāuai, e vē foki e i ei hona itū hāuai. Fanatu ai te vaka o Taetagaloa, koi fanatu te vaka kua lata atu ki gāuta, kae lea atu ia Taetagaloa ki tona fāoa: "Ko koutou lava ke uhitaki mai kia te au. Ko te itū e lea atu au ko koutou kalo ki ei kafai e tuhi ifo te tuhi i gāuta a Likāvaka oi kalo ki ei. Nahe tino e kalo kehe kae oti." Fanatu te vaka kae tuhi ifo ia Likāvaka i gāuta o Hāmoa. Kae lea atu ia Taetagaloa: "Kalo ki ama." Kalo te fāoa ki ama, oi hē oti i te tuhi a Likāvaka e fai ifo i gāuta. Toe tuhi ifo ia Likāvaka, lea atu ia Taetagaloa: "Kalo ki katea." Kalo te fāoa ki katea e hē oti foki. Kae vē ake lava te kupu a Likāvaka: "Ko ai nei lava tēnei tagata kua ia faia mai te vaka nei!" Kae kalaga atu ia Likāvaka i gāuta: "Hua." Kae tali mai ia Taetagaloa i gātai:

> Hua ma tukutuku
> Mata-fenua mata-haua
> Kae mulihau ki te katomea—Hua!
> Lauputuputu laumānunu
> Fauhia ki he kaho lakulu
> Ma noa koi tua o manunu—Hua!
> Tū kita i he kava
> Tatalo kita ki he kava niumata
> Keli ake te ika he pālaoa
> E tatao ma te taotao a Makula.

Vēake lava ia Likāvaka: "Ko ai nei tēnei tagata kua ia iloa mai nei oku hāhā nei?"

Fanake fanake lava te vaka kua pā ake ki gāuta kua hē oti te fāoa. Fanake lava. Ko Likāvaka tēnā nofo ifo i gāuta o Hāmoa e vē kua mātaku ia Taetagaloa. Fanatu loa lava ia Taetagaloa fakafetaui ma Likāvaka. Uga ai lā ia Likāvaka ke nofo i te tahi itū o Hāmoa, ka kua nofo ia Taetagaloa i te mea nae nofo ai Likāvaka.

Kua uma ai lā te kakai.

English Translation

THE TALE OF KUI AND FAKATAKA

There is a couple residing in one place named Kui and Fakataka. After the couple stay together for a while Fakataka is pregnant. So they go away because they wish to go to another place—they go. The canoe goes and goes, the wind roars, the sea churns, the canoe sinks. Kui expires while Fakataka swims. Fakataka swims and swims, reaching another land. She goes there and stays on the upraised reef in the freshwater pools on the reef, and there delivers her child, a boy child. She gives him the name Taetagaloa. When the baby is born a golden plover flies over and alights upon the reef. And so the woman thus names various parts of the child beginning with the name "the plover" [*tuli*]: neck [*tuliulu*], elbow [*tulilima*], knee [*tulivae*].

They go inland at the land. The child nursed and tended grows up, is able to go and play. Each day he now goes off a bit further away, moving some distance away from their house, and then returns to their house. So it goes on and the child is fully grown and goes to play far away from the place where they live. He goes over to where some work is being done by a father and son. Likāvaka is the name of the father—a canoe-builder, while his son is Kuikava. Taetagaloa goes right over there and steps forward to the stern of the canoe saying—his words are these: "The canoe is crooked." Instantly Likāvaka is enraged at the words of the child. Likāvaka says: "Who the hell are you to come and tell me that the canoe is crooked?" Taetagaloa replies: "Come and stand over here and see that the canoe is crooked." Likāvaka goes over and stands right at the place Taetagaloa told him to at the stern of the canoe. Looking forward, Taetagaloa is right, the canoe is crooked. He slices through all the lashings of the canoe to straighten the timbers. He realigns the timbers. First he must again position the supports, then place the timbers correctly in them, but Kuikava the son of Likāvaka goes over and stands upon one support. His father Likāvaka rushes right over and strikes his son Kuikava with his adze. Thus Kuikava dies. Taetagaloa goes over at once and brings the son of Likāvaka, Kuikava, back to life. Then he again aligns the supports correctly and helps Likāvaka in building the canoe. Working working it is finished.[8]

As for that land it is a land of skipjack, but the thing is that not a single skipjack is caught by any canoe. The canoe is finished, the canoe is readied to go off to go to sea. Taetagaloa goes in it, goes to direct the canoe of Likāvaka. So the fishing canoe sets off, going going going the canoe encounters a school of skipjack. The crew says: "Taetagaloa, let's go to the school over there." But Taetagaloa replies: "No, black-noddy are marking the school." Likāvaka shouts: "Those skipjack, smelly skipjack, scruffy skipjack, skipjack which have never frolicked in Lākulu's trap."[9] The canoe goes on rejecting that school and going. The canoe goes goes another school appears downwind. The crew says: "Taetagaloa, let's go over to that school of skipjack." Taetagaloa looks over as before, the school is marked by black-noddy too. While Likāvaka speaks as before: "Those skipjack, smelly skipjack, scruffy skipjack, skipjack which have never frolicked in Lākulu's trap." The canoe goes off not entering among the flock of birds. The canoe goes goes and the crew says: "Here the school is being marked!" Taetagaloa looking out sees the school is marked by sanderlings and terns. Taetagaloa speaks out at once: "Those skipjack, fragrant skipjack, biting skipjack, skipjack which frolic in Lākulu's trap." They go right down to the school and before Taetagaloa's canoe reaches the swarming birds the skipjack rise in abundance. Taetagaloa hooks hooks hooks skipjack, swamping the canoe. It

---

[8] Tokelau canoe hulls are constructed of three logs hollowed, shaped, and lashed together upon which irregular timber planks are lashed to build up the sides. Before final shaping the logs are set in supports to hold them in their correct position, so that they can be shaped to one another and lashed.

[9] Schools of skipjack rising to bait-fish are recognized from afar by flocks of birds feeding upon the same tiny fish. The trap (or bay) of Lākulu is an esoteric reference to another *kakai* that relates how a primeval pearlshell lure was recovered from a fishtrap for skipjack set in the sea by the fisherman Lākulu.

returns to shore. Returning there and distributing the skipjack to the village so that all have an equal share.[10]

Staying staying until one day suddenly now Likāvaka wants to go and journey to Samoa. So the canoe goes off going to Samoa. But there is the man who is like an ogre living in Samoa whose name is also Likāvaka. No canoe is able to reach shore safely. A canoe approaches there and Likāvaka's finger points down and the crew expires. As for Taetagaloa he also has some spells, he also is wise about things ogre-like, it seems that he is part-ogre. The canoe of Taetagaloa goes along, the canoe is still going along coming near to shore, when Taetagaloa speaks to his crew: "You all must obey me. The side I tell you that you must dodge to when Likāvaka points down his finger from shore you must dodge there. No one must dodge otherwise or he dies." The canoe approaches and Likāvaka points down from ashore in Samoa. But Taetagaloa says: "Dodge windward." The crew dodges to windward, and is not killed by the pointed finger of Likāvaka ashore. Likāvaka points again, Taetagaloa says: "Dodge to leeward." The crew dodges to leeward and again is not killed. Likāvaka says to himself: "Now just who is this person who directs that canoe?" Likāvaka shouts out from shore: "Turn." But Taetagaloa replies from the sea: "Hua ma tukutuku...."[11] Likāvaka says to himself: "Now who is this person who even knows my spells?"

The canoe goes up goes right up to shore and not one of the crew is dead. They go right ashore. Now that Likāvaka who lives down inland in Samoa seems to be afraid of Taetagaloa. Taetagaloa goes immediately to encounter Likāvaka. He dispatches Likāvaka to live at the other side of Samoa, while Taetagaloa stays at the place where Likāvaka formerly resided.

The tale is finished.

Narrative 2 (by Palehau)

—Ka fai atu taku tala. He tala e ō te atu Tokelau tēnei ka fai atu.

KO TE TALA O TAETAGALOA

Ko Taetagaloa nae nofo i Nukunonu. Hau ai te folau i Atafu oi fano ai lā ia Taetagaloa ki Fakaofo. Kua hopo ai i te malaga ki Fakaofo. Ko te folau na kaumai e nā toeaina ko Fakatakā ma Pāua. Fano fano te folau, tau ki tua o Motuakea, ki te Ava-o-te-Hue. Ko te Ava-o-te-Hue e i lalo o Motuakea. Oi lea atu te tahi tino o te tokalua toeaina na ki lā kaumaia te malaga: "Ko te vaka ka fano i lago o te Alofi." Kae lea atu te tahi toeaina: "Hēai. Fano i te pine. Tuku ake te vaka ki nā kaupapa." (Ka fai pea te tala. Fakalogo mai, kāmea heu mai.) Ko te Ava-o-te-Hue e i lalo o Motuakea. Ko nā lago iēnā e fanatu e fetaui ma te

---

[10] This is the ordinary and proper way of handling a catch of skipjack.

[11] This chant is included (with some variation) in all versions of the narrative. I have taken a stab at translating it in Palehau's *tala* that follows, since it was he who gave me the clearest explanation of its words and meaning.

Utua o Fenualoa i Fakaofo. E kite loa ia Fenualoa, tau tonu te vaka ki gāuta. Ko lago o nā kaupapa (o lototonu) e fanatu, e tau ki Fenuafala. Kae ko lago o te tuafenua, ko te Fatu-o-Kava. Ia, tēnā. Fano ai te folau tēnā, pā atu loa ki te Ava-o-te-Hue, fai te miha. Kua lea atu te tahi toeaina o Fakatakā ma Pāua: "Ko ki tātou ka fano i nā lago o te Alofi." Kae lea atu te tahi toeaina: "Hēai. Tuku ake kī na lago o lototonu." Kua hē mau tonu te tokalua, kae kua miha. Ko te mihaga tēnā, oi tūtaoho ki lalo i te tai. Kua fano ia Fakatakā kua liu fahua-taka, kae fano ia Pāua oi liu pāua. Kae kua kave te folau e iētahi toeaina fakamātuatua. Fano fano fano te folau, tau ki Fakaofo. Kua ōifo foki ia aliki o Fakaofo oi tali te folau. Kua kavake ki gāuta oi kave ai ki te fale e fai ma ō latou faleapitaga. Kua nonofo ai te kau folau ma Taetagaloa.

Nonofo nonofo i te tahi aho, kua fano ia Taetagaloa oi takamilo i te fenua. E fanatu, e fai te faigā-vaka. Ko te tufuga e ia faia te vaka ko Likāvaka. Fano ai lā ia Taetagaloa oi nofo i te mea e i ei nā tino fai-laukafa. E nofo lā ia Taetagaloa kae vēatu lava ki nā tino: "Ko te vaka e piko." E lagona mai lā e Likāvaka oi lea mai ai: "E, vēhea ake kō te tama?" Kae lea atu nā tino i tafa o Taetagaloa: "Heā kō te tokaga ai koe? Fai te tātou gāluega." Kae nau mai lava te tufuga: "E vēhea ake tana kupu?" Oi kua lea mai nā tino: "Heā kō! Ko te mea nei e lea mai ko te vaka e piko." Ia. Kua lea mai loa ia Likāvaka kia Taetagaloa: "Tama. Tū mai ake." Oi kua lea atu ia Taetagaloa: "Fai kō te galuega." Kae nau mai lava te tufuga: "Tū tahi mai ake!" Oi kua tū atu ia Taetagaloa. Olo ai, tutū mai i te haumi mua kae kikila. Kua lea atu ia Taetagaloa: "Ko te mea tē, ko te mea tē." (Ko te mea e i ei tana kupu—ko te vaka e piko.) Kua olo ki te haumi muli oi lea atu ia Taetagaloa: "Ko te mea tē, ko te mea tē. E piko." Oi kua lea atu ia Likāvaka ki te kau faigaluega: "Ā, e tonu te tama nei—e tonu."

Io. Tuku ai lā te gāluega, kua fai e Taetagaloa. Ko te vaka nei kua kafamate nā lakau. Kae na toe vete uma lele e Taetagaloa, auā ko te gāluega kua tuku kia te ia. Vete vete vete te vaka—uma. Fakatātitia nā lago—uma. Tuku te lākau matua ma kua fakatātia tonu. Toe nei ko nā haumi. Kae hau nei lava te ataliki o Likāvaka e igoa kia Pepelekava. Kua hau nei lava oi tū ki luga i te lago. Puke atu lava ia Taetagaloa oi tūlua te ataliki o Likāvaka i te toki kae lafo tana kupu: "Ko te mea nei he mea e hā! Ka fakatakoto lelei nā lago o te vaka, e hēai lele he tino e lalakā, pe he tino e tū ki luga. E hā te mea tēnā." Ko te ataliki o Likāvaka, ko Pepelekava, na tā e Taetagaloa, toe puke atu lava ia Taetagaloa. Tapō tapō te itūmanava oi tapō tapō te itūmanava oi kua toe ola te tama. (Kae tēnā lā tana tautalaga na fai... i te mea nei... ka tātia nā lago o te vaka, nā he tino e toe tū ki luga i he lago, nā he tino e toe lalakā he lago. Tēnā lava e ki tatou lagona kafai e lalago he vaka. E lea mai te toeaina—te tufuga: "Te lago nā toe gaoi! Nā he tino e toe tū ki luga i te lago! Auā lā kua uma te fakatātia tonu.")

Ia. Fai fai te vaka—kua uma. Hiki ifo ai ki te Afagā—te Afagā tēnei i Fakaofo. Kave ai te vaka kua fakakatea. Kua fufuli te taumua ki Hākavā kae fufuli te taumuli ki Haumā. Kae uku ake te momoipu i te Afagā oi fakauta ki luga, popoga ifo ma te mokomoko i te niu oi fakauta ki luga. Kae tāvelovelo te vaka ki Fenualoa ma Fenuafala i loto lava i te Afagā. Io. Kua uma te vaka oi kua lea atu ia Taetagaloa: "E lelei nā lago." Ia. Kua uma te galuega tēnā.

Nonofo nonofo te kau folau, pā ki te tahi aho tū atu foki ia Taetagaloa kua fano oi takamilo i te fenua—i Fakaofo lava. Tāmilo tāmilo, fanatu foki e i ei te huigālā. Ko te lā e ō Moa. E hui foki e Moa te lā. Kua fano foki ia Taetagaloa oi nofo i te mea e nonofo ai nā tino e fai-laukafa kae kikila ki te huiga o te lā. Nofo nofo oi vēatu foki ki nā tino a failaukafa ki latou: "Ko te lā e hehē te huiga." Na lagona mai foki e Moa, kae vēmai lava: "E vēhea ake ko te tama?" Kae lea atu foki nā tino e failaukafa: "Heā kō te tokaga ai koe?" Kae nau mai lava ia Moa: "E vēhea ake tana lea?" Oi kua lea atu nā tino nae nonofo fakatahi ma Taetagaloa: "Heā kō! Ko te mea nei e lea mai ko te lā e hehē te huiga." Kua lea mai foki ia Moa? "Tama, tū mai ake." Oi kua lea atu foki ia Taetagaloa: "Heā kō. Fai vēnā." Lea mai ia Moa: "Tū mai!" Oi kua tū atu ia Taetagaloa. Kua fanatu nei ia Taetagaloa kua tutū ma Moa i te ululā, kua fakahino: "Ko te mea tē e kino, ko te mea tē e vēia." Toe olo ki te mulilā, toe fakahino: "Kikila ki te tilātū, kikila ki te tilālalo." Kua fakahino vēnā e Taetagaloa. Oi kua lea mai foki ia Moa ki tana vāega: "Ha. E tonu te tama nei!" Lea atu loa ia Moa kia Taetagaloa: "Hui e koe te lā." E hēki ai lele ni kupu e lahi ma Taetagaloa. Tago atu loa ia Taetagaloa oi toe vete uma lele te lā. (Ko nā lā o tātou i nā aho anamua ni moega.) Ia. Tui tui tui te lā—uma.

Ko nā aho iēnā e fai te taumanu i Fakaofo. Ko te taumanu e fanaifo i matagi mai te Utua i Fenualoa. Pā ai ki te tahi taeao, fano ai ia Taetagaloa oi nofo i te Papa o Tautai. (Te papa lava tēnā i tua e koutou iloa uma lele.) E fanaifo he vaka oi lea atu ia Taetagaloa: "Hopo atu au ma hoa o te vaka." Kae ko te tautai e hē tokaga lele mai kae fano lava te vaka. Ia. Hao atu tēia vaka. Kua fakaholo vēnā lava te fuāvaka. E fanaifo he vaka e vēnā lavā. E fanaifo he vaka e vēnā lava. E nanau lava ia Taetagaloa ko ia ke hopo atu, kae hē amanakia lele e ki lātou. Fanaifo loa te toe vaka oi kua tapa mai ia Taetagaloa: "Hopo atu au ma hoa o te vaka!" Io. Kua lea mai te tautai: "Tuku atu mua ke hopo mai te toeaina." Kae lea mai te fāoa: "Aua! Nāhe fakahopo ifoa." Oi kua tū lava ki lalo te tautai, kua tāofi mai te vaka, kua fakakatea mai ki te mulipapa e i ei ia Taetagaloa. Kua hopo lā ia Taetagaloa, kua hopo i te liu. Oi kua fano te vaka.

Fano fano fano te vaka, hovē lava e pā atu te vaka ki tua o Nukumatau kae kitea atu kua fanaifo te taumanu. Kua tapa mai lā te foemua: "Te manu te kua fanaifo nei." Oi kua lea atu ia Taetagaloa: "Kikila atu pe kavaifo e te manu ā." Kua lea mai te fāoa: "E kavaifo e te takupu ma te lakia ma te katafa." Kae tali atu ia Taetagaloa: "Nāhe avea autou foe.... Ko atu nā, ko atu manuheku, ko atu nā ko hēki tiu i faga o Lākulu." Kae kua ifo ki ei te fuāvaka tēnei na fano muamua. E fanatu nei te fuāvaka tēnā—ko kakahi, ko takuo. Kua tagau nā kofe, tamotu nā pā, tagau nā maga. Kae fanatu lava to lātou vaka e hē papale ki ei. Fano fano fano te vaka, toe lea mai te fāoa: "Te manu tēnei e tau pakū ifo." Kua fehili atu foki ia Taetagaloa: "Kikila atu ake pe ni manu ā." Kae kua lea mai te fāoa: "E kavaifo nei e te akiaki ma te lefulefu." Lea atu loa ia Taetagaloa: "Tāofi atu lā autou foe.... Ko atu nā, ko atu manogi, ko atu tutuha. Ko atu kua tiu i faga o Lākulu, ko atu kakala."

Ia. Kua fano. Ko te inafo e......! Te mātolu! E lea mai, e fakaulu te vaka i te potu i mua, hula i te potu i muli, kae hēai lele he atu e vēvēake ki te pā. Liliu mai te vaka. Hau kui luga mai ō atu, e hēai lele he atu e kalopā. Toe liliu atu, e vēnā foki. Oi kua lea atu ia Taetagaloa: "Fanatu au lā oi faitaki?" Kae lea mai te fāoa: "Aua! Aua! E fano koe ki fea!" Kae lea mai te tautai: "Hau kō te toeaina oi faitaki." Lea atu te fāoa: "Aua!" Toe fai foki ta lātou gāluega i te tuliga o te inafo—ki te potu i mua—ki te potu i muli. Fano fano oi kua lea mai te tautai: "Hau kō te toeaina ke faitaki." Kua mālilie foki lā te fāoa. Kua lea mai foki ia Taetagaloa, auā e nofo i te liu: "Mai ake kia te au te kofe i kinei." E lea mai, e hēki pā tonu atu ona lima ki te kofe kae halafaki te atu. Ia. Ko te inafo na hī lava i te liu. Na fai ai te tūlaga i kinā. Na kave kave kave kave lava oi goto te vaka. Oi kua lea mai te fāoa: "Hoia kō auā te vaka ka goto.' Ia. Kua fakauta te kofe ki luga i te ama kae kua hau te vaka ki Falē.

Ko te fuāvaka tēnei e hēai he atu, kua maumau uma ō latou kope. Kua tagau nā maga, kua tagau nā pā, kua tagau nā kofe. Kae kua hau te vaka o Taetagaloa, hau hau hau te vaka oi ofi i te ava. Kua tū ake ia Taetagaloa. E lua ana atu na fano ma ia, kua fanake ma ia. Fanake ai ma te tahi atu oi togi ki te vao, kae fanake ma te tahi atu kua kave oi huhulu ki te tala o te Tolugafale. Ia. Tēnā nā atu e lua. (Tēnei lava e koutou lagona, e mau ai te hikupā o te atu, e mau ai te hikupā o te pāla. E vēnā foki nā taipāla i te nofo-a-pui-kāiga i Fakaofo. Ko te tautai e mānumalō i ta lātou fefaiakiga, e lea mai, nae fano lava ma te kaukaiga o ai. Hovē kua koutou iloa, e hē kō takua atu.)

Nonofo nonofo i te tahi vaitaimi, kua tāupō te malaga e fano ki Hāmoa. Kua fakamoe nei ko te vaiaho ka fano ai te folau. Kua fano foki ia Taetagaloa oi nofo i te Papa o Tautai, kae kua fakaholo atu lā te fuāvaka. Lea atu ia Taetagaloa: "Hopo atu au ma hoa o te vaka." Kae lea te fāoa: "Aua!" Kae lea ifo foki te tautai (te tino matua) i luga i te vaka: "Tuku ifo kō te toeaina ke hopo." Lea atu te fāoa: "Aua! Tiaki ma te mamafa." Ia. Fano tēia vaka. E fanatu he vaka, e vēnā foki. E hē fakahopoa lava ia Taetagaloa. E vēnā lava ana mihi, ke fanatu ia ma hoa o te vaka. Fanake foki te toe vaka oi kua lea mai foki ia Taetagaloa: "Fanatu au ma hoa o te vaka." Oi kua lea atu te toeaina i luga i te vaka: "Tuku mai te vaka." Kua tū ifo te toeaina matua oi tataki ake te vaka ki te papa e nofo ai ia Taetagaloa. Oi kua hopo.

Kua fano lā te vaka, kua fano te folau. Fano fano fano te folau, kua mao gātai, kua galo nā fenua. Fano fano fano, kua pō tahi, kae kikila atu—ko te aho! Kua hēai he tafatafakilagi e kitea, kua pōuli kautatau. Oi kua atu foki te folau ki te aho kua fai vēia, oi kua vēake te fāoa: "Tēfea nei kō lā te tino na lea mai ke hau ia ma hoa o te vaka? Heā nei tana e fai? Ko ki tatou nei lā ka maui vēhea?" Kua lea atu ia Taetagaloa: "Io, kua lelei." Tū ai lā ki luga ia Taetagaloa i luga i te vaka. Auā ko nā vaka ni fualua, kua tū lā i luga i te fola o te vaka. Kua hiki tona tokotoko kae taufōlua. E vēnei ia taufōlua a Taetagaloa:

O! Fakauliuli kae ni taefeke, fakauliuli kae ni taefeke!
O! Tafi ake, tafi ake lau malama!
Tūlia! Honia!
Kā ni loloau, fai ki te utāfenua!

E kikila atu nei te folau, tatafi te itūlagī tatafi te itūlagī, kae kua mālama lele te aho. Io. Kua teka te mea tēnā.

Kua fano pea te folau. Fano fano pe kua fia ake foki ni pō, kae kua hēai he oho oi kua mihi foki te fāoa. Kua vēake foki: "Heā nei kō tā te tino? Na lea mai foki ko ia e fanaifo ma hoa o te vaka. Ni ā nei tāna ka fai? Kaumai ke kai!" Ko Taetagaloa ka kai e te fāoa auā kua uma te oho. Ia. Kua lea atu foki ia Taetagaloa: "Io, kua lelei." Kua tū foki ki luga kae hiki te tokotoko ki te lagi. Na hiki ake loa lava te tokotoko o Taetagaloa ki te lagi kae malili ifo—ko te popo, ko te uto, ko te takataka, ko te hua, ko te mokomoko—ki luga i te vaka. Oi kua faimatahi foki te fāoa: "Hoia! Te vaka ka goto! Te vaka ka goto!" Io. Kua kakai mākokona ai te fāoa o te vaka i te mea tēnā a Taetagaloa na fai. Ko te fuāvaka tēnei na fano muamua, e hēki i ei he vaka e ake. Na gōgoto uma i te moana. Kae nā ko te vaka tēnā nae i ei ia Taetagaloa, ko te vaka tēnā na hao i te matagi.

Fano fano fano lava te vaka, tau ki Hāmoa. E lea mai te tala a nā toeaina, ko te vaka na tau tonu lava ki Apia. Ka ko hēki tau atu lā ki gāuta kae kua fai te tukutukuga a Taetagaloa. Kua lea vē atu: "Kikila! Ko ki tātou kafai e fano ki gāuta, e i ei te tino e nofo ifo i gāuta e igoa foki kia Likāvaka. Kafai ia au e lea atu—Ko ki tātou ke fakatulolo ki katea, ko ki tatou uma lava ia. Ka lea atu au—Ko ki tātou ke fakatulolo ki ama, ko ki tātou foki ia." Io. Kua vēnā lava. E fano lā te vaka kae mātau atu e Taetagaloa, kae tū ifo lā te tagata mai gāuta. Ko te tino e tū ifo i gāuta e fai ifo tana tuhi, ko Likāvaka foki te igoa. E fakapoi ifo te lima kae kalaga ia Taetagaloa: "Fakatulolo ki katea!" Kalo uma ia tagata ki katea. Toe nofo tonu kae kikila atu foki kua fakapoi ifo te lima o Likāvaka. Oi lea atu foki: "Fakatulolo ki ama!" Oi fakatulolo foki ki ama te fāoa. E lea mai lā ko te tino i gāuta kua vēake tana kupu i gāuta: "Ko ai tē i gātai nei?" Auā lā ko te uiga o te tuhi e vē ni hāhā e o ia, ia Likāvaka, e mamala. E mamate uma te fāoa kae kua hao te vaka tēnei. Lea atu ai lā ia Taetagaloa: "Ia. Kikila! Kikila ki gāuta!" Tuhi atu ia Taetagaloa i gātai, fano uma te itū tēnā ki te Vāimauga. Tuhi atu foki i gātai lava, e lea mai, ko te itū foki tēnā ki Faleata, e tokalahi foki te kau na feoti ai.

Ia. Kae fanake te vaka ke gāuta. Kua ake ki gāuta, ōake ai kua nonofo i kinā. E lea mai—Ko te folau na nonofo i Matafele. Nonofo ai nonofo ai nonofo ai nonofo ai, e i ei te tagata e igoa foki kia Likāvaka e nofo i nā motu i te Alofi Aana. E i ei foki ona hāha. E fano lā ki ei nā malaga matamata. Kafai lā e fanatu nā malaga māimoa ki ei, kae hē ki lātou taliagia nā taufōlua foki a te tino tēnā e igoa foki kia Likāvaka, ko iēnā tagata e mamate uma foki. Kae ko nā aho foki iēnā e tāupō ai foki te malaga tēnā e i ei ia Taetagaloa. Pā ai ki te tahi aho kua fano te malaga. Fano ai lā ia Taetagaloa, kua fano i te malaga tēnei—ko ia lava tē i te muli-malaga, auā ko te malaga he malaga hāvavali, ko ia lava te tūpito ki muli. Fano fano te malaga, tau ki te fenua. Kua iloa e Taetagaloa kua tali pā ki te fenua. Fano fano, kikila atu ko te tagata e nofo mai i he fale maualuga. E fai mai tona tiketikega e nofo mai ai. Io. Oi kua tau atu nei te mua-malaga ki te mea e nofo mai ai ia Likāvaka, kae kua kalaga mai lā ia Likāvaka mai luga i tona nofoaga. Kua kalaga mai: "Hua!" Kae hēai he tino e tali. Toe kalaga mai:

"Hua!" Ia. Ko Taetagaloa e fakalogologo lava ki te kau malaga, e hēai he tino e tali. Toe kalaga mai: "Hua!" Fakatafa ake loa lava ia Taetagaloa, kua fakahula kae kalaga:

Hua ma tukutuku
Mata-fenua, mata-haua
Kae mulihau ki te katomea—Hua!
Lauputuputu, laumānunu
Fauhia ki he kaho lakulu
Ma noa koi tua o Manunu—Hua!
Tū kita i he kava
Talo ki uta i he kava
He niumata
Keli ake he ika he pālaoa
E tatao ma te taotao a makulu.

Kua hao te malaga tēnā. Ko lau iēnā a Taetagaloa kua fai kua hao ai te malaga, auā ko hāhā o Likāvaka kua iloa kia Taetagaloa. Ko te uiga tēnā o ana taufōlua e fai—Hua, tēnā foki nae lau atu.

Ia. Nonofo ai foki lā i kinā kua tali foki te malaga e te fenua. Kae i ei lā te mea e fai e te fenua tēnā i nā aho iēnā. I nā aho tonu o te māhina fanake, te fakatahi ma te fakalua o namo, e i ei te tino e taka ai i to lātou kakai. Oi ko te tino kua fai ma a lātou mahani te tuli, e tuli ke popoki. Kua āhoa foki ta lātou faiga. He aho, hula te tino. Kua ki lātou iloa lava tēnei te tino. E tuli nei, e hē maua. E hē iloa lele te mea e mou ki ei. Oi tuli ai kae i ei te malaga. Lea atu loa ia Taetagaloa: "Tuli!" Ko te tino e takua vē he mānaia, ko Pepe te igoa o te mānaia. Tuli ai lā i te pō tēnā na tuli ai. Na fano ai lā ia Taetagaloa oi tuli. Tuli tuli, mou te tino. Kua hē iloa e te nuku kae iloa e Taetagaloa te mea kua fano ki ei. E lea mai—Ko Pepe e fano oi ulu ki te tūgamau o te mātua o tona mātua. Ko tēnā te mea e mou ki ei. Na tāofi lā e Taetagaloa i te pō tēnā. E ulu atu ia Pepe i te tahi tuliga, e nofo mai ia Taetagaloa i luga i te tūgamau—oi kua talanoa. Talanoa talanoa, vēatu loa te kupu a Taetagaloa—auā ko Taetagaloa, vae atu, ko te kili, e hē tākua foki te kili o nā manu te māfiafia, ko te mageho, te kili kino atili o te tagata. Kua fai lā ta lā talanoaga ma Pepe. Kua lea atu ia Taetagaloa kia Pepe: "Kaumai foki kō to kili ke kō faitakia, kae kavatu foki toku kili ke kē faitakia." Oi kua mālie ki ei ia Pepe. Kua ui te kili o Pepe, kua fōki mai kia Taetagaloa, kae ui te kili o Taetagaloa, kua fōki kia Pepe. E lea mai lā—E hēki uma te fakamauluga o nā lima o Pepe ki te kili o Taetagaloa, kae kua vē he mea e lolomi i he fatu fuaefa. Kua kokoma ai ia, ko ia foki ka mate. Na iku lava ina mate ai ia Pepe, kae fano ia Taetagaloa ma tona kili mānaia—ko te kili o Pepe.

Ia. Ko te tala faka-Tokelau tēnā kua uma.

Manuele Palehau Leone, 1968

English Translation

—I shall relate my *tala*. This is a *tala* of the Tokelau islands that I shall recount.

The Account of Taetagaloa

Taetagaloa was living in Nukunonu. The voyaging party comes here from Atafu and Taetagaloa goes with it to Fakaofo. He joins it on the journey to Fakaofo. The voyaging party is guided by the elders Fakatakā and Pāua. The voyaging party goes goes, coming to the oceanside of Motuakea, to the Passage-of-the-Pufferfish. The Passage-of-the-Pufferfish is on the leeward [western] side of Motuakea. There one person of the two elders who have guided the voyage speaks out: "The canoe shall proceed by the route markers of the Alofi." But the other elder speaks out: "No. Go to the mark. Point up the canoe to the reefs." (I will explain the matter further. Attend to me, stop me if I am wrong.)

The Passage-of-the-Pufferfish is to leeward of Motuakea. From there the markers go off to meet with the Fenualoa Reef Shelf of Fakaofo. As soon as one sees Fenualoa, the canoe heads straight to land. The markers of the linking reefs (of inside) go off, heading to Fenuafala. While the markers of the backland, they are to the Fatu-o-Kava.[12]

---

[12] The "markers" referred to here are land-marks at Nukunonu which by back-sighting provide direction to particular land-marks at Fakaofo, though in the middle of the voyage neither Nukunonu nor Fakaofo can be seen. Motuakea, an islet on the easterly side of Nukunonu's southern reef, is an appropriate departure point to Fakaofo, which lies to the southeast.

Well, that's it. That voyaging party goes then, arriving right over at the Passage-of-the-Pufferfish, the quarrel breaks out. One of the elders Fakatakā or Pāua speaks out: "We will go by the route markers of the Alofi." But the other elder responds: "No. Point up to the markers of the inside." The two of them do not consult properly, rather they quarrel. That is the quarrel, and they plunge down into the sea. Fakatakā going is transformed into a large clam, while Pāua going is transformed into an abalone. Then the voyaging party is guided by other elders rather less old. The voyaging party goes goes goes, getting to Fakaofo. The chiefs of Fakaofo come down directly and receive the voyaging party. They are taken up inland and taken to the house assigned as their billet. Here the voyaging party and Taetagaloa reside.

On one day after staying awhile, Taetagaloa goes and strolls around the land. Going along a canoe is being built. The craftsman who is making the canoe is Likāvaka. Taetagaloa goes over there and sits at the place where there are the people making sennit line. Taetagaloa sits there and just says to the people: "The canoe is crooked." Likāvaka senses something and speaks to them: "Hey, what did the boy say?" But the people next to Taetagaloa reply: "What is bothering you? Just do our job." But the craftsman keeps insisting: "What were his words?" So the men reply: "Not to bother! The creature here tells us that the canoe is crooked." Well. Likāvaka speaks forth immediately to Taetagaloa: "Boy. Stand up forthwith." Then Taetagaloa replies: "Just do the job." But the craftsman is insistent: "Stand up here at once!" So Taetagaloa stands forth. Going then, he stands right at the bow and inspects. Taetagaloa speaks out: "The place there, the place here. It is crooked." Then Likāvaka speaks over to the working party: "Eh, the boy here is right—it's true." Yes the work is halted right then, Taetagaloa takes over. Here is the canoe with the timbers aligned and roughly bound. But it is all completely taken apart by Taetagaloa, because the job has been handed over to him. The canoe is undone undone undone—done. The supports are set in place—done. The main timber is positioned and laid straight. Still to come are the bow and stern timbers. But now here comes the son of Likāvaka named Pepelekava. He comes right here and stands on top of the support. Taetagaloa seizes hold and splits the son of Likāvaka in two with his adze while he proclaims his statement: "This thing is a thing forbidden! When the supports of the canoe are all laid in place, not a single person may step over, or a person stand on top of them. That thing is forbidden." As for the son of Likāvaka, Pepelekava, who has been struck by Taetagaloa, Taetagaloa takes hold of him again. Pressing pressing the side of the belly and pressing pressing the side of the belly and the boy is again alive. (That then there was his statement given... about this matter... when the supports for the canoe are laid, a person must never again stand on top of a support, a person must never again step over a support. That truly we feel when a canoe is supported. The elder—the craftsman—tells us: "The support must not be moved! No person must ever stand on top of the support! Because the canoe has already been set properly in place.")

Well the canoe is made made—done. It is lifted down to the Bay—the Bay here at Fakaofo. The canoe is taken here its clear side [the side opposite the outrigger] to shore. The bow is turned towards Hakavā and the stern is turned towards Haumā. Then a broken coconut shell is brought up from the Bay and placed upon the hull, a drinking nut from a palm is twisted down and placed upon the hull. Then the canoe is thrust back and forth towards Fenualoa and Fenuafala right inside the bay.[13] Yes. The canoe is complete and Taetagaloa speaks out: "The setting is good." Well. That task is completed.

The voyaging party stays and stays on, until another day comes when Taetagaloa again steps out and goes and strolls about the land—right in Fakaofo. Strolling strolling, a sail also is being sewn. The sail belongs to Moa. Moa too is sewing the sail. Taetagaloa goes as before and sits at the place where the people making sennit line are sitting and watching the sewing of the sail. Sits sits and says as before to the people who are making sennit: "The sail is being sewn wrong." Moa too senses something, and he speaks out at once: "What did the boy say?" But again the people making sennit reply: "Why do you pay any attention to it?" But Moa keeps insisting: "What is it he says?" So the men who are sitting together with Taetagaloa reply: "What's this! The creature here tells us the sail is being sewn wrong." Moa speaks back: "Boy, do stand up." So Taetagaloa replies as before: "It's of no matter. Just carry on." Moa replies: "Come here." So Taetagaloa stands up. Going over now Taetagaloa stands with Moa at the head of the sail, he points out: "The place here is wrong, the place there is too." Also going to the foot of the sail, again pointing out: "Look at the standing boom, look at the boom below." Then Moa too speaks out to his company: "Damn. This boy is right!" Moa says to Taetagaloa: "You sew the sail." Yes. Taetagaloa does not waste words. Taetagaloa simply takes over and takes the sail completely apart. (Our sails in those days past were mats.) Well. The sail is laced laced laced—done.

In those days there are birds circling in Fakaofo. The feeding birds are going down to windward from the Reef Shelf of Fenualoa. When one morning comes, Taetagaloa goes over and sits at the Rock of Fishing Captains. (The very rock at the ocean-side you all know very well.) As a canoe goes down Taetagaloa speaks out: "Let me come aboard as crew of the canoe." But the captain does not pay any attention to him and the canoe just goes. Well. That canoe passes out through the channel—the fleet of canoes proceeds past just like that. A canoe goes down Taetagaloa speaks out: "Let me come aboard as crew of the canoe." But the captain does not pay any attention to him and the canoe just goes. Well. That canoe passes out through the channel. The fleet of canoes proceeds past just like that. A canoe goes down the very same thing. Taetagaloa keeps insisting he be allowed to come aboard, but they pay no heed to him. Finally the last canoe

---

[13] The Ahagā or Bay at the lagoon shore of Fakaofo is a broad, sloping beach where canoes are drawn up, protected by reclamations on either side. The built-up land to the south is called Hakavā and that to the north is called Haumā. Correspondingly, Fenualoa is an islet at the southern tip of Fakaofo atoll and Fenualoa islet lies at the most northerly point. The hull is tested in the calm bay to see if its movement is steady and true.

is going down and Taetagaloa calls out: "Let me come aboard as crew of the canoe!" Yes. The captain speaks forth: "Let us steer over and take the elder aboard." But the crew replies: "Rubbish! Don't let him board." But the captain stands right down, halting the canoe, bringing the clear side over to the reef edge where Taetagaloa is. So Taetagaloa comes aboard, boarding at the center. Then the canoe goes.

The canoe goes goes goes, perhaps the canoe has just reached offshore of Nukumatau when the feeding birds are seen going downwind. The bow paddler then calls forth: "The birds over there are descending now." So Taetagaloa speaks out: "Look at what kind of birds are marking it." The crew replies: "The red-footed booby and the white-capped noddy and the frigate bird are marking it." Then Taetagaloa responds: "Do not bend to your paddles.... Those skipjack, scruffy skipjack, those skipjack have not yet frolicked in the trap of Lākulu."

But this fleet of canoes that went before run down there. That fleet now enters them—yellow-finned tuna, giant tuna. Poles are broken, lures snapped, hooks broken. But their canoe goes right on not altering course to them. The canoe goes goes goes, again the crew of the canoe speaks out: "A bird here is diving down to feed." Taetagaloa asks over as before: "Do look out at what kinds of birds are marking it." And the crew replies: "White terns and sanderlings are marking here." Taetagaloa speaks out at once: "Bend then to your paddles. . . . Those skipjack, sweet-smelling skipjack, fragrant skipjack, skipjack who have frolicked in Lākulu's trap, stinging skipjack."[14]

Well. They go. What a school...! The multitude! I am told, the canoe enters at the front side, passes to the back side, but not a single skipjack rises up to the lure. The canoe turns back. Coming passing right over skipjack, not a single skipjack rises to the lure. Again coming around, the same thing again. Then Taetagaloa speaks out: "Might I go over and have a try?" But the crew responds: "No! no! where do you think you're going!" But the captain replies: "Let the elder come and try." The crew speaks out: "No!" Yet again they bend to their paddles to keep up with the school—to the front side—to the back side. Going going and the captain speaks out: "Let the elder come and have a try." The crew are finally agreeable. Taetagaloa speaks out too, for he is sitting in the center of the canoe: "Pass me the pole here." I am told, his hands are not yet properly settled on the pole when skipjack converge. Well. The school is hooked right there at the center of the canoe. He makes his stand there. He carries on carries on carries on carries right on and the canoe is almost submerged.[15] Then the

---

[14] See Kave's *kakai*, note 9.

[15] A *tūlaga* in skipjack-fishing is a single session of continuous casting by one fisherman. A pearlshell lure with an unbarbed hook is attached to a pole about 500 cm long by a strong line. The lure is made to skip along the surface, resembling the tiny bait-fish. A hooked fish is brought towards the canoe with a single motion and caught by the fisherman, releasing the hook, so that the lure may be immediately cast again, while the caught fish dropped in the bottom of the canoe thrash about. "Stands" are taken at the stern of the canoe and a fisherman who has taken 100 skipjack (or more) in a "stand" is renowned (see Macgregor 1937:110-12 and Hooper 1985).

crew says to him: "You better stop or else the canoe will swamp." Well. The pole is placed on top of the outrigger and the canoe returns to shore.

As for the rest of the canoes not a single skipjack have they, all their fishing equipment is completely ruined. The hooks are broken, the lures are broken, the poles are broken. So the canoe of Taetagaloa returns, the canoe coming coming coming enters the passage. Taetagaloa stands up. Two of his skipjack go with him, go up with him. He goes up with one skipjack and tosses it into the bush, then he goes up with the other skipjack and inserts it in the gable of Tolugāfale. Well. That is what he does with the two skipjack. (This you all know well, the tail of skipjack is testimony, the tail of wahoo is testimony. It was like that too in wahoo season at the time when the original families resided in Fakaofo. The captain who triumphed in his endeavors, it is told, this continues right on within his family. Perhaps you all know it, I will not tell you.)[16]

Staying staying for another period of time, there is a counting of nights to the departure of a voyaging party going to Samoa. It is now determined the week in which the voyage will depart. Again Taetagaloa goes and sits at the Rock of Fishing Captains, while the fleet proceeds past there. Taetagaloa speaks out: "Let me board as crew of the canoe." But the crew says: "No!" But the captain (the eldest man) upon the canoe says as before: "Turn down so the elder can board." The crew replies: "No! Reject him because of the weight." Well, that canoe goes. A canoe goes over, like that again. They will not let Taetagaloa board. He keeps repeating his same wish, that he go along as crew of the canoe. The last canoe finally goes along and again Taetagaloa speaks out: "Let me go along as crew of the canoe." Then the elder in charge of the canoe speaks out: "Halt the canoe." The old elder stands down and guides the canoe up to the rock where Taetagaloa is sitting. And he boards.

The canoe goes then, the voyaging party departs. The party goes goes goes, far to sea, land had disappeared. Going going going, one night passes, but look out—what a day! There is not a horizon to be seen, all is in darkness. And the voyaging party is very anxious about what such a day bodes, and the crew speaks up: "Where now then is the person who asked to come as crew of the canoe! What now will he do? What now shall become of us?" Taetagaloa speaks out: "Yes, all right." Taetagaloa stands up right there above on the canoe. Because the canoes are double-hulled ones, he stands there upon the platform of the canoe. He raises up his staff and shouts. The shouting of Taetagaloa is thus:

> Oh! Black as octopus ink, black as octopus ink!
> Oh! clear up, clear up bright sky!
> Chase away! Pour down!
> If there be torrents, make them on the land![17]

---

[16] This parenthetical aside is meant to be enigmatic; Palehau "knows" but he is not telling all. Tolugāfale was formerly one of the *falepā* (men's houses) in Fakaofo; today the name refers to a family homestead.

[17] This chant, as is the case with many chants, is opaque. The gist of it has perhaps been captured in my translation.

The crew looks out now, one side of the sky clears the other side of the sky clears, and the day is dazzling bright. Yes. That difficulty is surpassed.

The voyage continues going. Going going uncounted nights pass, and there are no more provisions and the crew appeals again. They speak up as before: "What now about the man? Did he not say before that he is going along as helper of the canoe? What now is he going to do? Bring him to eat!" Taetagaloa will be eaten by the crew because the travel provisions are finished. Well. Taetagaloa speaks out again: "Yes, all right." Again he stands above while raising the staff to the sky. As soon as Taetagaloa's staff is lifted to the sky then spills down—mature coconuts, sprouting coconuts, dried coconuts, drinking coconuts, sweet coconuts—on top of the canoe. The crew chorus together: "Stop! The canoe will swamp! The canoe will swamp!" Yes. The crew of the canoe eats their fill from the thing that Taetagaloa did. As for the fleet that departed earlier, not a single canoe survived. They all sank in the sea. But that canoe that Taetagaloa was on, only that canoe escaped with the wind.

The canoe just goes, reaching Samoa. By the account of the elders, the canoe fetched up right at Apia. They had not yet reached the land when Taetagaloa gave his instructions. He spoke out thus: "Look here! When we go towards shore, there is a person staying down inland who is also named Likāvaka. When I speak out—All of us lean to windward—every single one of us do so. When I say out—All of us lean to leeward—all of us must do so." Yes. It is just like that. The canoe goes along with Taetagaloa gazing ahead, and a man stands down there at the shore. The man standing down on shore points down his finger, Likāvaka is his name too. As the finger aims down Taetagaloa shouts: "Lean to windward!" The men all dodge to windward. They are sitting straight as before when looking out again the finger of Likāvaka is aiming down. So speaking out again: "Lean to leeward!" And just so the crew leans to leeward. I am told that the man on shore said to himself ashore: "Who is that offshore now?" That is because the result of the pointing which is really a spell of his, of Likāvaka, is disaster. It kills all other crews but this canoe has survived. Taetagaloa speaks out then: "Yes. Look! Look to shore!" Taetagaloa points to shore, all are gone from that side towards Vaimauga. Pointing over again right at sea, I am told, towards that side of Faleata, again a great many people were killed there.[18]

Well. The canoe goes up to shore. They go up inland, they go up then and stay there. I am told—the voyagers reside at Matafele. Staying here staying here staying here, there is the man also named Likāvaka residing at the islands in the Alofi A'ana. There are his spells too. Sight-seeing parties often go there. Now when the curious travellers go over there, but do not reply to the calls of that man, who is named Likāvaka too, those people too are all killed. When in those very days such a trip is anticipated Taetagaloa is there. The day arrives when the traveling party goes. Taetagaloa goes along with it, he goes on that visitation. I am told —he was right at the back of the traveling party as the party is traveling by foot, he is right at the very rear. The journeyers go go, reaching the place.

---

18 Vaimauga and Faleata are districts to the east and west of Apia, respectively.

Taetagaloa realizes they have nearly reached the place. Going going, looking out
there is a man seated at the front of an elevated house. It is said there is his stool
on which he sits. Yes. And now the forward party has reached the place where
Likāvaka is sitting, and Likāvaka shouts out to them from his high sitting place.
He calls out: "*Hua!*" Well. Taetagaloa attends closely to the traveling party.
Not a person is responding. Again calling out: "*Hua!*" Taetagaloa quickly slips
towards the front, shouting as he approaches:

> Turn towards swells coming off the land
> Reflections of land smells of land
> And shortly the reef is reached—Turn!
> Cluttered bush lucid bush
> Bound to a breadfruit rafter
> And still tied at the seaside of Manunu—Turn!
> We stand at a reef passage signal landwards a kava a drinking coconut
> Dig up the fish a wahoo
> Set with the pipe-fish of Makulu.[19]

That traveling party is spared. That speech made by Taetagaloa has saved the
traveling party, for the spells of Likāvaka are known to Taetagaloa. That is the
reason for the responding calls he made—*Hua*, as was recited above.

Well. Staying here too the traveling party is hosted by the community. Now
there is the thing that happens in that place on certain days. On the exact days of
the rising moon, the first and the second nights of lagoon rising, there is the man
who roams about in their village. And their custom is to chase the man, to
overtake and capture him. They have tried for many days to catch him. A day,
the man appears. They recognize clearly this is the man. Now they chase him,
but do not catch him. They have no idea where he vanished to. And they chase
him while the visiting party is there. Taetagaloa immediately calls out: "Run!"
The man is spoken of as a handsome person, Pepe is the name of the handsome
one. Here he is pursued on that night he is regularly chased. Taetagaloa went
along then in pursuit. Pursued pursued, the man vanished. The villagers do not
know where but Taetagaloa knows the place that he goes to. I am told—Pepe
goes and enters the grave of the mother of his mother. That is the place to which
he disappears. He is intercepted there by Taetagaloa on that very night. During
one chase as Pepe approaches, Taetagaloa is sitting down on top of the grave—so
they have a chat. Chatting chatting, Taetagaloa suddenly voices his
proposal—because Taetagaloa, do pardon me, as for the skin, it is not even

---

19 This is not a definitive translation of the chant that is central to the narrative and always
articulated very fast. There is some variation in its recitation (see Lili's *kakai*) but the
comparable lines can always be identified, even if they are differently interpreted. Palehau gave
me the fullest, most coherent interpretation of the lines and stanzas present in all versions, which
is the basis of my translation. He explained that the first stanza refers to signs of land yet
unseen, the second to the sighting of land, and the third to arrival at land—an appeal for
refreshment. The final line is an oblique reference to the last episode of Palehau's *tala*—to the
hiding place of Pepe. Although this line appears in all recitations of the chant, the episode
Palehau said it refers to is unique to his telling of the narrative. See Lili's *kakai*, note 23, for
another stanza.

comparable to the skin of animals the thickness of it, the itchiness, the absolutely disgusting skin of the man. During the course of his chat with Pepe, Taetagaloa suggests to Pepe: "Why don't you give me your skin to try on, while I hand over my skin for you to try on." And Pepe is agreeable to this. The skin of Pepe is stripped off, given over to Taetagaloa, while the skin of Taetagaloa is stripped off, given to Pepe. It is told thus—Not even before the arms of Pepe were completely inside the skin of Taetagaloa, it was like being pressed beneath a huge rock. It squeezes him, he is completely paralyzed. In the end Pepe expires, while Taetagaloa goes off with his beautiful skin—the skin of Pepe.

Well. The Tokelau account of Taetagaloa is finished.

Narrative 3 (by Lili)

KO TE KAKAI TENEI O TAEATAGALOA

Ko Kui ma Luafatu, ma Fakataka ma Paua, ko te vāega tēnā na olo ki moana, oi agi ai e te afā. Kua tō ma ua, goto ai te vaka. Fanaifo lava ia Fakataka, goto ki lalo o te akau i te moana. Tēnā lā e i ei ai nā fahuataka i te moana. Vēnā foki ia Paua, goto foki ki lalo. Tēnā lā e i ei ai nā paua e pipiki i nā akau. Vēnā foki ia Luafatu, na goto foki ki lalo o te moana. Tēnā e i ei ai nā fatu. Kae tagi kakau ake tahi ia Kui, nā ko ia lava tautahi. Fano fano ia Kui, oi kua fai tana momoko e vēnei:

> Ko au ko Kui e oku luga e oku lalo
> Ke akahi ifo oku vae ke tū ki he kauāfua.

Na akahi ifo lava te vae o Kui kae tū ki te kauāfua. Fanake nei ia Kui ki guta, he motu. Ka ko Kui kua tali fānau. Na pā atu loa ki gāuta i te ologahu, fakapakū loa ki lalo, fānau loa tana tama, kae oti ia Kui. Ko te tama e tātia, e fānau ifo e kafua, e ufiufi i he mea e vē he kafukafu.

Oi kitea ifo ai e Tagaloalagi mai te lagi, oi uga ifo ai e Tagaloalagi te Tuli ke tatui e ia te kafukafu ufiufi ai te tamaiti: "Kae kē lea ki ei: Ko koe na uga ifo e Tagaloalagi ke fanaifo ke fakaola koe. Io, ko tā igoa foki ko Taeatagaloa. Ka ko Tagaloalagi tēia, ko te tamana ia, e nofo ifo i luga o te lagi." Ia. Fanaifo loa te Tuli, tatui tatui tatui. Oi kua tū ake te tagata, he tagata kua matua. Oi fōki ai te meaalofa a Tagaloalagi ki te tama, na fanaifo ma te Tuli. He ualoa ma he atupa (ni toki), ko tana meaalofa tēnā na ia Tagaloalagi.

Pā ai ki te tahi aho, fano ai te folau, ni vaka e olo oi hīhī atu i moana. Fano ai ia Taeatagaloa oi tū i te Papa o Tautai, kae kalaga ki nā vaka: "Fanatu au lā." Kae tali mai te fāoa o te vaka: "E fano koe faia? Te mea papahu, te mea pona, te mea lalagoa. E fano koe ki fea? Ni ā te kē iloa? Nofo ko koe e hē fano." Ia. Toe fanaifo te tahi vaka, e fai lava te faiga tēnā a Taeatagaloa, nā ke pā lava ki te toe vaka. Oi toe kalaga ifo foki ia Taeatagaloa: "Fanatu au lā." Oi mumuna mai foki te fāoa o te vaka, kae lea atu te tautai: "Tuku vē mua keinā fanaifo, pe he ā te fia fano ai oi tāfao i moana." Fanatu lava te vaka ofi ki moana.

Kae lea mai te fāoa o te vaka (te vaka tēnei e i ei ia Taeatagaloa): "Ko te fuāvaka nei kua kalele mai, kua hī mai nā atu." Kae lea atu ia Taeatagaloa: "Aua,

nā hē taua ki ei. Ko atu nā, ko atu e manuheku, e hēki tiu i te faga o Lākulu."
Ia. Toe fano te vaka, fano fano te vaka. Toe lea mai te fāoa: "Te inafo tēnei e
fanaifo." Fehili atu ia Taeatagaloa: "Ni manu ā?" Tali atu te fāoa: "E kaumai e
he katafa, ma he akiaki, ma he lefulefu." Lea atu loa ia Taeatagaloa: "Io, tau ifo
lā ki ei te vaka. Ko atu nā, ko atu manogi, ko atu kakala, ko atu kua tiu i te faga
o Lākulu."

Fanatu loa te vaka, fakaulu atu ki loto. Tū atu te tautai, ki kō ki ei, e hēai he
atu fokotahi e kai. Kae vēatu lava ia Taeatagaloa: "Fakamolemole kō ke fanatu
au, ke kō faitaki tahia." Oi kua mumuna mai te fāoa ki ei, kae lea mai te tautai:
"Tuku ake mua ke hau." Fano loa ia Taeatagaloa ki muli, na tago atu lava ki te
kofe, togi te afo ki te tai, kae teki lava kua gugulu mai te mulivaka, kua hī mai te
matuā atu. Toe togi atu te afo, vēnā foki. Tūlaga tahi ia Taeatagaloa. Kave kave
lava, tumu te vaka i atu. Kua kalalaga mai te fāoa: "O! Ko te vaka ka goto, te
vaka ka goto!"

Io. Oake loa ki gāuta, fanake te vaka, pā ake ki gāuta i te mea e tutū ai ia
tautai. Oi tū ake ai ia Taeatagaloa ma nā atu e lua e kuku i tona lima. Fanatu
lava ia Taeatagaloa, fano ki te ologahu e tātitia ai nā ivi o tona matuā oi togi ai ki
ei te tahi atu. Kae fano ma te tahi atu, kua kave ma tona afafine. Ko te igoa o
tona afafine ko Lemalamafitikia.

Ia. Toe pā ki te tahi aho kua laga te folau, ka fano ki Fiti. Fano foki ia
Taeatagaloa oi tū i te Papa o Tautai, kae kalaga ifo ki nā vaka: "Fanatu au lā."
Lea mai te fāoa: "E fano koe faia?" Tali ifo ia Taeatagaloa: "E fanatu au ma oho o
te vaka." Lea mai te fāoa: "Ha, te mea papahu, kae kave vēhea koe ma oho o te
vaka?" Ia. Fai vēnā, fai vēnā lava, pā foki ki te toe vaka. Kalaga atu foki ia
Taeatagaloa: "Fanatu au kō." Oi kua lea atu te tautai ki te fāoa: "E! Tuku ake
mua ke fanaifo. Ke fanatu la ma oho o te vaka." Fanaifo, tigā lava te fāoa e ita
mai ki ei, ka kua fano lava e tuha ma te kupu a te tautai.

Fano ai te folau, ka fano, ka āgai ki Fiti. Hovē lava kua tali hula ia Fiti, kae
vēake lava te fāoa o te vaka: "Tēfea ko lā te mea na kaumai ma oho o te vaka? Ko
ki tātou nei kua fia kakaia. E hili te kaumai o Taeatagaloa ke fīnau." Vēatu lava
ia Taeatagaloa: "E! Na ke koutou popole i te itū tēnā." Puke ifo lava ia
Taeatagaloa, oi fālō tona tokotoko ki te lagi. Ola! Kua malili ifo ia meakai
kehekehe kua tumu ai i loto te vaka. Ia. Tatago atu loa te fāoa, kua kakai kakai
kakai, kua totoe, oi kua toli ki te tai. Oi toe lea mai te fāoa: "Kikila mai, ko ki
tātou ka oti i te fia inua." Oi lea atu ia Taeatagaloa: "Tatago ki te hua liu tēnā o
te vaka oi feinu ai." Tatago ifo te fāoa oi inu ake, e māgalo.

Ia. Fano fano te vaka, kua kite ia Fiti. Oi kua vēatu lava ia Taeatagaloa:
"Kikila, kafai koutou e fakalogo mai kia te au, ko koutou manuia to tātou fāoa
ma to tātou vaka. Kae kafai koutou e hē fakalogo mai, ko te ikuga o nā vaka
muamua e pā atu ki tātou, ko luga o nā fagautua kua opeopea ifo ai ia tagata kua
oti, kua fai ifo i nā mea faka-taulaitu a Tui Fiti i gāuta. Kae kafai koutou e
uhiuhitaki mai kia te au, ko ki tātou e manuia. Kafai lava toku lima taumatau e
hiki ki luga, ko outou lima foki ia. Kae kafai e hiki ki te itū tauagavale, ko
outou lima foki ia."

Fano fano te vaka, kua pā atu nei, kua i gāuta i te uluulu. Kikila atu nei kua tū ifo ia Tui Fiti, ka ko luga o te tai kua opeopea ia tagata kua oti ma nā vaka. Tū atu lava ia Taeatagaloa ki luga, kua fālō tona lima ki te itū taumatau kae kalaga. Kua tū i luga o te puke o te vaka, vēnei:

> Hua. Hua ma tukutukua
> Mata-fenua mata-haua
> Kae fakamuli ma te tokamea—Hua.
> Hua lauputuputu laumānunu
> Keli ake he ika he pālaoa
> Fakatatau ki he tapatapa ma ula—Hua.
> Tuku ifo kō aliki keinola
> Ko au ko Taeatagaloa.

Ia. Hēlekaleka atu te vaka ki gāuta, oi tū foki ia Taeatagaloa oi kalaga vēnā foki:

> Hua. Hua ma tukutukua
> Mata-fenua mata-haua
> Kae fakamuli ma te tokamea—Hua.
> Hua lauputuputu laumānunu
> Keli ake he ika he pālaoa
> E fakatatau ki he tapatapa ma ula—Hua.
> Tuku ifo kō aliki keinā ola
> Ko au ko Taeatagaloa.

Kae fakalogo atu nei ki gāuta i Fiti, kua pā ifo te lauaitu, kua mate te tupu o Fiti i nā mea faka-taulaitu a Taeatagaloa. Oi kua fanatu te vaka o Taeatagaloa, fanatu fanatu, pā ki gāuta. Oi kua lea atu ia Taeatagaloa: "Omai lā olo, olo oi matamata. Olo foki oi kikila ki te oti tēnā, ko te tupu o Fiti kua oti, kae ke nofo au i kinei oi fakatali atu ai."

Ia. Olo uma te fāoa, kae nofo ia Taeatagaloa. Ko te afafine o Taeatagaloa na kave, oi e tau i tona tua. Oi kua lea atu nei ia Taeatagaloa ki tona afafine, e tau mai i tona tua: "Hau lā oi fano ki gāuta, ko koe ka fano oi fakaola te tupu. E fanatu lava koe, e tū ifo te niumuli, he niukafaui. E fanatu loa koe fetaui ma te niu tēnā, tago loa koe oi gagau mai te hikuhikulauniu, popoga ma te mokomoko, fano loa ma koe ki te fale tēnā e i ei te oti. Kāfai lava koe e ulu atu ki loto fale, kae kikila atu koe e i ei ni tino e hē mālie mai kia te koe, oi ko koe e hē tokaga lele ki ei. E ulu atu loa koe ki loto, fakavāvā i nā tino, fanatu loa koe nofo ki ulu o Tui Fiti. Oi tago ai oi pepē te mokomoko ki te ulu o Tui Fiti, kae tapilipili i te hikuhikulauniu. Kae lea vē:

> Tui Fiti ala mai, Tui Fiti ala mai,
> Ko au ko Lemalamafitikia.
> Ko au na uga mai e toku tamana i tai nei
> Ko Taeatagaloa.
> Io, nofo mai ki luga!

Fanatu lava te teine, kua fai tana gāluega tēnā, kua tā te mokomoko ki te ulu o Tui Fiti, kae kalaga:

Tui Fiti ala mai, Tui Fiti ala mai,
Ko au ko Lemalamafitikia.
Ko toku tamana e nofo i tai nei
Ko Taeatagaloa.

Oi kua taufōlulua ia tagata o Fiti: "O! Ko Taeatagaloa, ko Lemalamafitikia ma Taeatagaloa!" Ia. Oi kua kikila uma lele mai te nuku ki te mea kua tupu. Ko te tupu kua nofo ki luga, kua vēake tana kupu: "He ā te mea na pā mai kia te au?" Oi kua lea atu nā tino, ko ia na oti. "E hē kō iloa." Oi kua lea mai nā tino: "He tagata e nofo i tai, ko Taeatagaloa, ko ia tēnei nae ia faia mai koe i ana mea faka-taulaitu."

Ia. Fekau loa e Tui Fiti ke fanake. Fanake ai ki gāuta, fai ai a lā tala. Kua lea atu ia Tui Fiti: "Ko au e fakafetai atu kia te koe, auā kua ola nei ia tagata uma talu ai koe. Ka na hēai he tagata vēnā ko koe, ko tagata uma e ōmai ki Fiti, e hēai he tagata e ola. Ka kua lelei. Hau keinā fano ki tō fenua." Fōki loa ma te meaalofa a Tui Fiti kia Taeatagaloa. Ia. Fano loa ia Taeatagaloa, kua toe fōki ma tona fāoa, ka kua nofo ia Tui Fiti.

Oi kua uma te kakai o Taeatagaloa.

English Translation

This is the Tale of Taetagaloa

Kui and Luafatu, and Fakatakā and Pāua, that party have gone to sea, where they are struck by a storm. Rain descends upon them, the canoe sinks. Fakatakā goes down, sinking below the reefs into the sea. That is why there are the giant clams of the oceans deep. Pāua like that too, also sinks below. That is why there are *pāua* (shellfish) clinging to the reefs. Luafatu like that too, also sinks below the sea. That is why there are rocks. As for Kui she alone swims along weeping, just she herself alone. Kui goes and goes, while making her wish like this:

I am Kui of the heights and of the depths
Let my feet be set down to stand upon a sandbank.

Lili Fakaalofa, 1970

Kui places the sole of her foot right down and stands upon a sandbank. Now Kui goes along towards shore, an islet. But Kui is just about to give birth. Just as soon as she reaches the grove of saltbush at shore, she suddenly collapses, immediately delivers her child and Kui herself dies. The child is left lying, delivered in a caul, wrapped up in something like a shroud.

When Tagaloalagi looks down at this from the sky, then Tagaloalagi dispatches the Golden Plover down there to prick the covering in which the child is wrapped: "Then you tell him, 'I was sent down by Tagaloalagi to come down and to give you life. Thus your name is Taetagaloa.' As for Tagaloalagi, the father himself, he remains above in the sky." So it is. The Golden Plover goes right down, pecks pecks pecks, and the man, fully grown, emerges. (According to the tale.) The gift of Tagaloalagi, which came down with the Golden Plover, is presented to the child. His gift from Tagaloalagi is a long-necked adze and short-handled adze.[20]

There comes one day when the fleet is going, some canoes are going to fish for skipjack in the ocean. Taetagaloa accordingly goes and stands at the Rock of Fishermen,[21] and calls to the canoes: "Let me go along." But the crew of the canoe answers him: "What are you going to do? Scabby thing, pimply thing, fly-blown thing. Where do you think you're going? What do you know? Stay there you aren't going." Well. Another canoe goes down, Taetagaloa does exactly as he did before, until the very last canoe comes along. Then again Taetagaloa calls down as before: "Let me go along." And the crew of the canoe abuse him too, but the captain speaks out: "Let's stop and let him come aboard whatever the reason he wants to go and play at sea." Going right off the canoe passes through the channel out to sea.

Then the crew of the canoe (this canoe with Taetagaloa) says: "The rest of the canoes are within a school of skipjack, skipjack are being hooked." But Taetagaloa replies: "No, the canoe must not join them. Those skipjack, scruffy skipjack, have never frolicked in Lākulu's trap." Well. The canoe goes on, the canoe goes and goes. The crew again speaks: "Here's birds diving to a school of skipjack." Taetagaloa asks: "What kind of birds are there?" The crew answers back: "A frigate-bird, a white tern, a sanderling are marking them." Taetagaloa responds at once: "Yes, steer the canoe down there. Those skipjack, fragrant skipjack, stinging skipjack, skipjack who have frolicked in Lākulu's trap."[22]

The canoe goes right over, entered into the midst of them. The captain takes his stand, over there over here, not a single skipjack rises to the bait. So Taetagaloa suggests: "Please let me go over, let me have a single try." But the crew abuses him, though the captain says: "Why not let him come?" Taetagaloa goes right to the stern, immediately takes up the rod, casts the line to the water, suddenly there is thrashing at the stern of the canoe, a huge skipjack takes the lure. The line is cast again, it happens again. Taetagaloa makes a single stand taking taking them in, the canoe is swamped with skipjack. The crew cry out: "Hey, the canoe will sink, the canoe will sink!"

Well. They go directly up to shore, the canoe goes on up, coming up to shore to the place where fishermen disembark. Now Taetagaloa stands up there with two skipjack grasped in his hand. Taetagaloa goes off directly, going to the grove of saltbush where the bones of his mother lie and tosses to them one

---

[20] The adzes are for making canoes. In her father's version the episode of canoe-building follows, as it does in other versions. Lili has deleted (or forgotten) this episode, but kept the necessary gift. I was told a lively version of the canoe-building episode by an accomplished Atafu carver as a *potu kakai* (part of a tale); he said he did not know the rest.

[21] The Rock of Fishermen (*Papa o Tautai*) is a sort of land's-end where senior fishermen (*tautai*) await their canoes that have been readied at the lagoon shore and guided over the reef by the crew to the point where they can step or climb aboard.

[22] See Kave's *kakai*, note 9.

skipjack. With the other skipjack he goes, taking it to his daughter. The name of his daughter is Lemalamafitikia.

Well. There comes another day when the fleet is readied, it is going to Fiji. Taetagaloa goes as before and stands at the Rock of Fishermen, and he calls down to the canoes: "Let me go along." The crew replies: "You are going to do what?" Taetagaloa answers them: "I shall go along as provisions of the canoe." The crew retorts: "Ha, scabby thing, who would want to take you as canoe provisions?" Well. It happens like that, just like that, until it comes to the very last canoe. Again Taetagaloa calls out: "Do let me come along." Now the captain speaks to the crew: "Hey! Do turn up so he can go down. Just go along as provisions of the canoe." He goes down, in spite of the anger of the crew towards him, but just going in accordance with the word of the captain.

The journey goes, goes on, proceeding towards Fiji. Perhaps Fiji is nearly in sight when the crew of the canoe starts muttering: "Where then is the thing brought along as provisions of the canoe? Now we are famished. It is just as well we brought along Taetagaloa to kill." Taetagaloa simply replies: "Hey! Don't get all fussed about that matter." Taetagaloa reaches down, and then stretches out his staff to the sky. Amazing! All kinds of things to eat tumble down filling up the canoe. Well. The crew just reaches out, they eat eat eat, and what is left over they throw into the sea. Then the crew speaks again: "Look here, we are nearly dead for thirst." So Taetagaloa says: "Take up the bilge water and drink it." The crew scoop down and drink up, it's sweet water.

Well. The canoe goes goes, Fiji is sighted. Just then Taetagaloa speaks out: "Look here, if all of you listen to me, then you will bring good fortune to our crew and our canoe. But if you all do not listen to me, we will meet the fate of previous canoes, for over the reef edges men who have been killed are floating down, done in by the extraordinary powers of Tui Fiji on shore. But if you all obey me, we will be fortunate. Whenever my right arm is raised on high, all your arms must be likewise. But when raised at the left side, all your arms must be likewise."

The canoe goes and goes, now approaching, they are inshore and within the channel. Looking out now Tui Fiji is stepping down, while upon the sea are drifting dead men and canoes. Taetagaloa steps forward to the front, stretching his arm to the right side calling. He stands upon the bow of the canoe, pronouncing:

Hua. Hua ma tukutukua...[23]

---

[23] See Palehau's *tala*, note 19. The chant here is similar to the others until the final stanza, which is present in all Atafu versions. Its meaning is absolutely clear; the English is:

Let down chiefs that they may live
For I am Taetagaloa.

The tale's ending is prefigured in this part of the chant, but is more explicit in Lili's father's version. Arriving voyagers (or chiefs) who have been killed by Tui Fiji's spell are strung up in trees, and Taetagaloa lets them down and revitalizes them.

Well. The canoe draws closer to shore, and Taetagaloa stands again and calls again as before:

Hua. Hua ma tukutukua...

But attend now to what is happening ashore in Fiji, the spell is cast down, the king of Fiji is dead from the extraordinary powers of Taetagaloa. So Taetagaloa's canoe proceeds, going going along, reaching shore. Then Taetagaloa speaks out: "Come why not go, go and look around. Be sure to go and observe that wake for the king of Fiji who is dead, while I just stay here and wait awhile."

Well. The whole crew goes, while Taetagaloa stays. Taetagaloa's daughter was taken along bound to his back. Now Taetagaloa speaks to his daughter, who is clinging to his back: "Come along and go inland, you will go and resurrect the king. As you go along, the young coconut palm, a palm of large green nuts, stands inland. You go straight along until you encounter that palm, you reach up and break off the very tip of the palm frond, and also twist off the immature nut, going with them to that house where the corpse lies. As soon as you enter inside the house, you will see there are many people who are angry at you, but you won't pay any attention to them. You just enter inside, you force your way through, and go directly placing yourself at the head of Tui Fiji. Then reach out and crack the coconut upon the head of Tui Fiji, while fanning him with the frond tip. Then speak thus:

> Tui Fiji awake, Tui Fiji awake
> I am Lemalamafitikia
> I have been sent by my father still at the beach
> He is Taetagaloa
> Yes, sit yourself up.

The girl goes off directly, does those tasks given her, striking the coconut upon the head of Tui Fiji, while calling:

> Tui Fiji awake, Tui Fiji awake
> For I am Lemalamafitikia
> My father still sits at the beach
> He is Taetagaloa.

Then the people of Fiji chorus: "Oh! It's Taetagaloa, Lemalamafitikia and Taetagaloa!" Well. Then all of the villagers gaze upon the thing that transpires. The king sits up, uttering his words: "What is the thing that happened to me?" And the people tell him that he was dead. "I did not know it." The people tell him: "A man is sitting at the beach, Taetagaloa who did you in with his extraordinary powers."

Well. Tui Fiji immediately summons him to go up. He goes up inland, they speak together. Tui Fiji speaks out: "I extend thanks to you, because all men shall now live on account of you. Were there not a man like you, all the men who come to Fiji, not one would live. It is just as well. Come you must go to your land."

The gift of Tui Fiji is presented to Taetagaloa. Well. Taetagaloa just goes, returning to where he came from with his crew, while Tui Fiji remains.

Thus the tale of Taetagaloa ends.

Analysis

The narrative structure is divisible into five episodes, each marked by at least one invariable image.

1. *Introductory episode*: While quite variable, as beginnings are apt to be, one or more people always disappear into the ocean depths.

2. *Canoe-building episode*: Taetagaloa's assertion, "The canoe is crooked," marks the episode. (As noted, this episode is missing in Lili's version, although it is anticipated by Tagaloalagi's gift, and is present in her father's version.)

3. *Skipjack-fishing episode*: The counterposed poetic descriptions of schools of skipjack epitomize the episode.

4. *Voyaging episode*: Taetagaloa's instructions to the crew in order to avoid lethal powers emanating from shore mark the episode.

5. *Arrival episode*: The long rhythmic chant—"Hua..."—within this otherwise highly variable episode is the enigmatic emblem of the whole narrative.

What Makes Palehau's Narrative a *Tala*?

Even a cursory comparison of the narratives as told by Kave and by Palehau reveals numerous contrasting features. In terms of content, their beginnings and endings are so different that they could be utterly distinct narratives if it were not for the protagonists Taetagaloa and Likavaka, and, although the episodes follow in the same order and contain the same marked images, Palehau's narrative incorporates episodes parallel to the central ones (for example: sail-making, dispelling of storm and provisioning, and the second encounter with Likavaka), as well as adding introductory sequences to episodes 3 and 4. Palehau's performance is embellished with authoritative asides and explanations, and specification of places; his narrative style is discursive and varied, incorporating sequences of dialogue. In short, his narrative is expanded, elaborated, and obviously much longer than Kave's.

But simple identification of how the two narratives differ, or even an intensive study of the differences between them, does not answer the question of why Kave's is a *kakai* and Palehau's a *tala*, or more broadly what features are salient in discriminating between the two genres. Raconteurs have characteristic narrative styles and strategies. Kave's style of narrating is direct and sparse, a string of short, punchy phrases separated by pauses. He does not waste words whenever he speaks. Palehau's style is discursive and varied, a complex series of rapidly articulated phrases contrasts with cryptic statements. He is known as an eloquent speaker and speaks with recognized authority. His asides and commentaries on the previous or lasting significance of actions and objects—whether direct or obscure—may be taken as assertions of his authoritative knowledge. His performance strategy is quite unique.

Raconteurs also tailor their performances to their audiences, and here I should note that Palehau told his *tala* to a small, select audience, while Kave performed for a diverse bunch of people who had gradually assembled from neighboring houses to listen to him and others tell *kakai*. Finally, the source or sources a raconteur has heard the narrative from and the matter of how "firmly stuck" (*mau*) the narrative is in mind may account for some variation. These factors I shall set aside for the moment.

By knowing the raconteurs and the context in which a narrative is performed, it may be possible to account for some features of difference, and I could go on to compare Palehau's *tala* with other *tala* to see what they have in common. Intensive comparative detective work might in the end answer my question, but is it not simpler (and sounder) to ask the expert (see Mead 1983:16)?

I asked Palehau and he answered without hesitation. His narrative of Taetagaloa was a *tala* because of its *pine fakamau* ("fixing signs/attached marks"), specifically, the naming of known places. Again comparing the two narratives, this difference is immediately striking. Palehau's *tala* is littered with place-names: all three atolls are named, reefs and islets of Nukunonu and Fakaofo are specified, areas and places in Fakaofo village are identified, as are districts and villages of Upolu (Western Samoa). These literally "ground" the narrative as an account of events that happened at known, named places. Kave names only one place, Samoa, as the destination of the voyagers, and this reference, like those to Fiti (Fiji) or Toga (Tonga) in other *kakai*, is simply to somewhere other than Tokelau where strange happenings can be anticipated. Thus, what makes a narrative a *tala* are specific place-names that "ground" it.

Once stated, the answer is obvious from other *tala*, and this feature of *tala* is common elsewhere in the Austronesian-speaking world. Take Roti (Eastern Indonesia), for example, of which Fox (1979:16-17) writes that "true tales" or "historical narratives" are "fixed" in place by geographical naming and in time by genealogical naming of past rulers. Tokelauans, unlike the Rotinese, are not particularly concerned to "fix" their *tala* in time. Although recent *tala* of the nineteenth century do feature named ancestors as actors, past *tala* at most make vague reference to genealogical personages. Genealogies and *tala* are not calibrated as they often are in Tonga (Bott 1982:89-155), Aotearoa (Grey 1855, Best 1976), and elsewhere. It is therefore irrelevant that Taetagaloa does not figure in Tokelau genealogies.

Another raconteur commented one day when I had my pencil poised to take a note, "The song is the Tokelau paper." That is, the song is the equivalent of a written record. This spontaneous remark did not refer to just any song, but to songs attached to memorable events and to accounts of memorable events, and extended to chants and phrases reputedly spoken by named actors in those events.

These fixed utterances, whether as short and straightforward as "The canoe is crooked" or as long and enigmatic as the "*Hua*" chant, do bring to mind events (or accounts of them). The fixed utterance is comparable to a quotation, and therefore should replicate the exact words of the original utterance, and may be faulted if it does not. However, although fixed utterances are always found in *tala*, they also appear in *kakai*, so they do not serve to discriminate between the two genres. In both, getting them right is evidence of accurate memory, of having firmly retained (*mau*) the narrative. In *tala*, where veracity is at issue, such utterances are also *pine fakamau*, which, like place-names, validate the account, so raconteurs and their audiences are more concerned that they are "right." But although getting them right is important, what they mean is often opaque. Raconteurs, especially in *tala* performances, may assert or allude to their meaning, but more often no explanation is given. As a translator I have frequently asked performers to explain their meanings, and have received quite different explanations or even admissions that they do not know, adding that this is what they heard from their forebears who presumably understood the meaning and they themselves neglected to ask what it was. We might conclude that getting these marked utterances right gives authenticity to a narrative, since if nonsense is accurately remembered then sense must surely be.

The emblematic chant of the Taetagaloa narrative is virtually identically rendered by Kave and Palehau, but Lili's (and her father's and other Atafu) versions are substantially different. An Atafu raconteur asserted that Palehau's rendering was incorrect, and this volunteered judgment would presumably invalidate Palehau's narrative as a *tala*. This, however, is of little consequence, since Palehau tells his *tala* to Nukunonu people who accept it as such because it is his version of the chant they know. But then what is the status of Kave's *kakai*?

Degeneration and Creation

The question impinges upon the old, outdated debate about the relationship between popular tale and heroic myth; are tales "broken-down myths," residues or survivals of great mythic traditions, or are epic myths the constructions of great raconteurs who have combined and elaborated simple tales? These two hypothetical processes may be labeled degeneration and creation, respectively, and Boas long ago marshaled abundant evidence that both happened, though he emphasized the role of creation in reaction to the bias of his time (1966 [1896]:429; [1914]:482).

The issue is readdressed in a rather different way, but one more germane to the problem at hand, in the scenario proposed by Fox (1979). He suggests that a memorable event involving known persons and places becomes abbreviated to a simple vignette as it is told and retold, but then gradually incorporates motifs and themes prevalent in fictitious tales, while retaining the personal and place-names which "fix" it. Thus it comes to be elaborated as a historical narrative or oral tradition, although in time it may become just an entertaining tale if the personal names (attested in genealogies) and place-names which "fix" it are forgotten. This trajectory from event to vignette to historical narrative to just a tale (*ibid*.: 23-25) is plausible and attractive, but is it so linear?

Returning to the question: is Kave's *kakai* a degenerate, "dwindled-down," unfixed version of Palehau's *tala*, or is Palehau's *tala* an artistically elaborated, imaginatively created version of Kave's *kakai*? Additionally, what is the relationship of them both to Lili's *kakai*?

I pondered these questions. Palehau had frankly told me that he contemplated the *kakai* he told and devised ways to make them more *mālie* ("entertaining") to his audiences. There was no doubt in my mind that he had the imagination to transform a *kakai* into a *tala*, but it would have been impertinent, if not downright insulting, to ask if he fabricated a *tala*. Yet, a quote from Boas seemed so apt—"the more thought bestowed... the more complex tales become, and the more definite are the local characteristics that they develop" (1966 [1914]:406). Palehau's narrative was indeed more complex and definite. But then Palehau had also told me who his mentors had been—two men reputed to have had great knowledge and wisdom—and Palehau himself is renowned throughout Tokelau as an "archive of tradition." Furthermore, Catholic Nukunonu had not suffered the intense denigration of local entertainment and art in the latter half of the nineteenth century, nor so heavy an imposition of Samoan forms via the Protestant Church, that Atafu and Fakaofo had (see Huntsman 1980:x-xxi for a fuller discussion of the effects of Christianity and of Palehau's background and reputation). So it could be reasoned that the *kakai* versions of Taetagaloa were simplified, degenerate versions of the *tala* Palehau told. Still, it seemed strange that Kave told the narrative as a *kakai* in the same small community where Palehau told it as a *tala*.

Again, an answer, or at least partial answer, to my quandary was provided by an expert, this time Kave. His response to my question about the two versions was characteristically direct and self-effacing. He explained that he had "read" the *kakai* (Mika's version) in Macgregor's book, of which a teaching Sister had a copy. (Kave is not an English-speaker, so his statement should be understood as follows: the Sister related the English translation of the *kakai* to him in Tokelauan.) Kave further explained that the tale had not been firmly fixed (*mau*) in his mind at the time, but from what he remembered he had developed his own version, and furthermore, since he had not obtained and retained the narrative from his knowledgeable elders as Palehau had, Palehau's version was undoubtedly more accurate.

This revelation, by way of an answer to my question that was utterly unanticipated, cast the relationships between the versions in quite a different light. Kave's inspiration for his own version had come from hearing Mika's version once. But if any version is degenerate it must be Mika's version, not as he told it in 1932, but as Kave heard it some decades later, for it is possible to trace a history from Mika's telling to Kave's hearing quite closely. Mika related the tale to Macgregor and an English-speaking Tokelau interpreter, who probably interrupted the narrative from time to time in order to translate it for Macgregor, who was jotting the translation down in his notebook. (It is in the early pages of his notes and obviously written with haste.)   The published version is an expanded and heavily edited version of the notes. (In both the skipjack-fishing episode is missing. Did the interpreter neglect to translate it? Did Mika forget it, what with all the interruptions, or did he just leave it out because telling the tale via an interpreter was so tedious? It is present in both Lili's and Ioane's versions.) Thus the Mika/Macgregor version, although the oldest recorded, is the least authentic; the recently recorded Atafu versions probably reflect more accurately Mika's rendering of the *kakai*. Finally, a Catholic Sister translated Macgregor's English version back into Tokelauan for Kave to hear.

In a real sense, Kave created his own version and it can be compared to the one he reports he heard. How does his creation differ from the Atafu version? Four obvious differences (or changes) have close parallels in Palehau's *tala*, indicating Kave's acquaintance with Palehau's version and perhaps other Nukunonu versions of which there is no permanent record. First, there is no mention of Tagaloalagi; he has no role in the birth of Taetagaloa, although the Golden Plover has a minor one. Second, both the canoe-building episode (missing in Lili's version) and the skipjack-fishing episode (missing in Mika's version) are included. Third, the destination of the voyagers is Samoa where Likavaka's powers are neutralized rather than Fiji where Tui Fiti is overcome. Fourth, the emblematic chant is identical to Palehau's rendering of it. Kave's version is thus, in several respects, a creative amalgamation of Atafu and Nukunonu versions, possibly in order to conform to the expectations of a Nukunonu audience. Yet Kave told the narrative as a *kakai*, and said that Palehau's version should be given precedence because Palehau had learned it from their elders, whereas he had only "read" it from a book. But was it just the mode of acquisition that made the difference? After all, people also learn *kakai* from their elders. Recall that Kave also said that he had developed his version from what he remembered. Logically his narrative could not be a *tala* because he created it. He had reshaped what he remembered from what he had heard once, drawing upon what he knew already and his own imagination. The conclusion of Kave's *kakai* is, as far as I know, unique.

Still unanswered is the question of the status of Palehau's *tala*. Did he, or one of his mentors, or someone generations ago create a *tala* by weaving *kakai* together and adding named places, as Boas suggested, or is the *tala* of Taetagaloa based on real "grounded" events that have been imaginatively elaborated, as Fox proposes? Whatever its past history, I would presume that the Tokelau creative imagination has shaped this *tala*, just as Kave shaped his *kakai*.

*   *   *   *

The study of versions of the same narrative raises questions, and pondering these questions throws light back upon the narratives, and more widely on human creativity and imagination. Scholarly experts can question and ponder in their studies and libraries, but their questions need not simply be subject to their own speculations, plausible and persuasive as many of their proposed answers are. The raconteurs are experts too, who are aware of what they have done and what they are doing. Consulted sensitively and specifically about the narratives they tell, I have found that they give frank, and often expansive, answers. Of course, some questions cannot be asked of them (for example, I could not ask Palehau if he had created his account of Taetagaloa), and they, for their own reasons, may avoid answering questions posed. Yet they should be consulted; they may often respond to our questions with answers we might have anticipated—but possibly with answers unimagined.[24]

References

Bauman 1977   Richard Bauman. *Verbal Art as Performance*. Prospect Heights, IL: Waveland Press.

Bauman 1986   _____. *Story, Performance, and Event*. Cambridge: Cambridge University Press.

Ben-Amos 1972   Dan Ben-Amos. "Toward a Definition of Folklore in Context." In *Toward New Perspectives in Folklore*. Ed. by A. Paredes and R. Bauman. Austin: University of Texas Press. pp. 3-15.

Best 1976   Elsdon Best. *Maori Religion and Mythology, Part 1*. Wellington: Government Printer.

Boas 1966   Franz Boas. *Race, Language and Culture*. New York: Free Press. Original eds. 1896, 1914.

Bott 1982   Elizabeth Bott. *Tongan Society at the Time of Captain Cook's Visits: Discussions with Her Majesty Queen Salote Tupou*. Auckland: The Polynesian Society.

---

24 Obviously this article could not have been written without the collaboration of Tokelau raconteurs past and present, and most of those who contributed directly to it have passed on. Mika Tinilau died the year I was born, so I know him only by his reputation in Tokelau and reports of Gordon Macgregor, who died in 1983. If I appear to slight Macgregor's contribution, it is only because times and technology have changed. His fieldnotes are invaluable and testify to his dedication and skill as an ethnographer, despite his short two-month stay in Tokelau. Both Alosio Kave and Manuele Palehau passed away in 1986, but I tend to write of them in the present tense because they are present to me in the narratives they told. For very substantial help in transcribing and translating the narratives I thank Ropati Simona, Pio Tuia, the late Toloa Poasa, Robin Hooper, and the raconteurs themselves. Recording and discussing *tala* and *kakai* have been entertaining evening diversions during my stays in Tokelau. These visits have been made possible by grants from the United States Institutes of Health, the Wenner-Gren Foundation for Anthropological Research, the New Zealand Medical Research Council, and the University of Auckland.

Burridge 1969   Kenelm Burridge. *Tangu Traditions*. Oxford: Clarendon Press.

Finnegan 1970   Ruth Finnegan. *Oral Literature in Africa*. Oxford: Clarendon Press.

Fox 1979   James J. Fox. "'Standing' in Time and Place." In *Perceptions of the Past in Southeast Asia*. Ed. by A. Reid and D. Marr. London: Heinemann. pp. 10-25.

Grey 1855   George Grey. *Polynesian Mythology*. London: John Murray.

Hooper 1985   Antony Hooper. "Tokelau Fishing in Traditional and Modern Contexts." In *The Traditional Knowledge and Management of Coastal Systems in Asia and the Pacific*. Ed. by K. Ruddle and R. E. Johannes. Jakarta: UNESCO Regional Office. pp. 8-38.

Hooper
  and Huntsman 1973   _____ and Judith Huntsman. "A Demographic History of the Tokelau Islands." *Journal of the Polynesian Society*, 82:366-411.

Huntsman 1971   Judith Huntsman. "Concepts and Kinship and Categories of Kinsmen in the Tokelau Islands." *Journal of the Polynesian Society*, 80:317-54.

Huntsman 1980   _____ . *Tales told by Manuele Palehau*. Working Paper no. 58. Department of Anthropology, University of Auckland.

Huntsman 1981a   _____ . "Butterfly Collecting in a Swamp: Suggestions for Studying Oral Narratives as Creative Art." *Journal of the Polynesian Society*, 90:209-21.

Huntsman 1981b   _____ . "Complementary and Similar Kinsmen in Tokelau." In *Siblingship in Oceania*. Ed. by M. Marshall. Ann Arbor: University of Michigan Press. pp. 79-103.

Huntsman
  and Hooper 1975   _____ and Antony Hooper. "Male and Female in Tokelau Culture." *Journal of the Polynesian Society*. 84:415-30.

Huntsman
  and Hooper 1976   _____ . "The 'Desecration' of Tokelau Kinship." *Journal of the Polynesian Society*, 85:257-73.

Huntsman
  and Hooper 1985   _____. "Structures of Tokelau History." In
                           Transformations of Polynesian Culture. Ed. by A.
                           Hooper and J. Huntsman. Auckland: The Polynesian
                           Society. pp. 133-49.

Macgregor 1932   Gordon MacGregor. Field Notebooks (manuscript).
                           Honolulu: Bishop Museum Library.

Macgregor 1937   _____. *Ethnology of Tokelau Islands*. Bulletin 146.
                           Honolulu: Bishop Museum.

Mead 1983   Sidney Mead. "Attitudes to the Study of Oceanic Art:
                           Some Introductory Remarks." In *Art and Artists of
                           Oceania*. Ed. by S. Mead and B. Kernot. Palmerston
                           North, New Zealand: Dunsmore Press. pp. 10-24.

Radin 1915   Paul Radin. *Literary Aspects of North American
                           Mythology*. Museum Bulletin 16, Canada
                           Geographical Survey. Ottawa: Government Printing
                           Bureau.

Wendt 1983   Albert Wendt. "Contemporary Arts in Oceania." In
                           Art and Artists of Oceania. Ed. by S. Mead and B.
                           Kernot. Palmerston North, New Zealand: Dunsmore
                           Press. pp. 198-209.

VIII

"THAT ISN'T REALLY A PIG": SPIRIT TRADITIONS IN THE SOUTHERN COOK ISLANDS

Christian Clerk

I don't know if it's true but—one night I was riding my motorbike on the rise by Te 'Utu o Apera. (You know, the one where the 'utu [Barringtonia] trees are by the Kingans' place at Tupapa.) Suddenly, there was a big pig right in front of me. The bike hit it and I fell off. The headlamp was broken. When I got up I couldn't see the pig.

Next day I told some people who live around there. They said, "You saw it. That isn't really a pig, it's usually a cow." They meant it was a *tūpāpaku*. There are plenty of stories about things that have happened at that place. When Stewart Kingan began to build his house there, people said it was a bad place to stay. Nothing happened to him.

But my brother-in-law also ran into two small pigs one night at the place where they say that thing goes.

(M.S., Rarotonga, 4/13/76)

The aim of this short paper is to propose the "ghost story" or "spirit account" as a particularly lively, continuously creative area of the Cook Islands' oral tradition that would repay more detailed study along a number of different lines. The data presented here as an introduction to the topic are in no way comprehensive. They represent information distilled from approximately fifty accounts, from full stories to fragmentary comments given in both English and Cook Island Maori. These accounts, from some thirty different informants, were mainly gathered during anthropological fieldwork on other topics in 1976-77, some during a briefer visit in 1983. The data were collected on the islands of Rarotonga and Mangaia, though informants also included residents from other islands of the Cook group, such as Aitutaki, Atiu, and Mauke.

Folklore studies are now in the age of the "urban legend." The responsiveness of oral tradition to social and cultural change in the modern world has become a key area of concern. In the Pacific context, Maranda (1978) could write a decade ago of Lau riddles of modernization, arguing the use of a traditional oral form as a tool for dealing with new external pressures. Yet we still have much to learn about the patterns of continuity and adaptation within the traditions of the region. I would argue that in the Cook Islands, and very probably elsewhere in the Pacific, accounts of spirit contacts and activities are a particularly fruitful area for

the examination of such patterns.[1] The account with which I opened (from an
Aitutakian of long residence on Rarotonga) suggests as much. It is firmly located
in the realities of current Rarotongan life, yet draws upon the forms and content
of older narratives of explanation to give an alternative perspective on the road
accident. The complexity of the relation between continuity and adaptation is
shown in the forms attributed to the spirit *(tūpāpaku)*. The idea of spirits in
animal form is deeply rooted in Polynesian culture history, yet the notion of a
cow as a suitable spirit vehicle is clearly one that can only have developed since
the introduction of such animals in the last century. Traditional story and new
experience have constantly embraced each other. A necessary starting point for
any consideration of spirit narratives must be the term *tūpāpaku* itself as well as
some of the historical background to its current usage.

The Nature of *Tūpāpaku*

Tūpāpaku, as represented in the oral traditions of the Cook Islands, are spiritual
beings or forces similar though not identical to the ghosts of Europe. As recently
pointed out by Baddeley (1985:130), writing of Rarotonga, *tūpāpaku* can be
located within a three-part division of the universe. They are the *aronga o te pō*,
"the company of the world of night or darkness," as opposed to the living people
of *te ao nei*, "this world," or the inhabitants of *te ao ra*, "that world"—God,
angels, *vaerua tangata*, "the souls of the dead." But the boundaries between
these worlds are not absolute and can be crossed.

A number of my informants, in fact, identified *tūpāpaku* with *vaerua tangata*
in the sense of the detachable human spirit, the part which is released when the
life-force is gone. *Tūpāpaku* also has the possible meaning of a dead person, a
corpse. Wandering spirits were featured in pre-Christian traditions, the ultimate
destination for most being the underworld of *te pō*. The nineteenth-century
missionary ethnographer William Wyatt Gill writes (1890:345, 1876:156):

> At Mangaia the spirits of those who ignobly died "on a pillow"
> wandered about disconsolately over the rocks near the margin of
> the sea until the day appointed by their leader comes (once a year).

> Many months might elapse ere the projected departure of the ghost
> took place. This weary interval was spent in dances and revisiting
> their former homes, where the living dwell affectionately
> remembered by the dead. At night fall they would wander amongst
> the trees and plantations nearest to these dwellings, sometimes
> venturing to peep inside. As a rule these ghosts were well disposed
> towards their own living relatives; but often became vindictive if a
> pet child was ill-treated by a stepmother or other relatives etc.

---

[1] Anthropological treatments of spirit beliefs and their transformations in Polynesia include
the extensive material on Tikopia provided by Firth (1970). Goodman's (1971) study of *aitu*
beliefs in Samoa provides interesting comparisons.

Eventually the spirits would depart from known *reinga*, spirit leaping-places. Such leaping-places also existed on other islands. Even after this departure some spirit intrusions from the underworld were possible.

The establishment of Christianity from the 1820s onward saw the emergence of new views of death and the afterlife, but these did not eradicate the idea of wandering spirits. Historically, the mission churches showed suspicion of local spirit beliefs, often condemning them, particularly in relation to the consultation of *ta'unga*, the medical/spirit experts. First among the mission-inspired Laws of Rarotonga of 1879 was a ban on the consultation of "sorcerers" to discover the cause of sickness or find a thief. A similar restriction was part of Mangaia's statutes until 1899. The churches clearly viewed such spirit contacts as reflections, or even a continuation of pre-Christian beliefs and practices in which ritual experts sought contact with the *atua*, the divinities/spiritual forces of the Polynesian religious tradition.

The *atua* have fallen before one and one-half centuries of Christianity. *Te Atua* is now the One God of the Bible. Stories concerning the old *atua* are mostly rooted in the past and classed as *tuatua ta'ito*, "accounts of former times." Yet, as I will suggest, there are continuities to be seen between these older traditions and recent "ghost" narratives. In a few cases there is even a continuity of personnel. The lesser Rarotongan *atua* Ta'akura has not been entirely consigned to the past. One Mangaian informant recalled a tradition that Ta'akura had appeared on Mangaia, in the form of a chicken, at the end of the last century. Her presence was linked with that of a "Frenchman" having connections with the Tinomana chiefly family of Rarotonga.[2] But there are far more recent accounts of encounters with "the red-headed woman" from Rarotonga itself, meetings with Ta'akura being said to occur in the Muri area of the eastern portion of the island. For instance, a Mangaian youth attending the Cook Islands Constitution Celebrations of 1974 is reported to have claimed a sighting of a beautiful red-haired woman in that area, seen when returning to his lodgings at night. It seems that Ta'akura is now regarded as a *tūpāpaku*. It is possible that other minor *atua* have been redefined as *tūpāpaku*, blocking further inquiry into their nature and limiting incompatibilities with Christianity.

As Baddeley (1985:131) notes for Rarotonga, most of those who give recognition to spirits of the dead do not see a real contradiction with strong Christian belief. While there is still some formal condemnation from the churches, spirit traditions cannot now generally be seen as a threat to their teachings. There is a fair degree of tolerance with acknowledgment of some deviation from the ideals of belief. In the words of a Mangaian pastor, "As good Christians we should not believe in ghosts. But in the body we do." In fact, declared attitudes to accounts of spirit action vary from general acceptance of literal truth to extreme skepticism. The pattern and extent of spirit belief

---

2 There are recorded myths which link Ta'akura, the Tinomana family, Rarotonga, and Mangaia. See, for instance, Tara'are 1919:188, 201-2. The "Frenchman" may have been a Belgian who was resident on Mangaia in the latter part of the nineteenth century.

represents a study in itself. Here I confine myself largely to the content of spirit account, yet the urge to use the word "accounts" rather than "stories" is a reflection of the extent to which many are expressions of experience.

There is, however, a range of *tūpāpaku* accounts, from the more formal and elaborate "ghost story" to fragmentary references to particular personal experiences which have been interpreted in terms of a *tūpāpaku* presence. The different levels feed upon each other. Because I am here interested in content rather than form, I will draw no firm distinctions. The Cook Islands "ghost story" is certainly a study in itself, and from my limited evidence may well be an important route for imported elements into the complex of spirit accounts. But the character of that complex is very much connected with the interrelation of story and experience. It is important not to identify oral tradition simply with the more formal "performances." Even the most skeptical in the Cook Islands' population are more or less aware of a body of ideas and conventions which are the basis for *tūpāpaku* narratives. My purpose in the rest of this paper is to outline some of these elements, and in so doing draw attention to some evidence of both continuity and adaptation in the narrative tradition.

The Elements of a *Tūpāpaku* Account

Visible Forms

A feature of recent Cook Islands spirit narratives is the considerable range of forms which the beings or forces concerned can adopt. In this they are consistent with the widely distributed and older Polynesian assumptions about the ability of spiritual forces to manifest themselves materially—assumptions which underlay the anthropological use of the possibly misleading label "totemism" in relation to Polynesian spirit beliefs.[3] This noted, it must be said that in some *tūpāpaku* accounts the spirits concerned are not seen at all, their presence being made evident in other ways, which are considered in the following sections. Further, a large proportion of narratives refer to *tūpāpaku* in human shape, from shadowy forms to complete likenesses of kin or friends. At the more formal end of the spectrum of accounts, there are stories of ghosts mistaken for living people. For instance, there is a tale from Rarotonga of a phantom card-player who is eventually revealed and reduced to dust by morning light.[4] When *tūpāpaku* are

---

[3] The idea of Polynesian totemism was clarified and refined by Firth 1930-31. He insists that Tikopian totemism can only be understood in relation to the general system of spirit beliefs. Spirit, totem (a form adopted by the spirit), and social group are the three corners of a triple relationship. Handy (1968) has argued that Hawaiian concepts concerning the embodiment of spirits in natural species and other objects should not be regarded as true totemism since they lack an emphasis upon the relation between the "totem" and a social category.

[4] Levy (1973:161) has pointed out that besides Biblical demonology, films such as *Dracula* have fed into Tahitian spirit belief. Equally, modern Cook Islands spirit narratives have fed on several decades of cinema and, in the last decade, video. Tales such as that of the phantom card player may well reflect this phenomenon.

described as appearing in dreams, it is normally in a form which is, if not completely recognizable, at least identifiably human.

However, as the opening example suggests, animal forms feature prominently. That they are part of a long-standing tradition is confirmed in the writings of Gill: "The spirits of the dead are fabled to have assumed, temporarily, and for a specific purpose, the form of an insect, bird, fish, or cloud" (1890:347). He contrasts this situation with the more permanent relationship between certain animal species and the gods, as, for instance, on Mangaia the *atua* Turanga was said to habitually take on the form of a gecko. However, whatever the nature of the spirits involved, an important function of the animal counterparts is that of communication. They are the media for supernatural messages. Often they are described as *'akairo*, "signs/omens." *Tūpāpaku* can be represented as temporarily resident within a real creature, or as simply adopting the semblance of an animal.

For example, large green crickets (Tettigonidae), both visually and audially striking, and intermittently appearing in houses, have widespread spirit associations in the Southern Cooks. While for older Mangaians these associations are negative (they are *manu tari maki*, "animals that carry sickness"), elsewhere there seems to be greater ambivalence. The crickets are spoken of as a form for either protective or harmful spirit presences, as positive sign (Davis 1952:190) or spying enemy. They are quite often referred to in stories of *ta'unga*, the traditional medical and spirit experts. A Rarotongan informant recounted how a *ta'unga* from Atiu had provided him with two protective cricket spirits who were addressed by the names of Old Testament prophets and whose distinctive sounds could be heard even when traveling by car.

Formerly there were extensive connections between *atua* and bird species. Some more restricted links between *tūpāpaku* and birds remain. In Mangaia and Rarotonga the *manu tūpāpaku*, "ghost birds," are *ūpoa* and *rākoa*, sea birds of the shearwater and petrel group (Procellaridae). They are nocturnally active and are noted for making disturbingly human cries—two factors which are significant in their spirit associations. Narratives concerning the *manu tūpāpaku* usually involve the deaths of chiefs, pastors, family heads, or other prominent figures. There are unusual patterns of behavior on the part of the birds, which foretell such events by flying around a village or family lands. A kingfisher species, *ngotare*, performs a similar function in Atiuan accounts.

Of particular interest is the appearance of introduced domesticates as spirit forms within *tūpāpaku* accounts. At the opening of the nineteenth century Mangaia apparently had no domesticated mammals, while pigs and dogs were found elsewhere in the Southern Cooks. Spirit narratives now encompass not only dogs and pigs but cows, horses, goats, and cats. On Mangaia the white sow of Araoa, a large pig followed by many piglets, is one of the most familiar of *tūpāpaku*, while there are stories of spirit horses seen galloping, as no real horse could, along the reef. On Rarotonga, tales of spirits in the form of cows were not restricted to the stories of the Te 'Utu o Apera area, which have already been referred to, but included some relating to the chiefly burial ground at Taputapuatea, and some concerning manifestations at a notorious accident black-spot near the international airport. From Atiu there are accounts of a spirit known as Iravaru, which is encountered near a tomb at the Ngatitiaka chiefly palace and is able to assume a variety of animal forms, principally those of cow, cat, or dog.[5]

That introduced species came to be so readily and completely incorporated is an indicator of the flexibility of the oral tradition. The possibility of a spirit-animal link was well established, and remarkable new creatures may have initially lent themselves to identification with supernatural forces. Missionary accounts (Gill 1876:91) suggest that the first pigs to be brought to Mangaia were for a time treated as manifestations of *atua*. Once the domesticates were established, identification with human owners may have helped to make them a particularly suitable form for ghosts. Apparently, in mid-nineteenth-century Mangaia a man's domestic animals were killed on his death (77).

Generalizing and simplifying, I would suggest that there are two common, broad patterns of behavioral comparison involved in animal-spirit accounts.

1) Wandering spirit detached from social world of the living—> Approaches human beings to communicate

   Wild animal (insect, bird)—> Approaches human beings/enters houses

2) Human spirit—> Normally leaves dwelling at death

   Domesticated animals strongly associated with human beings—> Seen unexpectedly (at night, behaving unusually) away from normal living areas

In both cases there is a sense of being "out of place," whether this involves an "outside" to "inside" or "inside" to "outside" movement. In addition, narratives suggest that domestic animals such as dogs are able to perceive *tūpāpaku* on occasions when human beings cannot, but that like human beings they are susceptible to spirit possession, such possession being revealed through erratic behavior. So domestic animals in their more usual settings may be presented as spirit-connected by virtue of such temporary indwelling, whereas those seen elsewhere are usually presented as a form assumed by a *tūpāpaku* rather than as a real creature which is occupied by a spirit.

The tradition of ghostly lights found elsewhere in Polynesia—for example in Tonga (Collocott 1923) or Hawaii (Luomala 1983)—is also well represented in the Cooks. These can be the static luminescent glow known as *pura* or moving lights seen either in the sea or on land (sometimes referred to simply as *turama*, a general term for that which gives off light). Even in the sea, such lights are often described as being like a flame. Mangaian narratives include accounts of rows of moving lights on the hills of the interior. These are the *aitu*, a term clearly cognate with the general spirit category *aitu* of Samoa, though in Mangaia apparently restricted to the one visible form of spirit activity.

---

[5] See, for example, Tangatapoto 1984:156, which refers to a black dog form.

Sounds

One night, when I was about thirteen, I heard the *ka'ara*. It was like people coming near, like a procession, beating drums. I woke up my mother. It was a loud noise, but she couldn't hear it. This time it was a sign—to do with a meeting of the *kopu tangata* (family/kin group) to say who would have a special title. That meeting was in our house.

(G.P., Rarotonga, 5/6/76)

In *tūpāpaku* accounts what is heard may be of equal importance to, if not more important than, what is seen. There are clear parallels with the importance of sound in the sports of ghost processions in Hawaii which have been recently discussed by Luomala (1983). Indeed, there are Cook Islands accounts relating to similar ghostly processions which are identifiable mainly by their sound. This phenomenon is usually spoken of as the *tīni*, the "band" or "company," or as the *tangi ka'ara*, "sound of the drum." Accounts more usually tell of individuals who at night, in out-of-the-way places, hear the sounds of a moving group of people talking, singing, and playing music. This is normally interpreted as a band of *tūpāpaku* moving between villages or other sites of significance to them. There are echoes here of the groups of undeparted spirits discussed by Gill, and of the wider Polynesian traditions of socially organized spirit groups.

Generally, ghost accounts attribute a whole range of unusual or unexpected noises to *tūpāpaku*. These range from sounds of weeping to otherwise inexplicable knockings around the house. As suggested above, the link between some animals and the spirit world seems to relate, in part at least, to the noises they can produce. The most extreme case of this phenomenon is that of the *vāvā* in Mangaia. One informant in his seventies, asked what a *vāvā* was, said simply, "*'E tangi, 'e tūpāpaku*," ("It is a sound, it is a *tūpāpaku*"). This sound, described locally as *tikerere tao tao*, a repeated, piercing metallic chirping often heard overhead, is in fact made by a small yellow cricket. Some, while recognizing the cricket *vāvā*, still maintain a link with spirit activity. *Vāvā* sounds are reported from places where no cricket is apparent nor would be expected, even from canoes fishing at sea. While the precise spirit associations have been revised to fit current conditions, the role of the *vāvā* offers one of the clearest examples of continuity in spirit traditions. Gill, writing in the last century of men killed in battle, states (1876:162):

A species of cricket rarely seen but whose voice is heard at night plaintively chirping "kere-kerere-tao-tao," was believed to be the voice of these warrior spirits sorrowfully calling to their friends. Hence the proverb, "The spirit-cricket is chirping" (Kua tangi te vava).

Further, an unpublished Mangaian text collected by Gill (n.d.) tells us that the chirping of the *vātā* was formerly associated with communications from the god Tane. As suggested earlier, accounts which refer to deliberate *tūpāpaku* approaches to humans often include the notion of a message to be passed on. Accounts of spirit activity merge with those of signs and omens. It can be argued that where these involve spirit/animal connections, the choice of an animal species is related to its behavior, particularly its ability to establish communication. Animals which from time to time seem to approach human beings and then call attention to themselves through the noises they make have been prominent among those with spirit associations (Clerk 1981:357-62).

Bodily Sensations

The presence of *tūpāpaku* is also linked with a range of bodily sensations. Several accounts refer to temperature changes. Ghostly presence can be associated with feelings of cold, and also with areas of unnaturally warm air. *'Uru vanavana*, the standing of the hair on end, may be referred to as part of the sense of unease experienced by an individual coming into contact with spirits. But some contacts are described as more violent. In particular there is the experience described as being squeezed or pressed, *ta'omi'ia*, or squatted on or brooded over, *pārai'ia*. This is usually said to occur when an individual is lying down to sleep. It involves the sense of a force pressing down on the body, preventing movement or outcry and making breathing difficult. There are clear parallels with the accounts of spirit (*tupapa'u*) assaults recorded by Levy (1973:394-98) among Tahitians and which he describes as being hypnoid hallucinations. Whatever their psychological origins, the description of events appears to be shaped by the oral tradition common within central eastern Polynesia. It is, nevertheless, very difficult to be certain whether close parallels in spirit traditions within the Society Islands and the Southern Cooks are part of an older shared heritage or developed through contacts, so extensive were those from the mid-nineteenth century on.[6]

According to some Mangaian informants, the ability to fight spirits that have come in dreams can be affected by the side on which an individual sleeps. Sleeping on the left side is better for this purpose. There are other suggestions of a connection between the left side and spirit activity. One account emphasized that in order to perceive its actions correctly, a *tūpāpaku* should be watched with the left eye. Less serious cases of spirit pressing may be presented as a sign from ancestors. A Mangaian informant described such an experience where the pressing had been preceded by images of his late mother and grandmother. The stories that tell of more active and dangerous physical encounters with spirits lead towards those that concern spirit possession and *tūpāpaku* as a cause of sickness. Again, the spirit contact may be presented in terms of communication, though in the case of such aggression the message is generally one of extreme displeasure rather than of warning.

---

[6] Tahiti was the major center of trade in the eastern Pacific with which Cook Islanders had frequent dealings. The Mangaian people even purchased land there as a permanent base for Mangaian residents. The potential influence of such contact is suggested by the framing of Federal Ordinance 30 in 1910 to counter a practice believed to have been introduced to Mangaia from Tahiti. This involved the digging up and burning of corpses to prevent spirit attack (*Cook and Other Islands, Continuation of Parliamentary Papers*, New Zealand, 1910).

Smells

A few accounts also made reference to smells suggesting the presence of spirits. For instance, a Maukean informant resident on Mangaia proposed a distinctive sweet mustiness as a sign of recent ghost activity. This 'aunga rīko he described as quite different from the 'aunga piro, the stench associated with physical decay. Two Mangaian informants spoke of the smell of pua (Fragraea) blossom around the house as a possible sign of the approach of a spirit. Apparently neither of them was aware of the role of the pua in the earlier belief system as a route for spirits to the underworld (Te Rangi Hiroa 1934:198-99).

Spirits and Time

Spirits are presented as approaching humans for communication when events in the human world provide a reason for doing so. But accounts often suggest another factor which conditions spirit activity. Tūpāpaku are seen as things of the night, yet also perhaps of particular nights. The pattern of spirit actions is linked with the arapō, the "paths of the nights" of the traditional lunar calendar. Few Cook Islanders could now provide a full listing of the arapō, the named nights of the lunar month. Nevertheless, particular pieces of knowledge connected with the lunar calendar are still used in activities such as planting, fishing, and crab collecting, and the links between specific nights and spirit appearances are sufficiently strong in some minds for the term arapō to be applied to both.[7]

Three nights strongly linked with ghosts are those with the name Rakau, usually said to be the eighteenth, nineteenth, and twentieth after the new moon, when the moon is beginning to wane. In Atiuan tradition, according to Vainerere Tangatapoto, the first of these, Rakau ta'i, is a night "when the spirits arise to reenact their past and remind us that they are still there" (1984:155). According to a listing of arapō published in the Cook Island journal Torea Katorika the subsequent nights are:

19 Rakau roto — Po ika kore. Maata te turuma[8] i roto i te tai.
20 Rakau akaoti — Kua aere te turuma ki runga i te maunga.

19 Rakau roto — Night of no fish. Many apparitions in the sea.
20 Rakau akaoti — The spirits go inland to the hills/mountains.

(Rickman 1931)

These descriptions suggest something of the way in which time, place, and event come together in tūpāpaku narratives. Many speak of recurrent appearances of particular tūpāpaku on particular arapō at particular locations. Some older

---

7 An example of this tradition expressed in modern Cook Islands literature can be found in Marjorie Crocombe's short story "The Healer" (1980).

8 Turuma is an alternative term for ghosts or spirits, though not nearly as commonly used as tūpāpaku.

Mangaians applied the term *mokoiro* to spirits that are highly consistent in form and in time and place of appearance.

Spirits and Place

Spirits are especially associated with places of burial, including formerly the burial site of the placenta (the *īpukarea*—a term also implying "ancestral land"). Old ritual sites, the *marae*, have powerful associations, as may "places where blood has been shed," as one man described the old battle grounds of Mangaia. Since death occurs in the sea, it is to be expected that the sea also holds spirits of the dead.[9] Current patterns and traditions of burial vary somewhat between islands. Tombs within a house compound are a common sight on Rarotonga. But on Mangaia the pre-Christian tradition of burial was in the caves and chasms of its coralline plateau, while burials alongside dwellings were later forbidden by an Island Ordinance. So, barring churchyards, burial has been largely outside or on the outskirts of villages. It is not, then, surprising that in Mangaian narratives particularly, *tūpāpaku* are not primarily creatures of human habitation, although they are drawn back to them at night by their feelings for the living or for a specific purpose. The encounters described may be in villages, but many are in lonelier and wilder places. This is, of course, significant in relation to the animal/spirit linkage.

Specific associations with death may vary considerably in their historical depth. The *tūpāpaku* accounts relating to the Black Rock (Tuoro) area of northwestern Rarotonga reflect both the traditional role of the heights at Black Rock as a *reinga*, a leaping-place for spirits of the dead, and the presence of the hospital in recent decades. Former Cook Islands Premier Dr. Tom Davis has suggested that initial use of the Black Rock sanatorium was discouraged by the older associations (Davis 1952:56-57). At the same time there were, apparently, fears concerning the ambulance as a potential ghost location (101), reflecting its current association with sickness and death. In 1976 there were still tales of ambulance doors mysteriously swinging open near Black Rock to deposit corpses on the road.

Sites of recurrent misfortune also became a focus for *tūpāpaku* narratives. The road-accident black-spot near the Meteorological Station at the west end of Rarotonga International Airport is a prime case. The importance of the explanatory function in many of the less formal spirit accounts becomes very clear here. Where there is a degree of uncertainty as to the more material causes, the presence of a spirit pathway, or of a *tūpāpaku* cow that drivers swerve to avoid, is invoked to account for the repeated pattern of disaster. To an extent, the stories linking *tūpāpaku* and accidents form a continuum with those suggesting links

---

9 Tangatapoto (1984:155) suggests that in Atiuan narratives the dead of the sea, identifiable by their fishy smell, may emerge to join the spirits of the land. Tales recorded on Mangaia refer to spirits emerging from fresh water. But, despite a few confusions, these appear to relate not to *tūpāpaku* but to a category of mythical beings, the *momokē*. Unlike *tūpāpaku* narratives, tales of the pale-skinned, fair-haired, slime-covered *momokē* seem closer to the legendary past than to personal experience.

with sickness. Clearly the former have a better chance of being localized, but specific *maki tūpāpaku*, "spirit sicknesses," can be related to interference with places or objects of strong interest to ancestral spirits—to which some *tapu* might still be held to apply:

> There was an engineer from New Zealand. He used a bulldozer to make the road at Arai te Tonga (the site of an old *koutu nui*, a chiefly court). He moved stones at another *marae* too. The *maori* workers wouldn't use the bulldozer at Arai te Tonga. He drove it himself and shifted some stones. Not long after that he got ill. His jaw was twisted and his eyes bulged. He had to go back to New Zealand. Later he came back to Rarotonga, but his jaw wasn't quite straight. The *maori* people said that this was because he had interfered with *marae*.
>
> My wife doesn't like me moving stones on one of the plots I work. It is from her family. I tell her her ancestors won't hurt me for feeding her.
>
> (M.S., Rarotonga, 5/18/76)

More tentatively, I would suggest as a possible area for consideration links between spirit accounts and land boundaries. Particularly in Rarotonga, I was impressed by the number of times that specific boundaries were referred to in locating *tūpāpaku* events. This is, of course, in part a reflection of the general importance of such boundaries in establishing location. But land and its boundaries carry an emotional charge which has probably been increased rather than lessened through the operations of the Land Court.[10] Ancestral rights and interests are of central importance. An informant speaking of the death omen provided by the "ghost bird" *rākoa* said that it flew the boundaries of the land belonging to the person who would die—the correct ones, not those established by the Land Court! It is interesting to note that two of the most storied *tūpāpaku* sites, Black Rock and Te 'Utu o Apera, lie at major district boundaries. Subject to more systematic collection and study, I would suggest that a dramatic underwriting of boundaries may be one of the functions that spirit narratives fulfill in the Southern Cook Islands.

Actions of and Reactions to Spirits

> There is a story about the shore near here (Araoa). A man came back from fishing, at night, you know. He got a fire to cook some fish. When he looks up, there are faces of little white pigs around him. This was before Andy Nola brought the *puaka tea* (white pigs) here. He knew they were *tūpāpaku*. He was scared. It was the fire which kept them away. When it went down the pigs got closer. He was really scared. He put on some wood, but soon there was no more, only his canoe. He was so scared of what would happen if those pigs came to him he started to cut up his canoe. He burned it, bit by bit. Lucky for him, when the sun came he still had one bit left.
>
> (N.T., Mangaia, 8/24/76)

---

10 Mangaia has always resisted the Land Court, using its *aronga mana*, a body of chiefly titleholders, as a forum for land dispute.

Tūpāpaku are potentially dangerous. Tales tell of fear of death, disease, and misfortune through spirit contact and spirit displeasure, although in many the specific threat is left vague. In stories of nocturnal encounters, avoidance or concealment is usually presented as the safest course for the observer. Harm may not be deliberate on the part of the spirit. One Mangaian account tells how a *ta'unga* diagnosed the twisted neck of a young, part-European boy as due to a chance meeting with the spirit of an old fisherman. The spirit, simply curious at seeing a *papa'a* (European), had touched him, causing the condition. On the other hand, some spirits, perhaps especially those of the young, are presented as malicious; they may engage in *kanga*, mischievous, injurious play. Many accounts do, however, rest on the assumption of more pointed spirit activity.

Much of this activity could loosely be labeled as "protective"—of places, objects, people, custom. The relations described between human beings and *tūpāpaku* then depend on whether the persons concerned are part of "the protected" or constitute a threat to it. A number of tales relate to spirits which are specifically *tiaki*, "guardians" of particular sites of significance. Certain of the old burial and depository caves of Mangaia are foci for accounts of protective spirits, such as the lizard-form guardian of Piri te umeume. Right of presence by virtue of family connection plays a part in a number of stories. What is protected for the family, the *kopu tangata*, may be a source of danger to strangers/non-kin. Attitudes then reflect relationship to the spirit concerned. Tales of *tūpāpaku* guardians underline continuities with the historical past of the caves and *marae* and also make assertions about particular family associations to land.

Individuals can have personal protectors, as in the case of the spirit crickets referred to above, while stories concerning *ta'unga* frequently ascribe to them the ability to consult or make use of spirits. The late *ta'unga* of Mangaia, Paia, was described as having three named *tūpāpaku* as helpers. In addition, parental or ancestral spirits, in their protective function, are presented as providing care and support for their families. As omen creatures they provide information about events to happen in the family:

> One night I and my wife heard a horse outside the house, eating banana leaves, making noises. In the morning we couldn't see anything. The banana leaves were all fine. We knew it was a sign that somebody in the family was going to die. That was right.
>
> (P.A., Mangaia, 12/16/76)

Yet family spirits can also be described as threatening in circumstances where they are interpreted as expressing disapproval of the actions of the living. Divisions within the kin group are sometimes presented as inspiring *tūpāpaku* intervention. Reflecting on stories heard on Rarotonga relating to spirit concern in disputes over family land and titles, it is tempting to suggest that, initially at least, the tensions of relatively rapid social change may create an environment suited to the generation of new spirit accounts. The use of spirit concepts in relation to informal social control has often been discussed with respect to other societies of Polynesia (e.g., Hogbin 1934, Shore 1978).

The Users of *Tūpāpaku* Narratives

Although a number of the accounts of *tūpāpaku* related to me were prefixed "Old people used to say...," it became clear that knowledge of the spirit traditions is very widespread, bridging age and gender. They can feature in children's games and pastimes. On Mangaia in 1983, an eight-year-old girl was able to demonstrate the weaving out of plantain (Plataginaceae) stems of a conical structure known as *tamaru tūpāpaku*, literally a "shelter for spirits," although she insisted it was really more of a seat (the same term is applied to some fungi). She also explained her fears of walking alone through the village at night in terms of what she had heard of *tūpāpaku* activity. Spirit narratives are part of the world of many children, with implications for their control. Equally, young men in their teens and early twenties often proved to be enthusiastic tellers of ghost tales, providing both simple entertainment and the thrill of the uncanny in their own nocturnal activities.

In the wider community, as I have suggested, for some people *tūpāpaku* accounts remain one explanatory option for events seemingly out of the ordinary, while such stories can also be used to dramatize what is valued, whether in terms of social relationships, proprietary rights, or historical associations. Others would insist that as objects of belief, the *tūpāpaku* are "going." However true that may be, a knowledge of the elements of spirit accounts is still very much present, and many accounts are of the present.

Conclusion

The "ghost" narratives of the Cooks have not as yet been given the same degree of attention as historical and legendary tales. From the collections of Mangaian stories made by the Culture Division of the Cook Islands Government, as it existed in the 1970s, accounts of *tūpāpaku* were notably lacking. This is an understandable situation, for a number of reasons. The focus of such collecting was on gleaning information from those most knowledgeable in tradition, the *tumu kōrero*, to ensure preservation for the future. It was selective, concentrating upon that which "experts" could provide. Ghost tales are not, in general, part of such specialist knowledge, even if *tumu kārero* might be able to enlarge upon the details of particular traditions. *Tūpāpaku* accounts have, then, not fallen so readily into the framework of "official culture" as some other forms of story, almost by virtue of their number and continuing vitality. But it is the scope of their distribution and their interaction with experience which makes them such a potentially interesting area of study. They have never been separated from the life of the community as a whole. They have adapted consistently to new circumstances, incorporating new experience, yet maintaining a continuity with traditions of great antiquity. They then invite detailed consideration in tandem with study of social and cultural transformations in the Southern Cook Islands.

Perhaps, as Sahlins (1987) has recently suggested, our firmly drawn contrasts between continuity and change, cultural structure, and historical processes are in themselves misleading. His view of an event as a *relation* between a happening and a structure is potentially very relevant to an understanding of oral tradition. The telling of a traditional narrative is an act of cultural reproduction. But as Sahlins would argue, "every reproduction of culture is an alteration, insofar as in action, the categories by which a present world is orchestrated pick up some novel empirical content" (144). The idea of a dialogue between received categories and perceived contexts is one to which many interested in oral tradition will readily respond. Narrated events may reflect "real world" happenings while at the same time the narrative provides frameworks through which happenings are constituted as meaningful events. To explore such a dialogue fully requires the kind of holistic approach to oral narrative proposed by Bauman (1986), tying together narrated events, text, and performance. It is through performance in a given context that the categories implied by a particular narrative are brought most clearly into the realm of action. There they are realized by specific individuals with specific experiences and interests and are made available to the audience to be assimilated to their own experiences and interests. If we are to appreciate the complex processes at work in the meeting of story and experience, the various aspects of performance cannot be omitted from consideration. An understanding of the nature and development of Cook Islands spirit accounts would then require detailed study going far beyond the introductory remarks on their content and social setting offered in this paper. But this storytelling tradition lends itself to the exploration of the relations between experience and narrative. The potential rewards of its study are considerable.[11]

References

Baddeley 1985   J. Baddeley. "Traditional Healing Practices of Rarotonga, Cook Islands." In *Healing Practices in the South Pacific*. Ed. by Claire D. Parsons. Hawaii: Institute for Polynesian Studies. pp. 129-43.

Bauman 1986   R. Bauman. *Story, Performance, and Event: Contextual Studies of Oral Narrative*. Cambridge: Cambridge University Press.

Clerk 1981   C. C. Clerk. "The Animal World of the Mangaians." Ph.D. thesis, University of London.

Collocott 1923   E. E. V. Collocott. "Sickness, Ghosts, and Medicine in Tonga." *Jnl. of the Polynesian Society*, 32:136-42.

11 Field research in 1976-77 was performed with the assistance of funding from the U. K. Social Science Research Council and the Central Research Fund of the University of London. I would also like to acknowledge the help of Mr. Rangi Moeka'a, then head of the Anthropological Division, Premier's Department, Cook Islands, and of my many informants.

Crocombe 1980   M. T. Crocombe. "The Healer." In *Lali*. Ed. by A. Wendt. Auckland: Longman Paul. pp. 3-10.

Davis 1952   T. and L. Davis. *Doctor to the Islands*. Boston: Atlantic Monthly Press.

Firth 1930-31   R. Firth. "Totemism in Polynesia." *Oceania*, 1:291-321, 378-98.

Firth 1970   _____. *Rank and Religion in Tikopia*. London: Allen and Unwin.

Gill 1876   W. Wyatt Gill. *Myths and Songs from the South Pacific*. London: Henry S. King.

Gill 1890   _____. "Mangaia (Hervey Islands)." *Australasian Association for the Advancement of Science*, 2:323-53.

Gill n.d.   _____. Unpublished manuscript. Polynesian Society Papers 1187, folder 59, Alexander Turnbull Library, Wellington.

Goodman 1971   R. A. Goodman. "Some *Aitu* Beliefs of Modern Samoans." *Journal of the Polynesian Society*, 80:463-79.

Handy 1968   E. S. C. Handy. "Traces of Totemism in Polynesia." *Journal of the Polynesian Society*, 77:43-56.

Hogbin 1934   I. Hogbin. *Law and Order in Polynesia*. London: Christophers.

Levy 1973   R. I. Levy. *Tahitians: Mind and Experience in the Society Islands*. Chicago: University of Chicago Press.

Luomala 1983   K. Luomala. "Phantom Night Marchers in the Hawaiian Islands." *Pacific Studies*, 7:1-33.

Maranda 1978   E. K. Maranda. "Folklore and Culture Change: Lau Riddles of Modernization." In *Folklore in the Modern World*. Ed. by R. Dorson. Paris: Mouton. pp. 207-18.

Rickman 1931   T. H. Rickman. "Arapo." In *Torea Katorika*, November 1931, Rarotonga.

Sahlins 1987   M. Sahlins. *Islands of History*. London: Tavistock Publications.

Shore 1978   B. Shore. "Ghosts and Government: A Structural Analysis of Alternative Institutions for Conflict

Management in Samoa." *Man*, n.s. 13:175-99.

Tangatapoto 1984   V. Tangatapoto, O.B.E. "Death." In *Atiu: An Island Community*. Ed. by N. Kautai et al. Suva: Institute of Pacific Studies of the University of the South Pacific. pp. 147-57.

Tara'are 1919   Te Ariki Tara'are. "History and Traditions of Rarotonga." Pt. 7. *Journal of the Polynesian Society*, 28:183-208.

Te Rangi Hiroa 1934   Te Rangi Hiroa (P. H. Buck). *Mangaian Society*. Honolulu: Bernice P. Bishop Museum, Bulletin 122.

IX

"HEAD" AND "TAIL": THE SHAPING OF ORAL TRADITIONS AMONG THE BINANDERE IN PAPUA NEW GUINEA

John D. Waiko

The main aim of this article is to provide some insight into the basic cultural perceptions and oral processes of the Binandere people, who evolved sophisticated oral art forms to register events, something which then came into contact with the *Kiawa* (European) system of writing in March 1894.[1] Although it is beyond the scope of this article to treat the difficult problem of selecting appropriate historiographical models for dealing with the contact between societies with a system of writing and societies with developed oral cultures as in Papua New Guinea, the detailed discussion of one particular culture in Papua New Guinea can throw some wider light on the nature of oral tradition and how it is conceived and transmitted.

The Binandere community numbers about 5,000 and its members are subsistence farmers; they live on the lower reaches of the Mamba, Gira, and Eia rivers in the Oro Province, Papua New Guinea. My intention is a detailed description and analysis of the method by which poetic oral tradition is passed from one generation to another and the reasons why distortions creep into the body of those traditions within a period of six to eight generations among the Binandere.

There are some conceptual problems associated specifically with tradition-bearers in Papua New Guinean acephalous communities in contrast to the stratified societies elsewhere. In this country, the essence of live oral tradition is, I think, that there is not one carrier above all others. This situation stems from the fact that in this Melanesian society there are no specialists who are set aside as carriers of traditions and made directly responsible to a chief or king, or members of a higher class, or even the state. The result is that the transmission of the forms and contents of oral tradition is not supervised, guarded, and controlled by

---

[1] The Binandere use the literal phrase *parara embo* for white men but the common term, *Kiawa*, comes from the word for an axe with a fluted blade. The foreigners were the *Kiawa embo*, the "steel axe men."

someone higher on the social scale than the carriers themselves. This presents a contrast to the way in which formal traditions in the highly structured or graded societies of Polynesia are not necessarily alive but are bent towards the yoke of a ruler, with the result that a specialist is the custodian of the chief's, king's, or state's tradition. What obtains in such milieus is not, then, a living oral tradition because once one ruler succeeds to the throne or chieftainship, his personal order of generations becomes established as the live one. In my view the live spoken word in the non-hierarchical culture of Papua New Guinea is, by contrast, not controlled by any individual, as if there were a single carrier above all others, so that one needs to take a different approach to understanding transmission from a situation in which the tradition is contained in and shaped by a unique vessel, and thus open to corruption, being tied to a leader.

Western concepts of the nature of "history" and the methods devised there to describe and explain oral traditions may be insufficient to penetrate the allusions of very rich oral art forms of non-Western cultures like the Binandere. Again, methods developed to analyze Western music may be inadequate when applied to describing and analyzing music from another culture, as V. Chenoweth explains for the Duna (1968-69:218):

> Descriptive linguistics offers useful tools for music analysis... [because] the vocabulary of our traditional Western music theory is directed chiefly at teaching or analysing and composing in one particular music, the European system. Western music theory provides little in the way of either terms or procedures for entering another music system, especially one which is unwritten. Descriptive linguistics in working with unwritten languages has developed both methodology and terminology for the analysis and description of diverse systems. These may appropriately be used in the analysis and description of diverse musical systems.

Native speakers, however, working with their own familiar and heretofore unwritten terms, concepts, and images may pose challenges and develop methodology which can provide access to oral traditions in other cultures.[2] This article therefore starts by outlining Binandere concepts and metaphors associated with oral tradition, as a prelude to a further analysis of their various forms of oral tradition and verbal art.

---

[2] I have written my Ph.D. thesis in two languages: *Be mi Jijimo* (270 pp.) is in the Binandere vernacular which is my mother tongue; and "*Be Jijimo*: A History According to the Tradition of the Binandere People of Papua New Guinea" (478 pp.). Both works were completed at the Pacific and Southeast Asian History Department, Australian National University, Canberra, Australia, 1982.

Oral Tradition and Binandere Concepts

Sirawa: Weaving Method

The fundamental Binandere concept of "Head" and "Tail" has to do with an idea of oral traditions "flowing" from the "head" of a *sirawa*, a conical-shaped fish trap, towards the "tail" (see Figure 1 on p. 181). This image appropriately comes from the basic technology of the Binandere themselves: the *sirawa* helps make graphic the sequence of composition, incorporation, and elimination in oral traditions. This process occurs within the limits of six generations between *opipi* (the first ancestor) and *mai* (the youngest descendant) as discussed below.

Now I want to describe the way in which the *sirawa* is made, because an understanding of its frame helps in grasping the basic elements of its application to the discussion of oral traditions. The "mother" *sirawa*, the main conical shape, is a weaving together of fifty to one hundred ribs with bark strings or vines of the mature palm of the sago tree. The beginning of the weaving (*jirari*) looks something like an open venetian blind. The second stage involves tying each rib to a ring of *mambu*, or lawyer cane, which is formed by cutting a piece of about one yard and joining its two ends together. This gives stability in the weaving and its circular form by binding it to the *mambu*. Thus the mouth or the wide end of the cone is formed and the weaving is continued in a spiral, gradually forcing the ribs closer together. The narrow or tail end becomes smaller and smaller until the hole is about six inches across; this section is called *kombera*, or tight binding, and completes the major fish trap.

The minor or inner trap is woven from the ribs of young sago trees shorter than those used to make the longer outer trap. The size of the *mambu* of the small trap is the same as the big body so that one can be fitted onto the other. The weaving of the minor trap is completed by leaving a tiny hole of roughly three inches. This tail end is woven in such a way that the hole is elastic; it pulls and stretches when bigger fish enter the *sirawa*.

Oral narratives are created and they enter the "head" or a mouth. They are pushed through the first aperture for the primary sorting of the material; here the great detail of an event is eliminated. The selected information is then kept "flowing" until it is being forced through another aperture where a secondary refining of oral traditions occurs. This involves a kind of filtering process, so that the material that comes out at the very end, or "tail," is the essence of the "pure" (residual) element. The "head" is the beginning with the detailed information. This may indicate "early" or "today," while the "tail" is the ending that is represented by *kiki opipi*, or the receding elements of legends.

"Head" and "Tail"

There are six terms that the Binandere use to designate the sequence of generations. They start with *opipi*, the terminal ancestor, and end with *mai*, the youngest living descendant of the clan. The four words that refer to the generations falling in between *opipi* and *mai* are *etutu, ewowo, apie*, and *mamo*.

The sources that derive from each generation of living people and recent dead may be called *ambo*, the "tail tradition," but here I want to discuss the *gisi*, the "head traditions," or those of the long-dead generations. Before I go on, however, let me briefly describe a paradigm in which the process of *gisi edo ambo*, the "head" and "tail," occurs.

The Binandere use terms that recognize junior and senior generations. In its simplest form this practice is evident in the words used between children and their parents. For example, *gagara/mai* or daughter/son are the terms used by parents to refer to the younger generation, while *aia/mamo* or mother/father are terms used by children to refer to the older generation. When the third generation appears and when the *gagara/mai* grow up and marry, the latter's children refer to the *aia/mamo* as *apie*, grandparents. And as soon as the fourth generation appears, what was *apie* becomes *ewowo* or great-grandparents. Over time *ewowo* becomes *etutu* with the appearance of a fifth generation, and when the sixth one emerges it refers to the individual known person(s) in a given lineage as *oro be as opipi*, or terminal ancestors.

In a clan history a body of traditions is remembered as from the terminal ancestor; beyond this ancestor, the traditions tend to be forgotten over time. In other words, as each new generation develops, the human memory no longer has the capacity to memorize specific names of individuals and places of the most distant generation, particularly those beyond the terminal ancestor. Therefore the events associated with those people become *kiki opipi* or legends. Then a new set, now ending at the current *opipi*, becomes the known "history" of the community.

I will illustrate this point with the terminal ancestor of my own clan, Ugousopo. My *opipi* was named Danato, who was said to live about six generations ago. I was the first person who put my *opipi* down in writing, having learned it in 1967 from my father. Neither my father nor anyone else in my village or other villages knew Danato's father or mother. As far as the Ugousopo clan is concerned, our *opipi* was Danato and his son Waroda was my *etutu*. The latter had four children, and we can trace the subsequent generations down to mine. Had it not been for the intervention of European contact, it would be highly likely that my children's generation would have forgotten Danato and Waroda would have become their *opipi* instead.

It is clear that for the Ugousopo clan history the terminal ancestor, Danato, and his son Waroda were born and died at Maji Hill on the Kumusi River. It is Waroda's children who migrated to Eraga on the Mamba River, perhaps when they were adults. The detailed activities of my *opipi* and *etutu* are blurred, although the history of the three succeeding generations is abundantly clear.

Let me use several analogies to illustrate this complex perception of the historical process. First, take a banana tree that has six leaves numbering 1, 2, 3, 4, 5, and 6. Place them along the terms of each generation from 1 to 6: as *opipi, etutu, ewowo, apie, mamo,* and *mai*. The number 1 is *opipi*; this is the dry banana leaf, too old to remain on the tree so it falls to the ground. This happens when the new leaf emerges right inside, first as a small shoot and later as a leaf.

That is, when the sixth leaf (*mai*) appears, the first one (*opipi*) dries and withers away. As soon as the new leaf or generation develops, *mai* becomes *mamo*, *mamo* becomes *apie*, *apie* becomes *ewowo*, *ewowo* becomes *etutu*, and *etutu* becomes *opipi*, which "pushes" the former *opipi* away like the old leaf.

For the second analogy, let me return to the metaphor of the conical fishtrap, *sirawa*. The outer *sirawa* represents the *embo matu* or *gisi badari*, the three older generations (*ewowo*, *etutu*, and *opipi*). The inner *sirawa mai* represents the *mai teka*, the three younger generations, the oldest of which is *apie*. In other words, *apie* or grandparentage is significant in terms of sorting out traditions worthy of retention or worthless and to be eliminated. It is against the knowledge of the living *apie* that the knowledge of the succeeding generation is tested and checked for its originality and the reliability of its sources.

This process is symbolized in the *sirawa* itself where "feeding," sorting, and elimination occur (see Figure 1).

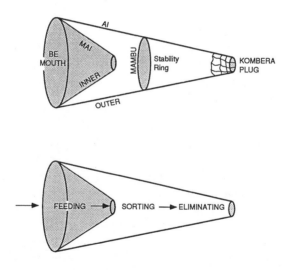

Figure 1. The Binandere Fish Trap

The diagram shows that oral traditions in the form of life experiences, incidents, and accidents are fed into the *mai* trap where they are sorted out with the store of traditions retained from the past. Some traditions that are not valuable, relevant, applicable, or practicable may have been discarded through time. Let us imagine that the third generation from the ego, the *apie* or grandparents, is like a repository for the oral traditions. But as the *apie* generation recedes into the past there occurs a critical point when traditions undergo changes: as a person separates the debris from the fish, so some traditions are selected and retained. This is neither a deliberate nor a conscious process but a slow and natural occurrence inherent in a society where oral communication is predominant. In short, the Binandere perceive time and sequences of events in a spiral form and not necessarily in a linear progression. There is repetition, as the *mai* generation changes into *mamo* and the *mamo* becomes *apie* and so on, but there is also movement forward in time; it is the endless cycle and advance of the spiral, it is both repetition and change.

This technique of using metaphorical language to represent changing detail is a way of condensing evidence into a form that can supplement the memory of man so that he can understand the past beyond the limit of six generations although he no longer retains detail. J. C. Miller puts it well when he distinguishes the historian who reads and writes history from written evidence and the historian who does not know how to read and write but seeks to explain events and draw evidence from oral tradition:

> Gradually forced by the limitation of the human memory to rely on abstract and condensed references to the original historical event, oral historians strive to retain historical accuracy (in exactly the Western literate sense) by eliminating the relatively unstructured details of proximate accounts from their performances. They substitute more easily remembered verbal formulae which indicate the event instead of dwelling on specific circumstances of the sort preferred by Western historians. They may embody significance in a proverb, in a stereotyped image or cliché, in a conceptual contrast drawn from their cosmological system, or in other symbol-laden verbal or mental construct and easily remembered form. It is this verbal nucleus that is historical in the sense that it conveys some combinations of a past event and its significance for oral historians and their audience down through time.[3]

Oral Traditions and Art Forms in Binandere Culture

The preceding discussion on how the Binandere metaphorically conceptualize the endless reflection and change of the past/present forms the background to the account in this section of the main types of Binandere oral tradition. It also helps to illuminate the processes by which these are formulated and transmitted.

In terms of an oral time-line, Binandere place legends beyond the *opipi*, the terminal ancestor. Thus *kiki opipi*, or stories having to do with terminal ancestors and beyond, contain precepts or ethical rules about the society. Moreover, the *kiki opipi* have a value as oral literature independent of their importance in transmitting values within the community. In spite of the changes that have taken place in the past one hundred years, the *kiki opipi* still reflect and enforce general Binandere morals and perceptions; they are still an "applied art."

The "Head": Legends as Oral Literature

It must be emphasized that *kiki opipi*, myths or legends, do not constitute a neat collection of straight threads making distinct patterns and portraying easily

---

[3] I am very grateful to Dr. Miller for kindly allowing me to quote this unpublished material from a manuscript I read in 1980.

understood moral lessons. Rather they are myriad tangled strands and weaving knots passing one on top of the other, mingling sacred and secular values, and leaving the listeners to unravel a small part of the mystery of right behavior.

In fact, among the Binandere there is a cultural warning that any legend contains puzzling and even contradictory elements. This feature is found in the standard opening phrases. The teller begins a myth with the following images: "*kiki akou pepeia papeia, bono jimi watawata; ato kirara karara; ango enune.*" This is literally translated as "story shell (coconut) flat; *bono* (a type of) lizard's tail wriggling; *ato* (a kind of an edible) plant's leaves with rattling noise; as it happened I am going to weave a story." This introduction contains two nonsensical things (the flat coconut and a crackling noise from the *ato* plant) and one which is sensible, and shows the weaving together of elements that are readily understood with those that are not easily comprehended. The opening phrases signal to the listeners that a legend is about to be told and may be interpreted as "there are many strands whose ends do not meet or make sense but I am going to tell it as it is—as a whole passed down from the past;" or, "I am going to trace the weaving of the story as faithfully as I can remember the version I have learned from my mother/father."

At the end of the legend the teller again recites a well known formula: "'*ro mai da, ra mai: iji vitari da, iji wotari da: rorae / wo isirari gido tedo orote tedo na rorae / wo etena.*" This means literally "men everywhere, from sunrise to sunset, find the existence of this thing/animal and tell a tale about it, so I have become a thing/animal." These standard opening and closing images are not used at all when the Binandere relate accounts of migration and warfare, although the narration starts with the *tugata*: "I am so and so; my father is such and such of Z clan, and I come from X village. It is I who am going to weave the story as I heard it from my father." Then he or she finishes by reidentifying the source of the story again as "I am . . . it is I who have told it." The stylized beginnings and endings clearly distinguish between the legends and the stories of warfare in terms of their validity as "history:" just as a Western scholar might ask how does this informant know, so the villagers question the reliability of the storyteller.

The context of the *tugata* is one way of keeping the oral tradition extremely "pure," since no one can tell a story without admitting and acknowledging his source. Anyone in the village environment can judge whether that person learned the story from a reliable person who really knows it or not. When he says "I know it from my father," he is actually declaring to someone who might challenge his authority by saying "my grandfather told me"—which may be a better version of it. This is how the oral history is kept so particularly well.

Thus Binandere have a clear distinction between myths or legends, which form an integral part of the body of literary tradition of those generations beyond the terminal ancestor, and history, which begins with the ancestor and goes down to the youngest living member of the clan. The litmus test for the distinction is to apply the basic rules underlying history: when, how, why, and who. If the answer relates to human beings or tangible things, then it is clear that one is dealing with history, particularly when the events relate to those generations on this side of the *opipi*. Beyond this point the test fails. In a nutshell, the terminal ancestor is an important landmark for much of clan history among the Binandere as they try to choose between myths and history.

I have on many occasions approached individuals who appear to know a certain tradition. They would not tell me any of it unless it is their story to tell. They would respond, "I am sorry, I know that story because I was there, but the central person who was involved with the events is Z, so Z is the right person to tell you." As a result, one avoids the poor version because the people keep referring the interested party back to the right person for a "correct" version; and that "reference," together with the fact that when they sing songs they must remember the words exactly, keeps the oral records intact. *Kiawa*, or Europeans, have literacy, but they have a poor memory of the activities of the members of their recent generations. Yet all peoples, *Kiawa* or otherwise, when they are not literate, have very good memories; and they are very concerned about keeping their traditions correct.

The "Tail": Art Forms

Earlier I mentioned that the "head" and "tail" concepts for traditions dealt with the way in which some testimonies are created, condensed, or codified, and I referred to the sifting processes. There are three filters, consisting of primary, secondary, and tertiary stages, through which oral traditions flow and by which they are distilled. This section takes up the specific oral sources that deal with what happened between *opipi*, the terminal ancestor, and the *mai*, the living generation. It also deals with the types of art forms that are arranged in the order of the distilling processes, beginning with the types of different primary art forms and the techniques of their creation and retention, then going on to the secondary art forms in which the primary is formalized; and then continuing with how the traditions are adapted into a tertiary art form to facilitate memorization and recitation among the Binandere. The section also concerns itself with the method by which all the three art forms are passed down from one generation to the other.

These different forms have different structures. For instance, that known as *ji tari* (see below) represents the spontaneous recording of an event that happened at the very time the event occurred, and the songs describe the persons or emotions in the immediate situation. The *ji tari*, like all traditions, start with an individual responding to a given situation and the individual expressing his emotions in song. A person may die and a relative burst into cry, and another close relative or perhaps a poet mentally records the chants; this may be called a primary art form because a chant is created over death. It is primary in the sense that the death creates a situation in which the original cry is composed by an individual. After the mourning period is over, with very careful recall of the exact words of the original cry, the gifted artist can turn the *ji tari* into *guru*, or more formal song with a standardized structure. The repeating of the original *ji tari* by such an artist may be termed a secondary art form simply because the artist adopts the *ji tari* into a formal set. This modulation simplifies memorization and recitation. The artist then embodies the chant and teaches other people, who may perform it on social occasions. The chant then becomes an item to reproduce as exactly like the original as possible, and it is in a form that can be recalled. This standardized *guru* I call the tertiary art form.

Thus there are three parts to the establishment of oral poetic tradition: an individual creates it in response to an emotional situation, a poet formalizes it to facilitate recall, and a group recites it in the form of *guru*. This evolution requires the cooperation of generations; creators, artists, and memorizers all play a crucial part in the repertoire of traditions for the next generation. There is a continuation and creation of things, as opposed to the static view of "old tradition" being handed down. But this situation creates vulnerability within each tradition. Among the Binandere, the members of each generation are taught to use the three art forms.

Each stage of primary, secondary, and tertiary art is marked by a filter through which oral tradition is distilled. This means that distortions are likely to creep in during the various stages, particularly between the secondary and tertiary art forms, because the composers of *ji tari* on which the later *ya tari* and *guru* songs are based may be dead. The chances of distortion increase when the *guru* passes from one generation to another because members of a given generation are more likely to remember traditions nearer to them than others from the deep past.

My analysis of the song form is, in fact, a decoding or de-condensing of the chants that includes the treatment of meaning and dating of the various art forms. This is because I have the advantages of being a speaker of the language and of knowing the method by which the Binandere encode their oral traditions, especially the *ji tari* chants and the *guru*, so that I am able to unravel the process by which condensing is done. I now turn to a detailed analysis of the structure and the rules that determine the creation of Binandere oral poetic literature, the *ji tari* and its associated *guru*, and how they are performed. The complexity of the composition and the allusions contained in the language make this type of oral art almost impenetrable to the outsider.

It is extremely difficult to take the terms of a Western discipline and apply them within a non-Western culture. The following attempt to simplify and describe selected poems, and then to present a detailed analysis of the composition and content of the *ji tari* and *guru*, may at least allow a person from another culture to see artistic order in what may otherwise be taken to be spontaneous, formless, or repetitive. I present types of different art forms and discuss their structures and meaning. There follow two examples of what I call primary art and the context in which they are created.

Ji Tari: Creation of a Primary Art Form

A *ji tari* is a kind of chant of lament, "a monotonous and rhythmic voice" uttered on occasions of death, loss, and pain. *Ji tari* express sorrow or happiness in a poetic manner, depending on the context in which they are composed. I start with the type of vocabulary that describes the lyrics and the complex or simple body movements that communicate meaning.

The *ji tari* is thus a cry. Chants take place when death occurs, over losses of items, at arrivals, and even at the temporary absence of loved ones. Indeed, people do "cry" on these occasions and another person listens carefully to the chant and mentally records it. Later the *ji tari* is adjusted to two kinds of songs. The listener decides whether the *ji tari* is *guru* or *yovero*; the former has meter and rhythm whereas the latter lacks repeating patterns of syllables.

The structure of the poem reveals three characteristics: images, meter, and repetition, each having a unique role for evocation, repeating pattern of syllables, and recurring themes, respectively. Thus, *ji tari* is poetry in the sense that poetry is a condensation of everyday language. A poem must contain a complete event, but this event is not described in detail; instead it is being evoked through a series of images.

The conversion of a *ji tari* to a *guru* is the work of gifted poet and singer. He (or she) takes the intensely felt emotion of a particular moment and makes it into art. It should be obvious that this careful memorization makes the *ji tari* a good source of history, provided that the material is deciphered properly, even though it is a register that keeps track of events and names of individual members of a lineage. It is a way of compressing events around a genealogy, of making them into a concise form for commitment to memory. The *ji tari* is also a technique for coding happenings that become a part of a body of traditions passed down from one generation to another.

Indeed, *ji tari* is the creation of the primary art form that involves the spontaneous recording of the event(s)—sung about the persons in the immediate situation. *Ji tari* is also the repeating of the songs by others, after the event is over, in a secondary form sung by an individual or a group. *Ya jiwari* is a tertiary form based on the primary *ji tari*. Therefore, it is significant that the source of all Binandere art forms is the musical expression given a particular real event or moment in time by someone who is very moved by strong feelings of some kind. This musical creation can then be used, if faithfully recorded by others, with altered forms and join a wider repertoire.

Ya Jiwari: Memorizing and Reciting Secondary and Tertiary Art Forms

In the art form known as *ya tari*, *ya* means both "song" and "dance," and *tari* is "to sing." The *ya* is derived from *ji tari*, a special term for it being *yovero*, a song sung by a single person; a group who sings a *ya*, especially while engaged in a physical labor, is given the name *tebuia*. The *ya* that expresses romantic love stems from *bote*, the songs lovers sing about each other. There is no aesthetic body movement—only the melodic voices. *Bote* and *ji tari* are spontaneously created songs about the person's own immediate situation; they are therefore primary art forms. *Ya tari*, on the other hand, are the repeating of those songs by others, sometimes after the event. *Ya tari*, in fact, is a secondary art form which involves some kind of formalizing of the songs.

The *ya jiwari* is a new form, although it is based on the *ji tari*. *Ya jiwari* has a formal structure in terms of verses and stanzas. It contains a standard form called *guru*. It may be termed a tertiary art form because of the way it is standardized for the purposes of memorizing and reciting on public occasions. *Ya jiwari* involves singing songs to the rhythm of drum beats. In the men's *ya jiwari*, sometimes called *guru*, the *ji tari* is adjusted to *embo da ya*, the men's dance. There are rules that govern the adjustment between *ji tari* and *guru;* the strict social sanction of remembering the members of a clan from senior to junior is a good example of the difference between the two. The *guru* requires accuracy. There are also rules that control the meter, image, association, cue, and repetition of the *jiwari* in songs. Two other conventions concern the order in which the *guru* is sung. There is the "first" *kumbari*, termed the *maemo*, by the male lead (equivalent to the precentor in Western music). This is followed by the "second" *kumbari*, often called the *be*. The second rule is that the man who follows the *maemo* must take his cue from the precentor so that the items in both *kumbari* match, or come from related categories of animals and plants. It is here that it is so important to remember to sing the names of a given lineage and not to confuse the sequence(s) of individual people in a given generation. The third rule is that the *jiwari*, or the rest of the men in the group, must repeat the *be* when they join in the singing; that is, they must give the names of individual items or human beings that the second *kumbari* has chanted.

During the final feast in honor of a dead relative, the *guru* takes place at night when men come together in the *arapa*, the center between the *mando* and *oro* of the family that holds the feast. The young men beat the drum, blow a conch shell, and join in the *jiwari*. The men of middle age and over sing the first and second *kumbari* by virtue of the fact that they are old enough to know the songs and indeed recite the genealogy. The men move to and fro within a space that may be a distance of about ten yards across. Also there are rules that govern the movement. The three sequential rules described above (first and second *kumbari* plus the *jiwari*) make up one complete *ya be*, and a *ya be* must be sung and danced twice before another *ya be* starts. It is sung the first time by the dancers moving through the *arapa*, and then repeated as they move back to their original positions. Each double performance of a *ya be* is followed by *kewoia*, a kind of buffer to give an opportunity for the elderly men to remember some more *ya be*, since one man leads and the rest join in; but it has also two stops before a new *ya be* begins.

A *ya jiwari* performed to a different kind of drum-beat is called a *kasamba*. By contrast this is *eutu da ya*, a women's song. It is often called *ba da ya*, or the Taro's song, so termed because it is performed at taro harvest times. The procedures that govern the singing of *kasamba* are simple: there is only one *kumbari* and the rest join in repeating the monotonous pitches; but the same *ya* has to be sung twice before another one starts. To sing *kasamba* both women and men sit around the fire. The conch-shell is the accompaniment to the men's *guru* and the women's *kasamba*, although each pitch is at different tempo.

Guru: Reciting a Tertiary Form

I have said earlier that the *ji tari* is a form of register; death is an important occasion to be remembered and the *ji tari*, and later the *guru*, serve to record such events as death and the emotion of the time. I have also shown how *ji tari* are changed to *guru* to highlight the creative method, the content, and the form of *ji tari*. The creative process is still going on and will continue in the foreseeable future. As one generation passes through time, deaths occur and new *ji tari* as well as *guru* are created and incorporated into the charter of traditional art forms, while the old *ji tari* and *guru* are forgotten. It is a creative and continuing process. A third point I wish to emphasize is the artistic use of image, meter, and repetition. It should be clear by now that *ji tari* is, in fact, a poetic way of recording an event with some details, while *guru* is a technique of condensing the same event into a precise form of recitation; in this precise form it can then pass to succeeding generations as part of the community's oral traditions.

The original chant is retained when it is changed into the *guru*. It is only the rhyme that is adjusted; everything else remains the same. The original *ji tari* is always a solo, the expression of an individual on a particular emotional occasion. *Guru*, on the other hand, is the work of a single creative person but performed by a group; it is the product of a gathering of men, young and old, singing with the repetitive drum beat. When sung in a social gathering, the *guru* in fact follows a different order from the one I have presented. The lead is given by the *ya kumbari* (literally the "song-taker"), who sings the first line, and he is followed by a second *kumbari* or solo singer before the *ya jiwari*, the group members, come along to repeat the lines of the second *kumbari* as a chorus in concert. The examples given a little later will make it plain that *guru*, or the tertiary art form, provides the entire recitation during the public performance.

Sequences of Events and Changes in Traditions

Earlier I have attempted to indicate the way in which Binandere relate the sequence of events that are determined or ordered by generations. Nowadays they talk about the past in terms of pre- and post-*Kiawa* (European). Indeed, the white man arrived during the time of my grandparents, so that the accounts of warfare and the initial contact histories described earlier—told from my father's generation and above—are one generation removed from me. The roots of the traditions that deal with the post-contact situation are very shallow because they extend over only two generations. Obviously, they are much more reliable than those of the pre-contact. The traditions associated with the earlier generations *ewowo, etutu,* and *opipi* are embedded in the deeper, although recent past, so that the chances of distortion are much greater than in the post-*Kiawa* times. I will give some examples to illustrate how the changes occur in the primary, secondary, and tertiary art forms, which also often usher in distortions.

The first is a lament uttered by an ancestress. Kaiae was an unmarried woman, probably of the Dowaia clan. But for some reason or other she determined not to marry Yaurabae, and avoided him at all times. As a warrior he was called to go on a war expedition to an enemy land. Decorated and armed for war, the warriors left by canoe. *Kokito*, a sea animal, attacked the canoe with its tentacles, sinking it and drowning all the warriors.

Kaiae lamented the loss of Yaurabae who was her *ru*, her "brother." She cried for him and regretted her lack of interest in him; and her *ji tari* was put into a *guru*. Her would-be husband was from the Dowaia clan. This is evident from the names of individuals: Bingoru, Gina, Gauga, Omena, and Barago; Yaurabae is not mentioned at all.

Iu Bingoru apie	Husband Bingoru grandson
Mimai eite	Catching sweet perfume
Iu o ru o	Husband brother
Mimane tae	I have lost the scent

Kaiae was more attracted to a man from her own clan than Yaurabae of Yopare clan, but perhaps deep down in her liver and lungs (said to be the source of love, rather than the heart) she desired Yaurabae as a potential husband. Perhaps she avoided him as a protest against those who arranged the marriage. The *guru* does not contain much information on the closeness of the kin relationship between the two, which might have been the reason for Kaiae's avoidance.

It is possible to say something on the dating of this *ji tari* because we have detailed information on Yaurabae's clan. A genealogical chart of Yopare clan shows that Yaurabae was one of the sons of Waiago. The latter was one of the five clansmen who migrated from the Kumusi to the Mamba via Daiago Swamp, a distance of about 30 miles, as a result of constant wars there. There have been four generations since Yaurabae lived: two have died and the members of the other two are living members of the clan. The oldest of the living generations, S. Teiane, was about seventy years in 1979 and the youngest of his generation is about forty-five years of age. The oldest of Teiane's children would be about thirty-five and the youngest about four years.

As yet I have not collected detailed genealogies of Kaiae's clan, but it would seem from the use in the chants of the suffix *apie* that her lover was a grandson of Bingoru and others. This means that Kaiae's *ji tari* has a time sequence of two generations prior to and four to five generations since she lived—a possible total of seven generations. This situation suggests that the *ji tari* and the sequent *guru* concern events that took place earlier than the time derived from genealogy alone; by using the information contained in *guru* still known today, it may be possible to go back further into clan histories than through genealogies. In other words, normally the *guru* gives the names of the parents and grandparents of the person lamented in the chant. Where the *guru* is set in a time at or beyond the limit of currently remembered genealogies, the chant effectively takes the listener a further two generations back.

The above example also brings out the subtle manner in which changes or distortions are likely to creep into the process of transmitting poetic tradition from one generation to another. In the original, Kaiae chanted Bingoru, Gina, Gauga, Omena, and Barago. It was clear that Kaiae was the third generation from her terminal ancestor, and so was Yaurabae; most elders know that and they recite his clan's names as well. Without the elders, however, the younger generation replaced the original names with people such as Ororo and Baude *apie*:

Iu Ororo apie	Husband Ororo grandson
Mimain eite	Catching sweet perfume
Iu o ru o	Husband brother
Mimane tae	I have lost the scent

But men such as Ororo and Baude in fact come after the Kaiae and Yaurabae generation. The younger people have fallen into the expected error of replacing distant ancestors with those more familiar to them. And this is precisely one reason why the old and the young dance and sing *guru* in which the genealogies are recited, dramatized, and passed on.

The songs of the Binandere not only record their people's history, but like all songs and poems, they also reflect what the composers find intensely moving. The *ji tari* are in this way history invested with a community's values and emotions. The value of the songs as sources for the historian is made apparent by connecting them to incidents in Binandere history. For the *Kiawa*'s writings there is a disadvantage in that they show cultural bias, but taken as a whole the songs do express the feelings of all the community.

I illustrate this point with two laments from my clanswoman, who was born before the *Kiawa* reached the area but died after the contact. On one occasion Gewara, a Bosida woman whose husband, Aveia, had passed away, put on a *boera*, a jacket of Job's Tears. During this period of mourning her *bi*, a term used by a wife to refer to her husband's sister, a woman called Mimbai, also died. Her body was buried when Gewara was not in the village. The chanter imagined what Gewara's dead husband would want to know as soon as the spirit of Mimbai arrived in the village of the dead. He would ask, "How is my wife?" Gewara, the chanter assumed, would wish her *bi* to answer him, "Your wife still loves you very much to this day, as is evident from the fact that she has not removed the jacket from her body; she has not made love to anyone." The pathos of the moment is increased because the absent Gewara had been unable to say anything to the dying Mimbai; she had missed a chance to have a message carried across the barrier between the living and the dead:

Teiano visido	I have not washed
Buie de teiko	She should say to him
Takimba aro	If he asks
Giwasi o teiko	How is my bonded wife, the wife once so tightly bound to me.

Binano visido	I have not removed my *boera*
Buie de teiko	She should say to him
Jijia aro	If he asks
Giwasi o teiko	How is my wife now held by time-loosened binding.

Domano visido	I have not abandoned him
Buie de teiko	She should say to him
Punduga aro	If he asks
Giwasi o teiko	How is my wife still held by the knots
	which never untie.

In the Binandere language the closeness of husband and wife is conveyed through the terms used when lashing fence poles together. *Takimba* in the first verse describes the tight, new vine; *jijia* in the second verse implies that the bindings have dried and loosened, but in the third verse *punduga* is the firm end knot that must hold, indicating that Gewara is still tightly bound to her dead husband. The sequence of metaphors is readily understood by a Binandere audience, but cannot of course be translated literally for outsiders.

The mourning jacket remained on Gewara's body until the final feasts. She climbed onto the display platform, and during the ceremony she wept that she was going to remove the jacket because she was still emotionally attached to him:

Iu bindedo	Am I to remove him with the jacket
Domain o enita?	And abandon my husband?
Iu gagara Koia da aie	I am Koia's mother.

Iu te'edo	Am I to wash my body
Domain o enita	And abandon my husband?
Iu gagara Upari o aie	I am Upari's mother.

Iu kokedo	Am I to cast off my old skin
Domain o enita	And abandon my husband?
Iu gagara Gori da aie	I am Gori's mother.

Kapura maia o	He hunted alone in Dapura's dense forest
Binain o enita	Am I to desert him?
Iu gagara Koia da aie	I am Koia's mother.

The Binandere ancient oral art which was developed prior to the arrival of *Kiawa* continued to record significant incidents in the post-contact period. Again the songs are worth close analysis to uncover the response to the demands of the new order:

Tangsia Wowore	Daring with pineapple clubs
Apie ito da	Were your grandparents,
Leveni embo de	But red-ribboned people
Dede gesiri e	Have frightened you.

Kepata wowore	Brave with *kepata* weapons
Ewowo o ito da	Were your great-grandparents,
Kaia embo de	But under the knife-people
Tosi e genteni e	You have submitted.

Taiko wowore	Courageous with *taiko* spears
Etutu ito da	Were your great-great-grandparents,
Benesi embo de	But under the bayonet-people
Siro e esiri e	You have suffered defeat.

Bunduwa worore	Fearless with disc clubs
Opipi o ito da	Were your ancestors,
Pausi embo de	But the pouch-men
Dede gesiri	Have humiliated you.

The red ribbon which was worn on the edge of the police uniform, the knife, bayonet, and pouch refer of course to *Kiawa* and the policemen. The poet contrasted these items with the traditional weapons, the *kepata*, the knife-like instrument, and the *taiko*, the spear, both made from black palms. Translation of Gewara's songs diminishes much of the power of the images. The historian who wants only the "evidence" may be satisfied with bare prose and a description of the context, but the "art" is no longer there.

"Emic" and "etic" are descriptive terms employed by linguists and anthropologists who study societies other than their own. K. L. Pike, a linguist, defines the words (1967:37):

> The etic viewpoint studies behavior as from outside a particular system, as an essential initial approach to an alien system. The emic viewpoint results from studying behavior as from inside the system.

This approach omits a third possibility that the colonized might use to describe their own society. This third approach is signaled by the Binandere term *tono*. At present I would use it to express my purpose in contrast to that of, for example, F. E. Williams (1969). I am inside the Binandere community that is itself changing, and share many of that community's values. I am also equipped with the techniques of the outsider—including of course the language—that I am applying as well as I am able to the culture of my own people. I have tried to "unwrap" some of the songs so that others can see right to the *tono*, to the very basis of their creation and meaning.

Williams, a sympathetic observer, did not have sufficient understanding of the language to appreciate the art of the *ji tari* and the *guru*. He praised the drama that was displayed before him, but the ear of the outsider is deaf to the subtlety and the allusions of the *ji tari* and *guru*. In addition, the *ji tari* and the *guru*, as compressed statements, retain much recent history and may provide clues to a more distant past. As I have shown in this article, the *ji tari* and *guru* as well as other oral traditions are still being created, but at the same time fragments are being lost. The *ji tari* and *guru* are fixed to no pages; they are part of a dynamic culture and move with that culture alone; the *ji tari* and *guru* are thus a continuing process.

Conclusion

The condensation process therefore changes the nature of the reconstruction of the past, in the real sense that it may also allow distortion and/or corruption to creep into the body of traditions, particularly the oral kind. The fact is that every generation tends to sort out its own traditions with great care in such a manner that what is passed down in a refined form through word of mouth is still something that is very useful in re-creating the past and indeed in interpreting the present.

By and large, in Papua New Guinea the egalitarian nature of the social structure provides great scope for developing methods to analyze the social history of the many communities in the recent past. However, the acephalous society also imposes severe limits on the social historians: one such constraint has to do with the seasonal and generation-bound time scale whose memory-span spreads within ten generations as a rule (although there are exceptions). The bearers of traditions are not necessarily specialists who are assigned the responsibility of the clan's or tribe's repository. This situation means that almost every member of each clan is obliged to learn and keep alive—as well as to pass on—the customs, traditions, and history of the clan.

Each member of the nuclear family—grandparents, mother, father, and children—listens to and learns stories, legends, and the history of the lineage and other traditions of their immediate and extended family in greater detail than do those outside the clan. Just as the mother and father transmit their knowledge to their daughters and sons, so that they in turn can preserve and transmit the history of the descent, there is no one person who is set aside or above as the unique carrier of traditions (possibly with the one exception of the sorcerer of the clan). Just as the authority and influence of the recognized "big man" of the group does not go beyond the clan, so too the detailed knowledge of history in each lineage remains within the bounds of the small society. In a nutshell, the sources of history for the group are not confined to a specialist but are spread around among the members of the group, as opposed to the situation in hierarchical societies elsewhere.[4]

References

Chenoweth 1968-69   V. Chenoweth. "An Investigation of the Singing
                         Styles of the Dunas." *Oceania*, 39:218-30.

---

[4] A version of this paper was presented at the Pacific History Association Conference held at the University of South Pacific, Suva, Fiji, 27 June to 2 July, 1985. Another version was delivered in the "Myth and History" section of the Sixth International Oral History Conference, Ruskin College, Oxford, England, 11 to 13 September 1987. I am grateful to Drs. Cliff Moore, Edgar Waters, and Ms. Inge Riebe for their comments, suggestions, and criticism. They are absolved from any error of interpretation or judgment, for which I am entirely responsible.

Denoon and Lacey 1981   J. D. Denoon and R. J. Lacey, eds. *Oral Tradition in Melanesia*. Port Moresby: UPNG Printery.

Inglis 1967   K. S. Inglis. "The Study of History in Papua New Guinea." Inaugural Lecture, Boroko.

Kolia 1976   J. Kolia. *The History of Balawaya*. Boroko: IPNGS.

Lacey 1975   R. J. Lacey. "Oral Tradition as History: An Exploration of Oral Sources Among the Enga of New Guinea Highlands." Ph.D. dissertation, University of Wisconsin, Madison.

Miller 1980   J. C. Miller, ed. *African Past Speaks: Essays on Oral Tradition and History*. Folkstone: Dawson and Archon.

Pike 1967   K. L. Pike. *Language in Relation to a Unified Theory of the Structure of Human Behavior*. The Hague: Mouton.

Stephen 1974   M. Stephen. "Continuity and Change in Mekeo Society 1890-1971." Ph.D. dissertation, Australian National University, Canberra.

Vansina 1965   J. Vansina. *Oral Traditions: A Study in Historical Methodology*. London: Aldine and Routledge & Kegan Paul.

Waiko 1972   J. D. Waiko. "'Oro' Orokaiva: A Binandere Response to Imperialism." B.A. (Honors) thesis, UPNG.

Waiko 1986   _____. "Oral Tradition Among the Binandere: Problems of Method in Melanesian History." *Journal of Pacific History*, 21:21-38.

Waiko 1982   _____. "*Be Jijimo*: A History According to the Tradition of Binandere People of Papua New Guinea." Ph.D. dissertation, Australian National University, Canberra.

Williams 1969   F. E. Williams. *Orokaiva Society*. Oxford: Clarendon Press.

X

EVERY PICTURE TELLS A STORY: VISUAL ALTERNATIVES TO ORAL TRADITION IN PONAM SOCIETY

James Carrier and Achsah Carrier

Those concerned with recording the history, the culture, and the tradition of village societies seek the sources of their information in the spoken word. Historians, folklorists, and anthropologists have sat down with their informants, pencil and paper in hand, and have urged them to *talk*. After all, these are the people and societies without history, the people and societies that do not produce written accounts that might contain the answers to the questions posed by investigators. These researchers have benefited from a change that has been taking place in western scholarship, unevenly in different disciplines, over the past quarter-century: the revaluation of the sources of tradition and local knowledge, a revaluation that elevates oral sources and oral traditions in relation to their written counterparts. In our own field, anthropology, evidence of this change is found in the growing interest in ethnohistory and ethnopoetics, part of a general turn toward more cultural concerns. This shift shows an increasing awareness that oral studies have a logic and validity of their own, that they are not merely inferior cousins to the study of written sources. Indeed, some scholars who espouse this viewpoint have theorized that the emergence of writing was not an unalloyed good, a leap out of the darkness (e.g. Goody 1977; Ong 1971). Instead, it comes to take on elements of a fall, as the spread of writing is associated with the growth of an oppressive state.

Such reconsideration of the centrality and privileged position of writing has, however, not moved to the next important step, a reconsideration of the centrality of words themselves. The idea that the Great Transformation was from speaking to writing is a statement of how much we focus on words, how much we see words as the key form of expression, the key to mentality, and even the key to humanity itself. The spoken word may be different from the written word, but there is nothing more. The gap between writing and speaking is but a small leap compared to the chasm between words and everything else.

One might object that such a judgment of the centrality of words is self-evident. And so of course it is. One cannot, we suspect, seriously imagine human existence in the absence of words. How could people make themselves known to each other? How could experience and knowledge pass from person to person, much less from generation to generation? But to say that the centrality of words is self-evident does not mean that the topic is closed, that words are all there is. The unthinking acceptance of this centrality of words has an unfortunate consequence that surely is unintended: other forms of communication are lost to view. Because we take the oral and written forms to exhaust the ways in which words can exist, we often take them to exhaust the ways in which communication can exist, that history and tradition can be maintained over time and passed from one generation to the next. But when this notion is stated explicitly, its falsity is apparent. We all know of many ways in which meaning can exist and be transmitted other than in written or spoken words. And when we reduce these other ways to inconsequence, we unthinkingly reproduce and impose on the people we study the Western valuation of verbal communication.

Our purpose in this paper is to demonstrate the partiality of the concern with words. We will do so by showing how one group of people described to themselves their history and organization and sense of themselves in a nonverbal way during the period we studied them. That nonverbal means is the arrangement of the display of gifts in exchange, and the people are villagers from Ponam Island, in Manus Province, Papua New Guinea.[1] In stressing the importance of nonverbal communication, however, we do not mean that an investigator could look at Ponam gift display and derive from it alone any sort of adequate knowledge of Ponam society or history. Certainly we had to undertake extensive oral work to elucidate the meanings embedded in the displays, and certainly Ponams themselves talked about their displays. We are not, in other words, arguing for the exclusivity of these displays in Ponam culture. Similarly, we are not arguing that they are self-contained. In fact, they were always accompanied by speech.

Such qualifications do not mean, however, that these displays were secondary to the speech that accompanied them. They were not some fumbling attempt at sign language, a poor effort to convey with nonverbal markers a meaning that actually resided in words. Neither were they derivative of some body of words that was culturally prior or more valued. They were not second-best, mere figures or embellishments that accompanied the real verbal work of transmitting Ponam history and tradition. Instead, it would be more accurate to say that the reverse was true: the displays were primary, they told the story. The words that accompanied them were secondary, deriving from and embellishing the displays. The *words* were second-best.

---

[1] Since our concern here is not ethnographic, we will dispense with the usual brief description of the society concerned. Those who are interested should consult J. and A. Carrier 1985, 1989. Ponam display in exchange is described in detail in A. Carrier 1987, and the relationship of Ponam ceremonial exchange and display to islanders' self-conception is discussed in J. Carrier 1987.

Nonverbal Representation of Social Relations

Although nonverbal communication is not a popular topic, it has attracted some interest among anthropologists in Melanesia, particularly people's use of display and decoration as a means of making statements about themselves. For example, in *Self-Decoration in Mount Hagen* (1971), Andrew and Marilyn Strathern describe the ways that Hageners paint and dress themselves as part of ceremonial displays. Also, they show that this decoration is a system of communication, more or less explicitly articulated by the people themselves. What Hageners usually communicate is their strength and solidarity as a group in relation to other groups; while this concept can be communicated verbally, spoken assertions do not carry the force of visual demonstration. More generally, such self-decoration serves Hageners as "a medium through which people demonstrate their relationship to their ancestral spirits, express certain ideals and emotions, in short make statements about social and religious values" (1).

Michael O'Hanlon (1983) also has described the use of display in the Highlands of Papua New Guinea, although his concern is less the symbolism of specific elements of decoration that attracted the Stratherns, and more the overall effect of the appearance of massed dancing clansmen. O'Hanlon says that the Wahgi groups he studied are concerned with their strength, especially their internal unity and amity. This strength is always threatened by the chance of betrayal from within the group, brought about by hidden anger among clansmen. The manifestation of this betrayal is in the appearance of the clan's dancers: instead of a mass of strong, unified, young, and shiny-skinned men, the betrayed appear to be few, weak, out-of-step, and dull-skinned. For the Wahgi, the appearance of the dancers communicates their moral state: "A group displaying its numbers cannot be regarded as displaying the neutral consequences of fertility and survival rates but must be seen as implicitly revealing the existence or absence of decimating fratricidal strife within the displaying group" (327). For O'Hanlon, then, as for the Stratherns, the physical appearance of ceremonial dancers is a nonverbal medium through which people tell each other about themselves, their histories, and their places in the traditional order. And thus these dances represented a way in which lore about the groups that constitute the society was passed from person to person and from generation to generation.

Just as some anthropologists have been attracted to the idea that there are nonverbal channels of communication, so too some have been attracted to the specific nonverbal channel that concerns us, the organization of space. Perhaps the best example of this is Pierre Bourdieu's analysis (1973) of the Kabyle house, put forward as part of his concern to show how traditional social arrangements are maintained over the course of time. Bourdieu demonstrated that the Kabyle house is constructed, divided, and organized in such a way that it makes concrete and immediately apparent some of the key concepts of Kabyle cultural lore: the distinction between and meaning of the two genders; the relationship of human, animal, and agricultural worlds; and fecundity and fertility. Another example is

Alfred Gell's description (1982) of the Dorai market, in which the spatial arrangement of sellers and their various products maps the geographic origins of the sellers, their status in the local social hierarchy, and the status of the goods they sell. The market thus provides "an indigenous model of social relations" that "gives tangible expression to principles of social structure" (471).

Display and Ponam Lore

The social model provided by the Dorai market and the cultural code contained in the Kabyle house, however, appear to be unconscious. In this paper we will investigate something different, the way that Ponam Islanders produced conscious, intentional representations of their history and social order. In the process of ceremonial exchange, islanders arranged gifts in displays that diagrammed the relations among the contributors or recipients, and so represented Ponams' conceptions of the existing relations among individuals and kin groups and the historical basis of these relations: the traditions that explain who Ponams are and how they are related to each other.[2] And these displays were important to Ponams:

> In May of 1979 Demian Self-Njohang was in his late 50's, short, heavy and hale. He was at the culmination of the ceremonies commemorating the death of his younger brother, Camilius Pari, six months earlier. The death was sudden, and rumors had it that the ancestors had killed Pari because of unresolved bitterness among Pari, Self-Njohang and their close agnates. Self-Njohang was renowned for his ability to perform ceremony, and because he was indirectly implicated in Pari's death, this was a crucial ceremony.
>
> Over a hundred adults, just about everyone on the island over 16 and not senile, formed a large semi-circle, as they sat in what shade they could find at the edge of the cleared area in front of Self-Njohang's low, thatched house. Self-Njohang himself sat on a bench under the eaves of his house. Next to him was a bony old woman who was his advisor on the fine points of kinship for this display. His wife stood in shadow just inside the doorway of his house, looking out.
>
> Watching villagers chatted amongst themselves until Self-Njohang began the hardest work of the funeral ceremonies, arranging the display that was the core of the distribution of cooked food to the dead man's relatives. He directed a young nephew to get three dishes from the mass of over eighty that were at Self-Njohang's left at the edge of the cleared area. At the man's direction, his nephew laid the first dish about ten feet away from the door of Self-Njohang's house. The second dish was placed about six feet beyond the first, the third a like distance beyond the second. The nephew got three more dishes and laid them beyond the first three, making a line of six. By this time

---

2 This representational, storytelling potential is inherent in the arrangement of gifts, and hence may be important anywhere else that the exchange of gifts is frequent. In Melanesia some anthropologists have suggested a vaguely representational aspect in the gift displays they describe (e.g. Foster 1985:192; Young 1971:200). However, there are no reports of the sort of explicit representation by gift exchange of the sort that existed on Ponam.

the only noise from the watching villagers was mothers murmuring to their infant children to quiet them.

Self-Njohang sat looking at the line. He leaned to talk quietly to the old woman and to listen to her when she, after some deliberation, answered him. Then he stood up and walked to the third dish. Hesitating and still considering, he picked it up. He then walked to the fourth dish. He picked it up as well, and looked quickly back at the old woman. Then he placed the third dish on the ground where the fourth had been, and the fourth on the ground where the third had been. He walked back to the bench and sat down.

For almost two hours, Self-Njohang continued. The nephew brought out two or three dishes and placed them singly on the ground where he indicated. At times he would direct him to move one to a new spot. At times he would heave himself up from the bench to move a dish or switch two.

The watching semi-circle of Ponams remained silent. This was the hardest work of the funeral ceremonies, and Self-Njohang was a master.

A common theme of traditional lore is that core issue of social life: what are the groups that make up society? This theme is important because it deals with two significant matters: who are we and how ought we to deal with each other? On Ponam, the displays that attracted so much attention, like the one Demian Self-Njohang was arranging, dealt with these matters by portraying the key sorts of groups in society and their relationships.

One of these sorts was the *ken si* (*ken* = base or origin, *si* = one), and each Ponam belonged to several of them. These were cognatic stocks, the descendants of a given person, reckoned without regard to sex. Thus, all the great-grandchildren of a person were members of the cognatic stock bearing that person's name, regardless of whether they were descended through sons or daughters, grandsons or granddaughters. These cognatic stocks were important economically, for they were a significant channel through which wealth passed from person to person. They were also important socially, for they provided the framework that defined how people identified their relationships with each other, and hence identified how they ought to act toward each other. Relations between cognatic stocks, and thus between members of them, were shaped not only by kinship and marriage but also by past acts of patronage, adoption, or defense that were remembered and passed from generation to generation.

The other important kind of group was the *kamal* (*kamal* = male), and each Ponam belonged to only one of these. These were property-holding, agnatic descent groups, which we will call clans. Membership in a clan, and the right to use clan property, passed from a man to his children. On marriage, a man's daughter would lose her rights to his clan's property and gain rights to her husband's clan's property holding. Clans were important economically in the past, especially before World War II, but since then the significance of the property they controlled had decreased, so that by the time of our fieldwork, clans and their property were significant primarily in terms of social identity within Ponam society. Although clans were much more autonomous units than were cognatic stocks, nonetheless some of them were related in different ways, relations that modified their formal equality and autonomy. In some cases the founders of clans were brothers, in others a man from one clan had been adopted to strengthen a failing clan, and in yet others one clan had acted as protector and patron of another.

What were the cognatic stocks? Who was in them? How were they related to each other? These were the issues that Ponams addressed when they produced their displays; thus these displays were social diagrams. As such, they were, for those who knew how to read them, visual presentations of the record of birth, marriage, and death, of patronage and alliance, that constituted Ponams' conception of their past and the present organization of their society. They were a view of one aspect of Ponam history. They were visual alternatives to oral tradition.

These displays were not restricted to infrequent, highly ceremonial occasions. Instead, the arrangement of gifts in genealogical diagrams was the central activity of almost all Ponam prestations—a term we use to mean the accumulation, giving, and distribution of objects, predominantly cooked food, raw food, indigenous and Western valuables, and minor household goods. And these prestations were a frequent occurrence. During our period of continuous fieldwork, a prestation involving essentially all adult Ponams took place about once every four or five days. On a few occasions of particular importance, such as bride-price, marriage, and occasionally funerals, people decorated, danced, and did things that were not merely instrumental to the process of gift accumulation and distribution; but in most prestations the accumulation and distribution of gifts constituted the focus. In other words, these displays were not rare or peripheral events involving arcane lore. Rather, they were common and attended by most islanders, and they provided an important means by which Ponam tradition was reinforced.

As one might expect, Ponams talked a great deal about the arrangement and meaning of the displays that people made. However, this does not mean that these nonverbal displays were subordinated to the talk that accompanied them. Instead, they dominated the talk. The displays, and the exchanges that informed them, were themselves the occasions that sparked the talk and gave it a focus and a content. Usually the talk did not bypass the display and refer to the social relations that it described or the position or interests of the person arranging it. Rather, the talk focused on the display itself, on the nonverbal representation of social relations and social history. Certainly we could make no sense of the talk until we saw that it was about the displays, and Ponams themselves understood the relationship in the same way.

Distributions to the Community

The first form of distribution that concerns us is to the community, to the island as a whole without regard to individual kin relationships with the person making the prestation. We describe this form before turning to distributions to kin, because it is the easier way to introduce the principles that islanders used to produce and interpret their displays. Distributions to the community always used dishes of cooked food and occurred whenever an individual or group wanted to give to others on grounds other than those of kinship. For example, this type often repaid people who had helped with some enterprise like house- or canoe-building, and was used as well whenever the intention was to distribute to the island as a whole, as occurred at public festivities and at weddings and mournings, when all Ponam was presumed to be involved. Most of these distributions took place in front of the dwelling or clan men's house of those making the distribution. Typically, the door of the building in front of which the arrangement was being made gave the arrangement an orientation. The gifts were arranged in parallel lines leading away from the door. The end of each line near the door was the base of the line, the more prominent position, and the end farther away was the crown, the less prominent.

Once the dishes of food were arranged, a public speaker (*sohou*), almost always a man, would address the crowd. He would stand near the base of the display and speak briefly, thanking people for attending and perhaps making some humorous or pointed remarks, but the overall tone of his speech was always sober. However, this address was not stylized or marked in any way that distinguished it from any other public address. *Sohous* tried to speak loudly and clearly, but so far as we could tell they used no special vocabulary, grammar, or style.

After the initial remarks, the speaker would walk through the arrangement. He would point to each set of dishes in turn and call the name of the category of people who should come to collect it. Like the opening remarks, this activity was not ritualized or formalized in any way. He then retired to the edge of the display. In a very small, informal, or hurried distribution the speaker did not always bother to walk among the dishes. He might simply shout out the names of the recipients and leave people to sort out for themselves which group was to get which dishes, something they could do by matching the pattern of dishes and the sets of recipients. As will become clear, with some forms of prestation this was not difficult. When the speaker stepped away from the display of food, a few members of each of the recipient categories would come forward to collect their shares and move them away from the center of the clearing for redistribution, or for eating on the spot.

Distribution to the community could take one of two general forms, but in each one the food to be distributed was arrayed as a map of the sets of people who were to receive them. The more complex form of distribution and display, *sahai*, was to clans. The simpler form was to moieties, to the residents of the northern (*Tolau*, North) and southern (*Kum*, South) halves of the island. Islanders had no special name for moiety distributions, and we call them simply Kum-Tolau distributions.

Kum-Tolau Distributions

In the simplest Kum-Tolau distributions, items given to the North moiety were laid out to the north of the items given to the South moiety. If there was enough food, the portions for each moiety could be subdivided into shares for men and women. Here the array was a simple map of the two island moieties.

Similarly, different categories of people could be added. Shares could be given to off-island visitors or the island's foreign schoolteachers or schoolchildren, or to sets of people who had contributed in some special way to the work being celebrated. Gifts for these sets of people were smaller than those given to moiety men and women, and their position in the display reflected the relative significance of their place in the occasion of the prestation. Figure 1 shows a distribution in which four shares were given to non-moiety groups: teachers, schoolchildren, and the young men's and young women's clubs, Posus and Nai.

	O	O	School
Teachers	OO	OO	Children
Kum	OO	OO	Tolau
Women	OO	OO	Women
Kum	OO	OO	Tolau
Men	OO	OO	Men
Posus	O	O	Nai
Club	OO	OO	Club

HOUSE OF THE LEADER   N →

Note: The relative size of a gift is indicated by the number of circles shown next to the name of the recipient, which represent objects given (dishes of food in this case).

Figure 1. An arrangement of gifts distributed to the men and women of the Kum and Tolau moieties and to other categories

Sahai Distributions

Sahai was the distribution of items to each of the island's fourteen clans, and it was seen as a difficult distribution: it normally took half an hour to arrange and was entrusted only to mature adults. Like the Kum-Tolau display we just described, this type of display was intended to produce a map of the village: shares for each clan were laid out in two lines almost exactly in the manner in which their men's houses were arranged in the village, perhaps with a few extra shares for others laid out at the head of the display. This distribution was difficult because the map had a social as well as a geographical aspect. Because clans were more complex and more sensitive politically than were moieties, they were more difficult to represent. Consequently there were differences of opinion about how *sahais* should be arranged and variations in their actual arrangement. These differences help to illustrate the way in which these displays recreated an important answer to the question, "who are we, and how are we related to one another?"

The *sahai* in figure 2 is illustrative. The man who arranged this distribution began by laying out one row of eight sets of dishes and then another row of six, one for each clan. Above these he placed a few sets for foreigners. Then, acting as speaker, he announced how they were to be distributed. He began by pointing to the set at the base of the North line (number 1) and calling out, "For Lamai," the westernmost North clan. Walking toward the crown of the line, he designated shares for each of the North clans in the order in which their men's houses appeared along the northern shore of the island. Then he designated the few shares at the head of the arrangement for special groups before announcing the clans of the South, beginning with Puyu in the east (number 12) and proceeding to Kayeh in the west. The speaker announced the clans just about in the order in which he would have encountered them had he made a circuit of the village, starting with Lamai in the northwest and finishing with Kayeh in the southwest. By arranging and announcing the clans in this way the leader produced an accurate representation of village geography.

			O School children	
			OO (10)	
Buhai	OO OO	O Anthropologist	O Teachers	
(8)	OO OO	OO (9)	OO (11)	
Nilo	OO OO		
(7)	OO OO		
Kehin	OO OO	OO OO Puyu	
(6)	OO OO	OO OO (12)	
Kosohi	OO OO	OO OO Kahu	
(5)	OO OO	OO OO (13)	
Toloso'on	OO OO	OO OO Lopaalek	
(4)	OO OO	OO OO (14)	
Lifekau	OO OO	OO OO Mahan	
(3)	OO OO	OO OO (15)	
Sako	OO OO	OO OO Lehesu	
(2)	OO OO	OO OO (16)	
Lamai	OO OO	OO OO Kayeh	
(1)	OO OO	OO OO (17)	

KOSOHI MEN'S HOUSE   S →

Figure 2. *Sahai* held for Pe-Nja Kapen, a Clan Kehin man, October 1979
(including separate shares for men and women)

If these displays were simply mechanical representations of agreed-upon facts about which men's house was where, there would be no significant variations among them. They might differ because the people arranging them erred, but they would not differ because the people disagreed. However, this was not the case. These displays were part of the continuing re-creation of Ponam tradition, the ongoing effort by islanders to recreate and redefine the social groups and social relations that constituted their society and the history that shaped those groups. This regenerative aspect of displays and the lore they present is apparent when we consider variations in *sahai* displays. These variations revolved around two related contentious issues: what are the Ponam clans, and where are they located in space? Although we present these as contemporary issues, issues of the state of society at the time the arranger laid out the display, such a perspective is somewhat misleading. What the clans are and where they are located in space clearly were contemporary questions, but at the same time they were historical matters, for they referred back to events in the past that shaped Ponam society, events that were recreated and perhaps given new valuation in the display that the arranger was to organize.

What are the Ponam Clans?

During the time that we have known Ponam the clans recognized in *sahai* did not change, but Ponams did not think that they were unchangeable. Island history records that new clans emerged by breaking away from existing ones; existing clans weakened, were absorbed as dependents, and ceased to build men's houses of their own; and sometimes these dependent groups regained strength and reappeared again. Earlier in this century, for example, Buhai, Kahu, Lamai, Lifekau, and Puyu were dependents of other clans. When a group of agnates had the land and strength to build a men's house, they could claim recognition in *sahais*. If they ceased to be able to do so, they could no longer claim recognition. It was when groups stood at the point of transition that there was room for dispute.

When the brothers of the sub-clan Molou attempted to declare themselves independent of Clan Nilo in 1985, they announced that one of the buildings in their hamlet was henceforth to be a men's house. However, as a small, impoverished group they did not raise a new men's house building, and consequently did not distribute the *sahai* that was part of men's house-raising, both being important markers of clan identity. Ponams reported that in the *sahais* distributed during 1985, no shares were designated for Molou. Molous, however, did not accept part of the *sahais* given to Nilo as they had done in the past. This was not, however, merely a marker of passing dissatisfaction. The position of Molou in Clan Nilo was historically anomalous, a fact signaled by the displays of Nilo sub-clans that accompanied distributions within the clan: Molou always went uncertainly at the most distant spot. In trying to induce a change in *sahai* display, then, Molou members were trying to redefine Ponam traditional lore about their link with Nilo.

Just as Molou was poised to emerge as a newly independent clan, so Toloso'on stood on the brink of extinction; the last man of Clan Toloso'on died in the 1950's and only women remained. The two surviving Toloso'on women kept control over their clan's property and recruited the descendants of previous generations of Toloso'on women to maintain the men's house and sponsor prestations. As a consequence, this clan continued to be represented in *sahai*. For the time being, then, Toloso'on continued to be a part of Ponams' understanding of who they were and how they were related to each other. For the time being, the absence of Toloso'on men was a minor inconvenience that would be overlooked for as long as the order of *sahai* included them.

Thus the fact that the clans included in *sahai* did not vary during our stay does not mean that producing a *sahai* was automatic, simply a repetition of the names of men's houses. Molou claimed to have a men's house, although everyone arranging a *sahai* ignored its existence; Toloso'on had no men's house, although everyone arranging a *sahai* ignored its non-existence. In every case someone had to decide how to handle the potentially tendentious clans, whether or not to be the first one to put Molou in or leave Toloso'on out and so on—in short, whether to be the first to redefine Ponam society.

Where are the Clans Located in Space?

Although we said that a *sahai* display represented the spatial arrangement of Ponam clans' men's houses, it was not always obvious just where the men's houses *really* were located. There were ambiguous cases, in which men's houses were perceived to be in the wrong place; they really should have been built somewhere else. In these situations the person laying out the *sahai* had to decide where to place the share for the clan in question: should it be placed according to where the clan was, or where it ought to have been?

For example, this conflict between geographically and socially correct positions appears in the placement of the share for Clan Kahu. Some put it to the east of that for Clan Puyu and some to the west. This reflected ambivalence about the proper location of the Kahu men's house. In the mid-1970's Kahu's leader decided to move his men's house and hamlet back to their precolonial site on the eastern end of the island. His clanmates formally supported him, but tended to remain in their old village houses except when the leader came home from work on his holidays. Most Ponams followed their lead, and thus when the leader was absent *sahais* gave Kahu its old village site rather than its new one, a maneuver that the arrangers of these *sahais* found amusing.

The case of Clan Buhai is more complex. The Buhai men's house stood in the South, Kum, although its ancestral land was in Tolau, and Buhai members acted as Northerners when moiety membership was important. In the *sahai* Buhai's share was normally put in the North line, reflecting its moiety membership. However, because Buhai had no men's house in its proper moiety, people were not sure where in the line it belonged. This allowed a certain latitude in the placement of the clan's share in *sahai*, and some Ponams arranging displays used this latitude to make assertions about the history and identity of Buhai. As we noted already, earlier in this century Buhai had no independent existence, but was a client of, and to some extent incorporated in, Clan Nilo. After World War II, Buhai began to reassert its independence, and by 1980 it was recognized once more as a fully active clan. Those who sought to commemorate (or reassert) this historical tie to Clan Nilo placed the Buhai share immediately after the Nilo share, while others commemorated its independence by placing it at the crown of the North line.

We said that clans were important as an element of Ponam identity, and these *sahai* displays were important for understanding Ponam clans. Islanders talked from time to time about their clans and their histories; however, this talk was not an important part of Ponam life. Islanders did not tell and re-tell these stories as part of an active body of oral tradition. (Indeed, as J. Carrier [1987] has pointed out, Ponams had relatively little *oral* tradition of any sort.) Instead, they presented and represented the nature and relationships of their clans in these displays. For it was in these physical arrangements of dishes of cooked food that islanders focused on and honed down their understanding of one aspect of who they were and how they were related to each other, and that understanding referred back to events in the past as much as it reflected events in the present. This same focusing and honing down occurred for family groups, Ponam cognatic stocks, in the individual-focused displays that we want to describe now.

Individual-Focused Displays

In the preceding section we described the way in which Ponams represented two types of social groups, moieties and clans, in the course of the distribution of gifts in ceremonial exchange. We did so to introduce these displays as a feature of Ponam exchange, to demonstrate some of the principles that govern the organization of display, and to show how display presents and recreates key elements of Ponam lore. We turn now to the representation of the relatives of the individual making the distribution. Instead of Ponam social organization taken overall, these displays represented that organization from the point of view of particular individuals—those making gifts to their relatives or receiving gifts from them.

Such displays used genealogy instead of geography as their theme, with the piles of gifts representing *ken sis*, stocks of people descended from a common male or female ancestor, rather than clans and moieties. The arrangement of piles represented the relations among *ken sis* as the stocks of an individual's kindred. Ponams could read these displays just as anthropologists can read genealogical diagrams, seeing in them relationships of ascent, descent, and siblingship.

There were a variety of possible ways of arranging these displays, as we shall show. However, they all had a common structure. Figure 3 is an idealization of one common pattern for the display of gifts being contributed by or distributed to an individual's kindred (treated here as a display of contributions). The gifts are arranged before the main door of the leader's house in a single line, made of piles, each contributed by a separate stock, or *ken si*, within the leader's kindred. The display of gifts for kindreds such as this one was thus completely different from those we described previously in this paper. Clans were not represented in these prestations, except as maximal *ken sis*; moieties did not appear at all, and no distinction was made between male and female recipients.

The line begins with gifts from the *ken sis* that are most closely related to the leader through his or her own patriline, starting with the leader (number 1) and proceeding to ever more distantly related stocks: first the leader's siblings, then

11	FM[11]
10	M[10]
9	FFFZ[9]
8	FFFB[8]
7	FFZ[7]
6	FFB[6]
5	FZ[5]
4	FB[4]
3	Z[3]
2	B[2]
1	EGO[1]

HOUSE

Note: The large numbers refer to the numbers in the genealogy in Figure 4, the superscript numbers are the order in which the speaker would announce the piles.

Figure 3. Hypothetical display of gifts for or from a person's kindred

the father's siblings. Often the latter were long dead, the gifts having been collected from the father's siblings' children and possibly affines. Next came gifts from the father's father's siblings, and so on, for as many generations as necessary to reach the founder of an individual's own clan, and occasionally to reach beyond to include other clans affiliated through ancient ties of patronage or common origin. After all of the gifts from patrilateral kin came those from people who are the leader's maternal kin, father's maternal kin, and occasionally father's father's maternal kin.

A single line was used only when the number of gifts was small or during bride-price prestations (when gifts were hung on a long rope). On other occasions the display was usually broken into several different lines. However, items were still announced by the speaker in the order in which we show them here, proceeding through the leader's patrilateral kin from closest to most distantly related, and then to his or her matrilateral kin.

The genealogical relations among these groups are illustrated in figure 4, the numbers on the genealogy corresponding to the numbered gifts in figure 3. The manner in which the genealogy is illustrated here is different from the bilateral branching-tree genealogy appropriate for representing English kinship, for example, since it is derived from the representations that Ponams made in their gift displays. And as this genealogy illustrates, displays were not simply muddled codifications of oral lore. The relationships that these displays celebrated were not passed down orally as a series of Biblical "begats" which were crudely translated into lines of dishes. In fact, it was difficult to elicit genealogies orally from Ponams. Instead, when islanders talked about these webs of kinship, they talked about them in terms of the spatial dimensions of their gift displays.

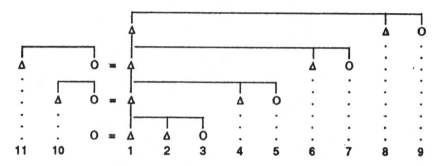

Figure 4. Genealogy of *Ken Sis* in Figure 3

The Return Prestation for an Engagement

We want to illustrate these displays in a real example, the accumulation and distribution of a single prestation, a *kahuwe tabac*, the return prestation for an earlier gift of tobacco and money that had marked an engagement. This prestation was not a complex one, nor was it trivial. On the contrary it was ordinary, illustrating what most prestations looked like most of the time.

In the first week of January 1986, Philip Kemou's family brought a gift of tobacco and money to mark his engagement to 18-year-old Sowahanu Tapo, who had given birth to his son just three weeks before. Sowahanu's parents discussed the distribution of this gift privately that evening. They proceeded the next day to divide the money and tobacco among their kin. Because of a dispute with his son, Michael Tapo gave him nothing, and as a result several of his closest agnates refused to accept the shares offered to them.[3] Despite admonitions from the rest of his kin, Tapo stuck to his original decision and announced that he would go ahead and make the return prestation without their help. This took place about three weeks after the initial prestation.

---

[3] The son and daughters had different mothers (one from Ponam, one not), a fact which made it possible to exclude the son from his sister's affairs.

16	Kuluah Pakou (FMB)[7]				
7	Sowapulo (FZ)[6]	13	Aluf Ndrakolok[13]		
6	Asaf Ndrau (FZ)[5]	12	Mwaka[12]		
5	Aluf Ndrau (FZ)[4]	11	Sapakol II[11]		
4	Sakati (FBD)[3,a]	10	Sapakol I[10]		
2	Sowahanu (Z)[2]	9	Kihian (FFFB)[9]		
1	Michael Tapo (ego)[1,b]	8	Ndrau Salin (FFB)[8]	15	Pisa'oh (M)[14]

MICHAEL TAPO'S HOUSE

Note: The large numbers refer to the numbers in the genealogy in Figure 6, the superscript numbers are the order in which the speaker announced the piles.

a   Michael Tapo's FBS's descendants refused to accept tobacco, so that there was no single contribution from his FB's descendants. His FBD's descendants took their place.

b   The bride's brother should have led this prestation and his gift should have gone at the base of the display. The bride's mother's gift was included with Michael Tapo's instead of being placed separately as it would have been if her son had led the work.

Figure 5. Accumulation of *Kahu* for engagement prestation

At about mid-morning on the appointed day, gifts were accumulated and displayed in front of Michael Tapo's house. He announced to the assembled company the names of the *ken sis* that had contributed to him by walking through the display, pausing briefly beside each pile as he called out the name of its contributor. He began with his own gift and concluded with his mother's. Figure 5 gives a schematic illustration of the display and figure 6 a genealogy of the groups involved.

Michael Tapo's clan, Mahan, included three sub-clans, descended from Mahan's two sons. One was Kihian, and one sub-clan bore his name. The other son was Michael Tapo's great-grandfather Tapo, whose only son Ndrau had two wives. Therefore, Tapo's descendants were divided into two sub-clans: Ndrau Salin (right Ndrau), the descendants of the first wife; and Ndrau Kamau (left Ndrau), the descendants of the second. The display of this contribution included in the left line the gifts from his own sub-clan, Ndrau Salin, and from Ndrau's first wife. The center included the gifts of Ndrau Kamau and Kihian, the other two sub-clans. At the end of that line were gifts of other groups associated with Clan Mahan: Clans Sapakol I and Sapakol II, which shared origins with Mahan, and two other groups that were once Mahan's dependents. The third line included only a gift from Michael Tapo's maternal kin. In other words, by means of this display of gifts Michael Tapo presented a graphic, nonverbal representation of the structure of his kindred and the state of relations among them: not just a record of who married whom and who begat whom, but also the old alliances and associations that had been created in the past and were remembered and celebrated in the contribution, display, and distribution of objects in exchange.

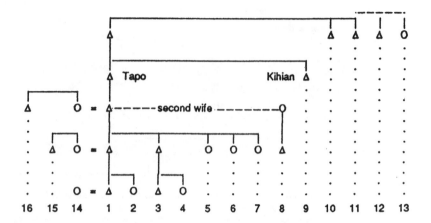

Figure 6. Michael Tapo's genealogy

When Michael Tapo finished his announcements, his kin took apart the display
and carried the gifts to the groom's house. After their arrival they retired into the
shade, and the groom's father, Chris Pelekai, came out of his house to speak. He
thanked Michael Tapo and his kin for the gift. Then the bride's relatives brought
out a gift of cooked food for the groom's relatives. A little while later, Philip
Kemou's family began their redistribution of the gift. They started by placing
single items on the ground, each to mark a pile of items, as they experimented
with different arrangements. Once they had decided that they liked the
arrangement, they began to distribute the remaining food appropriately among
them. Figure 7 shows the arrangement of the distribution and figure 8 the
genealogy of the recipients.

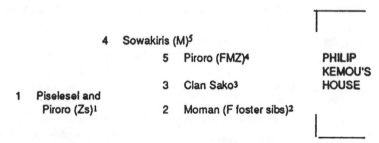

Figure 7. Distribution of *Kahuwe Tabac*

Philip Kemou's sisters led this distribution, although as women they did not
speak. The left line included their gift only, for aside from Chris Pelekai (Philip

Kemou's father) they were the only adult members of their sub-clan within Clan Sako. The right line included gifts for other groups of Philip Kemou's kindred: first, a gift for the sub-clan that had fostered his father when he was orphaned as a child; second, a gift for the remaining Sako sub-clans; and third, a gift for his father's mother's sister, his father's mother's only sibling. Philip Kemou's mother's gift was placed rather indeterminately between these two lines.

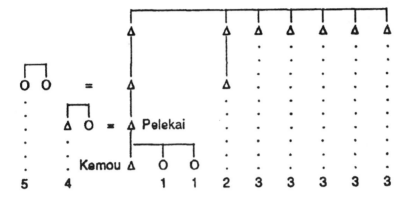

Figure 8. Philip Kemou's genealogy

Philip Kemou's genealogy was remembered in a simpler form than that of Michael Tapo, and the display accompanying the distribution of the gift was correspondingly simpler. But as was the case with the more complex genealogy, here display is not merely a way of distributing gifts. Instead, it recreates a history of the relations that constitute a kindred and so defines for one set of people who they are and how they are related to each other. And again, the display did not recreate merely some agreed-upon succession of births and marriages. To be sure, the sisters who arranged the display recorded the genealogical relationships that were involved. Equally, however, they celebrated and recreated the fostering of Chris Pelekai, Philip Kemou's father, by Moman, a sub-clan within Clan Sako.

Display as Social Commentary

In our discussion of *sahai* we noted that displays were something more than neutral representations of the geography of Ponam clans. The same observation applies to individual-focused displays, which were shaped not only by the agreed-upon history of marriage and childbirth, alliance, patronage, and fostering that became the structure of a person's kindred. In addition, they were the means of presenting, and thus inevitably commenting on, the state of social relations among the people who were the living representatives of the dead ancestors whose names were called out when the display was announced.

This function is illustrated by the arrangement of the contributions to the return prestation for Sowahanu Tapo's engagement gift (figure 5). Under normal circumstances, this prestation would have been led by Sowahanu's elder married brother, whose gift would have been placed at the base. Sowahanu's mother's contribution would have been placed separately, probably in the far right line next to Sowahanu's father's mother's gift. But because Sowahanu's father, Michael Tapo, was in dispute with his son, he refused to allow him to participate in the exchange and he arranged the display in such a way as to make this situation very clear. Michael Tapo's display suggested that he, Tapo, was Sowahanu's brother: his contribution was placed at the base of the line, and Sowahanu's mother's contribution was included with his rather than being placed separately. He and his wife could have chosen to place his gift at the base and her gift in the line with his mother's, an arrangement that would have implied some sort of openness to compromise. But instead, by contracting the genealogy and placing her father in her brother's place, they laid out an arrangement that completely eliminated Michael Tapo's son from the bride Sowahamu's kindred.

Although this display deviated from the genealogical rules we have described, and although it did not accurately portray the kindred according to convention, it was not in any sense wrong. No one made an error or a social *faux pas*. In fact, given the circumstances of the prestation, the arranger would have been wrong to put together the display in a conventional manner. Ponams could, and did, use display in this way because it was its own form of cultural transmission with its own rules and conventions. It was an independent way of passing information, of making statements about who Ponams were and how they were related to each other.

Conclusion

We have had one simple goal in this paper: to show that people can communicate significant parts of the past and present—and so transmit and recreate what could in a sense be regarded as one form of oral (unwritten) tradition—in ways that do not use words. Although Ponam prestation required talk, we have demonstrated that its core was the visual display of gifts that occupied so much time and attracted so much attention in Ponam exchange. Possibly Ponams could have simply heaped their gifts into a big pile as they were accumulated and then taken apart the pile again gift by gift for distribution.[4] But such a simple procedure would be tediously uninformative when compared

---

[4] They did not think that they could. They said that the process of arranging displays is, in addition to being expressive, an essential step in figuring out how distributions should be made—figuring out to whom and how much to give. In view of the complexity of these distributions, some sort of procedure such as this one does seem necessary. Pre-planning with pen, paper, and calculator had become more important, but working out distributions on the ground in the way that they did will probably always be easier than planning them on paper. It would be interesting to know how other people who make complex distributions like these manage to keep track of what they do without such forms of display.

with what gift displays actually provided. The arrangement itself conveyed considerable information about the structure and composition of Ponam society generally and, more particularly, about individuals' kindreds, about who was related to whom and how, and about the actual state of social relations among kin and clans.

We do not mean that these displays were in any sense self-contained representations of social organization and social relations, and certainly they are not self-evident. It took the two of us almost six months of fieldwork to come to realize why so many villagers spent so much time attentively and quietly watching other villagers set out piles of gifts or dishes of food, pause, think, change their minds, and set them out in a slightly different way. And in spite of close study over an extended period, we never mastered enough knowledge of Ponam kinship and gossip to be able to decipher and understand, without help, any but relatively simple displays. We suspect that the most complex and subtle displays even bemused some of the less attentive villagers. In other words, we always needed to be told, we always needed the medium of words to clarify what was being related visually. However, this discrepancy does not invalidate our point. Ponams understood themselves and their past through nonverbal representation. The word, spoken or written, that figures so strongly in what we know and in how we go about getting others to describe themselves in no way exhausted the ways in which Ponams described themselves.[5]

References

Bourdieu 1973	Pierre Bourdieu. "The Kabyle Household." In *Rules and Meanings*. Ed. by Mary Douglas. Harmondsworth: Penguin. pp. 98-110.
A. Carrier 1987	Achsah Carrier. "The Structure and Process of Kinship: A Study of Kinship and Exchange on Ponam Island, Manus Province, Papua New Guinea, 1920-1980." Ph.D. dissertation, University of London.
J. Carrier 1987	James Carrier. "History and Self-Conception in Ponam Society." *Man*, 22:111-31.

---

5 Fieldwork on Ponam Island between 1978 and 1980 was carried out with the assistance of the University of London Central Research Fund and the Papua New Guinea Ministry of Education; field trips between 1980 and 1986 were assisted by the University of Papua New Guinea Research Committee. We are grateful for their support. Also, we want to acknowledge the kind permission of the governments of Papua New Guinea and Manus Province to pursue this research, and especially the patience and good humor of Ponam Islanders. Portions of this paper are taken from A. Carrier 1987.

J. Carrier and
  A. Carrier 1985   _____ and Achsah Carrier. "A Manus Centenary: Production, Kinship and Exchange in the Admiralty Islands." *American Ethnologist*, 12:505-22.

J. Carrier and
  A. Carrier 1989   _____. *Wage, Trade, and Exchange in Melanesia: A Manus Society in the Modern State.* Berkeley: University of California Press.

Foster 1985   Robert Foster. "Production and Value in the Enga Tee." *Oceania*, 55:182-96.

Gell 1982   Alfred Gell. "The Market Wheel: Symbolic Aspects of an Indian Tribal Market." *Man*, 17:470-91.

Goody 1977   Jack Goody. *The Domestication of the Savage Mind.* Cambridge: Cambridge University Press.

O'Hanlon 1983   Michael O'Hanlon. "Handsome Is as Handsome Does: Display and Betrayal in the Wahgi." *Oceania*, 53:317-33.

Ong 1971   Walter Ong. *Rhetoric, Romance and Technology.* Ithaca: Cornell University Press.

A. Strathern and
  M. Strathern 1971   Andrew Strathern and Marilyn Strathern. *Self-Decoration in Mount Hagen.* London: Duckworth.

Young 1971   Michael Young. *Fighting with Food.* Cambridge: Cambridge University Press.

XI

WINGED TANGI'IA: A MANGAIAN DRAMATIC PERFORMANCE

Marivee McMath and Teaea Parima[1]

With the arrival of Europeans rapid and far-reaching social change occurred in Polynesia, and a number of observers predicted that the oral tradition of the area in which they were living was about to disappear. Yet over much, if not all, of Polynesia an oral tradition continues to flourish, much of it a synthesis of old and new elements. The purpose of this article is to examine something of this creative and ongoing process as it can be viewed in the tradition of dance-drama on the island of Mangaia. An example of a dramatic performance recorded in 1973 is chosen, and the recorded text and a translation are given. The performance is placed in its immediate social context, and attention is paid to the relationship between the performers and their audience. At the same time it is shown that the play also requires a careful consideration of Mangaian history and culture. Because the Mangaian dance-drama is a highly flexible art form that readily combines new and old elements, a sophisticated understanding requires the adoption of a number of different approaches.

Mangaia is the most southern of a group of fifteen islands now known as the Cook Islands. The oral tradition of present-day Mangaia can be viewed against a well-recorded past, in that a great many Mangaian texts of songs and narratives were collected and published by William Wyatt Gill, of the London Missionary Society, who lived on the island from 1852 to 1874. He describes the kinds of occasions on which festivals were held, and speaks of their importance to Mangaian oral tradition and history (1876a:ix, 269-73; 1876b:65; 1894:243-58). However, the only eyewitness accounts of festivals held at Mangaia last century are of two occasions focused exclusively on the church: the May missionary festivities (1876b:52-56), and the May school gathering (56-69). All the written accounts lead the reader to believe that the indigenous Mangaian festivals, together with their associated performances, had been suppressed prior to Gill's arrival on the island (W. Gill 1856, 1880; W. W. Gill 1876a, 1894).

---

1 This article is the result of an association between the two authors which has developed over a period of 15 years as a result of our mutual interest in Mangaian culture and history.

In this century, the ethnologist Te Rangi Hiroa (Peter Buck), who in 1929 lived on Mangaia for some five months, quotes from Gill in asserting that with the introduction of Christianity, the old festivals together with their associated traditions of dance, song, and drama had ceased. According to him, by the time of his visit "the old time amusements" had been replaced by church-based activities, particularly the part-singing of hymns, and the old traditions were no longer being taught; they were in danger of being either forgotten or completely transformed to fit a Christian mold (Buck 1939 and n.d.:688).

While doing ethnographic fieldwork on Mangaia in 1973, McMath observed the Nuku, an annual festival which commemorates the arrival of Christianity (Mark 1976). Although the festival was church-centered, Mangaian tradition and culture were clearly apparent, and in spite of much change there appeared to be more continuity in Mangaian oral tradition than had been expected from a reading of the earlier writings. During the day McMath's interest was taken by the performance of the legend of Tangi'ia, which featured, among other things, a simulation of the preparation and use of kava—this in spite of the fact that the use of the *kava* root (*Piper methysticum*) in Mangaia ceased soon after the arrival of the missionaries.[2] As the performance was clearly a Mangaian art form, and this indicated the existence of a larger dramatic tradition complete with dance, song, and drama, the situation cannot have been as simple as Gill and Te Rangi Hiroa indicated.[3]

In this article we argue that contemporary Mangaian national festivals represent a new synthesis, a syncretism containing elements of traditional Mangaian

---

[2] The plant itself was nearly absent from the island by 1973 (Sykes 1980:61).

[3] The question might be asked as to whether the old tradition may have died out and been re-introduced to Mangaia from another island at a later date. While it may not be possible to give a definitive answer, for several reasons it seems most unlikely. Firstly, Mangaia was relatively isolated, compared with, for example, Rarotonga. Secondly, Gill's accounts focused primarily on the activities and testimonies of persons who had converted to Christianity, but according to information which is contained in his writings, and made explicit by Te Rangi Hiroa (n.d.), there was a politically active "non-Christian" faction on the island as late as 1878. So although the Christians were holding exclusively church-focused festivals, and their activities have been relatively well documented, we do not know what the others were doing. Thirdly, although Gill assumed that with the deaths of his informants all the old knowledge would be lost, Te Rangi Hiroa tells us that while much was gone, much still remained—although he, like Gill, was of the opinion that when certain of the old men he knew died, all would be gone. On the basis even of this information it is clear that a continuity of transmission was still possible, in that the old men (and women) who were involved in selecting the stories and directing the activities in 1973 would have been aged about twenty-one when Te Rangi Hiroa was on Mangaia.

Adaptation to new circumstances inevitably involves change if a culture is to survive. Perhaps it was as a result of wishful thinking or nostalgia that some observers confused ideas about social change with ideas about extinction. There is an alternative, and that is to view social change as part of a creative process of adaptation, and to see changes in oral tradition as specific examples of that process.

society, Christianity, and modern-day society.[4] Dramatizations of old legends (*peu tupuna*) are highlights of these festivals, and also provide evidence of syncretism. (Indeed, they are described by some Mangaians as being made up of old stories with new words.) Whether one argues that Christianity has been changed to fit the Mangaian mold, or the Mangaian tradition has been altered to fit a Christian mold, may depend entirely on one's point of view. It is in either case certain that oral tradition still has a role to play in Mangaian society.

The Festivals

At least twice a year Mangaians take part in major festivals during which dramatizations of old legends or other items are performed. One of these festivals is the aforementioned Nuku, held annually on October 26. Nuku celebrations are held on most, if not all, of the twelve inhabited islands in the Cook group; they are specifically local affairs, the audiences, with few exceptions, being locally resident Cook Islanders.[5] The Nuku are one-day events during which, generally, different social groups compete in the following events, in this order: ' *imenetuki* (a Cook Islands form of hymn-singing), choral items, biblical pageant, enacted legends (*peu tupuna*), action song, and drum dance.

The other major festival is the Constitution Celebrations, held annually in August to mark the anniversary of the Cook Islands Independence in 1965. This event takes place on Rarotonga, the central island in the group and also the capital. In this case the performers and the audience include people from all over the Cooks, and overseas visitors are present. In fact, from very early on it was expected that the activities associated with the Constitution Celebrations would become a tourist attraction.

The Constitution Celebrations share a generally similar pattern with the Nuku observed at Mangaia; but while the Nuku is a one-day event, the Constitution Celebrations' activities span at least a week. On the first night there are

---

[4] According to W. W. Gill's description of the May missionary festival, none of the traditional dramatic arts played a part in either of these annual festivals, although many traditional Mangaian values, customs, and accoutrements were present: for example, the concept of a national festival which involved feasting, competition, and the use of specially constructed long shelters (1876b:52-59). These church-based festivals have undoubtedly influenced the development of the contemporary Nuku celebrations. But the festivals described by Gill involved only a lengthy church service (up to three hours!), much hymn-singing, and feasting. The Nuku observed in 1973 did not follow that pattern; it had at least as much to do with Mangaian history as it did with the Church. In addition to commemorating the arrival of Christianity to the Cook Islands, it was a celebration of Mangaian identity. And the rehearsals of the dramatized legends, together with their performance, communicated many aspects of Mangaian culture and history at the same time as they entertained.

[5] Rarotonga and Aitutaki are the only two islands in the Cook group regularly visited by tourists.

competitions in *'imenetuki* and choral items, and on the remaining days groups
from different islands compete, in no set order, in enacted legends, song
performance and composition (*'ute*), action song, and drum dance. Most of these
items are the same as those performed in the Nuku, except that the Constitution
Celebrations include *'ute* (which in this context are often satirical and/or political)
and do not include the biblical pageants.

Additional festivals are also held on Mangaia to commemorate a special event,
such as the arrival of an important visitor on the island or the opening of an
airport or a school. As well, items are performed when Mangaians travel
together, around the island or overseas, in large parties; in this case, a broader
range of traditional items may be performed, in part for the benefit of overseas-
born persons of Mangaian descent.[6] All Mangaian festivals tend to follow the
same kind of pattern, although the number, type, and range of the items
performed may vary. Whatever the occasion, these activities are always associated
with an atmosphere of festivity and competition.

Here we will describe the 1973 Nuku observed on Mangaia, concentrating upon
the dramatic performance of the story of Tangi'ia. We will discuss the Mangaian
dramatic tradition in general, describe the Nuku at which the Tangi'ia play was
performed and the performance itself, give the text and translation of the
performance, and then make some concluding remarks.

The Dramatic Tradition

The word *peu* generally means "activity, behavior, custom." In 1972-73, one
of the writers heard the term *peu 'etene* (literally, "heathen activity") used to refer
to the dramatic performance of legends. Some others prefer the term *peu tupuna*
(literally, "ancestral activity"). Since the term *'etene* carried negative
connotations, this may be more than a casual difference. For example, the use of
the term *tupuna*, which conveys ideas of wisdom and values that are to be
respected and treasured, may indicate that the speaker takes a particular pride in
things Mangaian. Since these terms appear to embody two rather different points
of view, they may be modern parallels to the social and political divisions noted
by Te Rangi Hiroa (n.d.). Mangaians, most of whom are bilingual, use the word
"legend" to translate the terms *peu 'etene*, *peu tupuna*, and *peu ta'ito* (literally,
"ancient activities"). They use the same word to refer sometimes to old stories,
and sometimes to dramatizations of such stories.

The *peu tupuna* nowadays appears to be structurally quite similar to some
performances described by W. W. Gill (see, for example, 1876a:225-50,
1894:243-58). It presents an entire story through a combination of solo parts and
choruses and may include old songs or poetic chants (*pe'e* or *mire*) together with
dances, chants, or songs especially composed for the performance. The *peu
tupuna* may encompass the entire range of the verbal and performing arts, and

---

[6] See Loomis 1984 for a discussion of performances by *tere*, or (traveling) parties.

conveys historical information concerning persons, places, events, and activities. In contrast to other, more conservative genres in Mangaian oral tradition, the performance of *peu tupuna* involves creativity and innovation and encourages a degree of artistic license on the part of the performers. Such license allows the actors to readily combine old and new ideas, especially with regard to interpretation and the use of humor, and thereby insures the continuing vitality and social relevance of this art form.

The Nuku

During the weeks leading up to the 1973 Nuku, each group practiced a choral item and an *'imenetuki* and their young people practiced action songs and drum dances. Each group also chose a biblical passage and created a pageant enacting it, and they selected, dramatized, and rehearsed a legend unique to the island, and in some cases unique to their own particular area.

In the village of Ivirua-Karanga, where McMath was living, some of the leaders met and discussed which legend they thought the village might perform. The recognized experts (*tumu korero*), who are considered to know the best stories and to be most knowledgeable about the language, are the ones who normally determine which items will be included at major festivals. On this occasion, they chose a story and then discussed it among themselves until they had agreed on all the important details.[7] Actors were subsequently chosen, and rehearsals were held in the open area between the church and the Sunday school. The performance that evolved was not the act of a single individual, but rather a dramatic presentation involving collective decision-making and the cooperation of many members of the village. The actors did not learn their lines from a set script, but made up their own words to fit the general theme and outline of the story; for this reason they had been chosen, in part, on the basis of their language skills. During the rehearsals many of their lines became set, especially those which proved particularly popular. There was a limit to the place that innovation occupied: while it was actively encouraged in relation to dialogue, it was not permitted in many aspects of the performance. Considerable attention was paid by various specialists to certain kinds of detail, such as the miming of action by individuals or groups.

The Nuku was held at the village of Oneroa. On the morning of the event, people from the other villages (Ivirua-Karanga and Tamarua) arrived at Oneroa by truck and gathered outside the Cook Island Christian Church. At this stage the three village groups were readily identifiable, for within each group the women wore identical dresses and hats. First, the groups performed their choral pieces and *'imenetuki* inside the main Cook Island Christian Church. Later in the

---

[7] According to what we have been told, the process at Oneroa, and the eventual selection and presentation of the Tangi'ia story, seem to have been similar.

morning, the groups staged their biblical pageants outside on a large playing field located across the road from the church; for this event, each group carried its own identifying banner as it walked on to the field, its members ingeniously and appropriately costumed. These performances marked the end of the religious part of the festivities. Following a break, during which visitors ate picnic lunches or had lunch with friends and relatives in their homes, each group performed its dramatized legend (*peu tupuna*). This also took place on the playing field, while the audience watched from the sidelines. Then in the evening the festivities concluded with a dance, in the course of which some members of the different groups presented drum dance and action songs. The dance took place inside the Sunday School building.

The Story of Tangi'ia

At this Nuku the crowd favorite was the legend of Tangi'ia, as performed by the people of the village of Oneroa: McMath's tape recording of the legend was borrowed until the tape broke! Small children could be heard for days calling out lines they remembered from the play. The Tangi'ia performance was so popular that it was performed again during the 1974 Constitution Celebrations held at Rarotonga, and it won first prize in the competitions.

The story of Tangi'ia is known to have formed part of Mangaian oral tradition in the early years of the nineteenth century. There are a number of versions of the story of Tangi'ia; one was published by W. W. Gill (1894:143-48), and one will be presented here. The central figure, Tangi'ia, is always a cannibal who demands children to eat, and he is usually killed by poison that has been added to the chiefly drink of *kava* (*Piper methysticum*) offered to him. In Gill's version Tangi'ia is a god who speaks through a priest of the same name. He occasionally demands human flesh in place of the usual offerings of taro and fish, and on one occasion he demands that a man named Marere, a member of the 'Akatauira clan, should bring his child to be eaten. Marere (who is regarded as the discoverer of three poisons used to kill fish) decides to kill Tangi'ia; he prepares all three poisons, adds them to the kava, then offers the priest the poisoned kava along with his little son. The priest decides to drink the *kava* before eating the child; it kills him, and the child is saved (143). Gill's version is similar in many respects to the version enacted at Oneroa in 1973. There are also several points of difference.

The Performance of the Story

During the 1973 performance of the story a large group of people at one end of the playing field made up a chorus for the songs. Two lines of dancers radiating out from this group defined an area within which the principal actors performed, and a small group of men provided the drumming that intermittently accompanied the action. In contrast to the biblical costumes worn for the pageants, the basic costume in the *peu tupuna* consisted of a skirt and cape made of the green leaves of the *ti* tree (*Cordyline terminalis*). Tangi'ia possessed, in addition, huge wings that were cleverly attached to his arms. He could open and close these at will, and he used them to good dramatic effect.

While many of the actors' lines had become set during the process of rehearsal, some improvisation was expected of them, so they all had to be on their toes lest they miss their "cues." Although the story is serious and deals with tragedy, in many places the actors used words or actions to please the crowd and keep them entertained. On this occasion all the actors appeared to get quite carried away with their roles, and they embellished the story more and more with each episode.

Drumming, on wooden slit gongs (ka'ara), was employed during the performance for two purposes. First, it marked transitions between scenes: a certain kind of short fast beat on the drum signalled a break between activities or a point where one activity ended and another began. In an open space where all the characters of the play can be seen by the audience, some such device is necessary to separate the different episodes. Second, drumming was employed to intensify meaning. In the episodes where the couples were about to lose their children, low continuous beating helped to create an atmosphere appropriate to the fear and grief they were experiencing. A certain quickening beat announced the arrival or presence of the main actor, Tangi'ia, and aroused fear in the audience, while a kind of running beat (referred to as a "traveling" beat) was used when Marere was collecting the poisons and the women were performing hand actions that mimed the making of kava.

The three songs sung by the chorus in the course of the action provide variety, and also help to explain the story and convey an atmosphere. The opening song introduced the story; the second communicated the grief of the families suffering from Tangi'ia's exploitation; and the final one summarized the story. The two lines of dancers accompanied these songs with hand actions that added further variety and meaning.

The Transcript and Translation

The text presented here was recorded in 1973 by McMath, and was transcribed and translated by Parima in 1988. Because it is a field recording, there are numerous places where it is quite difficult to hear the actors over the laughter and comments of the audience, and some words may have been missed. The cast list that precedes the text was compiled from the tape and with the help of two of the participants. Audience reactions are given in square brackets. The three choral songs are printed in bold type; while the second song was being sung, some dialogue was being spoken.

The text of the play, with the recorded responses of the audience and the accompanying photographs, may give the reader some feeling for what these performances are actually like. The text is also of value in its own right, as representing a neglected area of Polynesian oral tradition: although dance-dramas were formerly performed in a number of island groups, and in some areas still are, only a very few texts of performances have been published.[8] The transcript will have a special value for the Mangaian people themselves, who now eagerly seek such records. Copies of the original tape recording, the Mangaian language translation and a literal translation into English, together with annotations, are to be placed in the collections of the library in Rarotonga in the Cook Islands and the Hocken Library in Dunedin, New Zealand.

TANGI'IA PE'AU

'Akatutu 'ia e te Oneroa Ekalesia

Nga tangata 'akatutu

Mataora Harry	*Tangi'ia*
Torotoro Kimipiiti	*Papa 1*
'Apaina Kareroa	*Mama 1*
Kite-'i-te-kata Harry	*Papa 2*
?	*Mama 2*
Ata'aere Papatua	*Papa 3*
?	*Mama 3*
Area'i Ngairua	*Marere*
Mareva No'oroa	*Va'ine-a-Marere*
Metu Samuel	*Va'ine-a-Tangi'ia*

Ki te iti tangata. Kua tata'ia teia tua e 15 mataiti i muri ake i te tuatau 'i rave 'ia tikai 'ia ai. Mei te mea e 'e koto'e anga teta'i no te au mea tei vare, tei tarevake te rauka nei ia maua te tatara apa atu no te reira.

'Akamataanga. Tangi te ka'ara

Va'atara.   Teia nei, te 'akamata atu nei te Peu 'Etene a te Oneroa ko te tua'oki teia no Tangi'ia Pe'au. Teta'i ta'ae teia tei tae mai 'i runga 'i to tatou nei 'enua. Thank you very much, ladies and gentlemen.

---

8 The only comparable text and discussion of a Mangaian performance to be published is a dramatic reenactment of the arrival of Captain James Cook (W. W. Gill 1894:251-58), although Gill elsewhere publishes some partial texts of performances and incidental information about them. The only other published text of a Polynesian play we have seen is a Tuamotuan text (Caillot 1914:95-109). Cook Islanders quite often now videotape such performances, and we have been told that recordings made during the annual Constitution Celebrations may be available for purchase through the Cook Island Government.

An audience view of Tangi'ia and another actor. They are framed by two lines of seated dancers backed by the village chorus. Three minor actors are sitting "off-stage" at the right. Apart from Tangi'ia's wings, costumes are made primarily of natural materials.

Photo: Marivee McMath

Imene Akamata.

> **Tangi'ia 'e rere mai nei, na te mareva 'o te ao**
> **Tangi'ia 'e rere mai nei, na te mareva 'o te ao**
> **To rima 'e pe'au manu te to mai nei e**
> **Tangi'ia 'e rere mai nei, ta'ae rikarika no te ao**
> **To rima 'e pe'au manu tei to mai nei e**
> **Tangi'ia 'e rere mai nei, ta'ae rikarika no te ao**
> **Tangi'ia 'e rere mai nei, na te mareva 'o te ao**
> **Tangi'ia 'e rere mai nei, na te mareva 'o te ao**
> **To rima 'e pe'au manu tei to mai nei e**
> **Tangi'ia 'e rere mai nei, ta'ae rikarika no te ao.**

Tangi'ia.   Ko taua ta'ae nei teia 'e karanga ia nei ko Tangi'ia Pe'au tei tere mai na te mareva. Kua tae atu teia ta'ae 'i Kiriapi, Tamarua. Kua no'o atu ana 'i te va'ine no roto 'i te 'oire Veitatei.

Tangi'ia.   E aka koreva toku. 'Ua kaki au 'i teta'i tamaiti ei katikati atu naku. Teia nei, ka tere atu au ka kimi 'i teta'i tamaiti ei katikati atu naku.

[Tangi te ka'ara]

Papa 1.   E 'oa!

Mama 1.   E ou, e Pa!

Papa 1.   'Ie 'akarongo atu e e a'a te tangitangi a te ka'ara?

Mama 1.   Aue! 'E ta'u 'oa e! 'E ka'ara tumatetenga teia.

Papa 1.   E a'a ia 'e ma? 'I tano mai 'oki 'ua 'ati ta'u pererau 'i te
                   tamaki.

Mama 1.   Akamaro'iro'i e ta'u tokorua.

Tangi'ia.   E, te ngutu'are, ei!

Papa 1.   E ou! E a'a to'ou tere 'i toku ngutu'are?

Tangi'ia.   E 'aere mai nei au, e tiki 'i teta'i tamaiti.

[Kata te matakitaki (no te tu 'i te tara a Tangi'ia)]

Papa 1.   Kite koe e te ta'ae, 'are a maua tamariki. Te no'o nei maua 'i
                   konei, 'angai puaka ta maua 'anga'anga.

Mama 1.   Aue, e Pa e.

Tangi'ia   I a'a koe e rave mai 'i teta'i 'anga'anga tarevake. Mei te mea e
                   te 'amo mai nei koe 'iaku ['i a aku]. Ko koe, ta'au va'ine e
                   ta'au nga tamariki, ka kai pau rava au 'i te reira.

Mama 1.   Aue, e Pa e! Kimi'ia teta'i ravenga 'ia 'oro tatou e . . .

Papa 1.   Meitaki e te ta'ae. Tano mai ra koe 'i te tuatau 'ua 'ati ta'u
                   pererau. 'Aere ra, naringa koe 'i tano mai e te vai nei ta'u
                   pukupuku patia 'ia atu koe e au 'i ta'u korare . . .

[Tangi te ka'ara. 'aere a Tangi'ia]

                   E, Ma?

Mama 1.   E ou, e Pa!

Papa 1.   'Ua rongo 'oki koe 'i te tara a te ta'ae?

Mama 1.   Aue, te rikarika e . . . aue e.

Papa 1.   Kakaro mai 'oki koe 'e 'apikepike teia. Me ka 'oro'oro 'oki
               taua 'i Tava'enga to'ona pererau oki.

Mama 1.   E tika 'oki ta'au, aue.

Papa 1.   Teia 'ua ka 'akakoromaki taua. 'Ua tangi rai au 'i a taua nga
               tamariki. E rua rai 'oki 'i te ora'anga.

       [Kata te matakitaki]

               Tera 'ua e 'akatika te pati 'akatenga a teia ta'ae. Ka 'apai ta taua
               mata'iapo.

Mama 1.   Aue ta maua nga tamariki e.

Papa 1.   Kite koe e a maua nga tamariki ka 'aere 'ia tika te 'akakoro'anga
               'o te ta'ae.

       [Tangi ka'ara]

Mama 1.   Aue e.

Papa 1.   E 'akakoromaki e 'oa. No tei 'ati ta'u vaevae 'i tuku ai au 'i ta
               taua tamaiti. Tangi rai au 'i a au e ta'u tamaiti. Naringa 'i a'a
               ta'u vaevae 'i 'ati.

Mama 1.   Aue e.

       [Tangi te ka'ara e motu]

Papa 1.   Tangi'ia ei! Tangi'ia ei! Teia mai nei au e kare 'i to va'apiro.

Tangi'ia.   Ahahaha, ahahaha, ahahaha.

Papa 1.   'Ua manuia ra koe 'i tano mai, 'ua 'ati ta'u pererau.

Tangi'ia.   Ahahaha, ahahaha. Iaaamu, iaaamu.

Papa 1.   Teia nei te tuku nei au 'i ta'u tamaiti 'ei va'apiro na'au.

Tangi'ia.   Ia koi e ia! 'ma'i. Ngaungau.

       [Kata te matakitaki]

Papa 1.   Aue ta'u tamaiti 'ua kainga e te ta'ae. E to te tapere ei! E to te
                   tapere ei! Tera te tangata 'i Tamarua, e tangata kai tangata! 'Ia
                   no'o te'ate'a mamao te au ngutu'are!

Tangi'ia.   'Ua roaroa ake nei, 'ua topa teia ki kopu.

Mama 2.   E Pa!

Papa 2.   E ou e Ma!

Mama 2.   Ka 'aere au ka 'angai 'i ta taua 'anau.

Papa 2.   'Angaiia ra ['angai 'i a ra].

Tangi'ia.   Teia nei, te manako atu nei au ka 'aere 'aka'ou atu rai au ka
                   kimi 'aka'ou 'i teta'i tamaiti potakataka 'i a 'ue'ue rava atu ta'u
                   kopu.

Mama 2.   E pe ma. 'Aere mai. E kai e pe ma.

    [Tangi te ka'ara]

                   Aue, Aue toe, aue.

    [Tangi 'uatu rai te ka'ara, e motu]

Papa 2.   E ma 'aua'a koe 'e mania. [Pakakina, pakakina]. 'Aua'a koe 'e
                   mania. [Pakakina, pakakina].

    [Kata te matakitaki]

Mama 2.   Aue, aue, aueee . . .

Tangi'ia   E te ngutu'are ei!

Papa 2.   E no'o 'i reira.

Tangi'ia.   E 'aere mai nei au . . .

Papa 2.   E a'a!

Tangi'ia.   E tiki 'i ta korua tama'ine potakataka rava atu, 'aua'a te mea
                   tuere, 'ei mea potakataka tikai. 'Ei kaikai atu naku.
Mama 2.   Aue.

[Tangi te ka'ara. 'aere a Tangi'ia]

Papa 2.   E Ma!

Mama 2.   E ou ee!

Papa 2.   'Are e tika 'iaku ['i a aku].

Mama 2.   Aue toe toe Pa e. 'I te tangi e.

Papa 2.   Teia ra te nga'i kino. Me kore taua e 'akatika ka kainga [kai i
                    nga] taua e ta taua 'anau katoatoa.

Mama 2.   Aue toe ee.

   [Kata te matakitaki]

                    E a'a atu te ravenga.

Papa 2.   Tera 'ua ka 'akatika taua 'i te 'inangaro 'o te ta'ae.

Mama 2.   Aue ta'u anau e! Ka 'akape'ea ra! Aue toe! 'Are e kino e.
                    'Apaina atu teta'i 'o ta'i 'ia ora ake taua 'e ta taua toenga mai 'i
                    ta taua tamariki. Aue e.

Papa 2.   E ma!

   [Tangi te ka'ara]

Mama 2.   Aue. Aue ta taua tamariki. Aue te tangi 'i te tamariki. Tera
                    ake te ta'ae puaka-taona.

   [Kata te matakitaki]

Papa 2.   Aue, aue.

Mama 2.   Aue ta'u tamaiti. 'I na ake ana ra. 'I na 'i karo atu ana au a
                    ngaro atu ei 'i roto 'i tena kopu e.

Tangi'ia.   Iaaa. 'Ua kite rai au e 'o au rai te ta'ae 'i runga 'i A'ua'u 'enua
                    nei.

Mama 2.   Aue toe. 'Aere ra 'e ta'u tamaiti e. A ngaro atu koe 'i roto 'i te
                    kopu 'o tera atu tangata neneva. Aue.

Tangi'ia.   A! 'Ua reka ke ta korua tama'ine. Mei te kiko 'o te kina
                   momona. Taviviki mai 'e 'ia, taviviki. Iaaa.

   [Ngau! Ngau!]

   [Kata te matakitaki]

Mama & Papa.   Aue.

   [Tangi te ka'ara]

Tangi'ia.   Aue te reka nei teia pae 'anga'anga. 'I teia nei ka 'aere 'aka'ou
                   rai au ka kai 'aka'ou rai 'i teta'i tamaiti naku.

   [Tangi te ka'ara]

Papa 3.   E ta'u 'rerau ['are rau] ei!

Mama 3.   E ou e Pa!

Papa 3.   Tera ake 'oa taua tuputupua kutekute nei 'e 'aere mai nei.

Tangi'ia.   'Oi!

Papa 3.   Aue toe te mataku e! Aue.

Tangi'ia.   'Oi!

Mama & Papa.   Aue. Aue.

Papa 3.   'Aere!

Tangi'ia.   E 'aere mai nei au.

Papa 3.   E a'a ta 'au 'i inangaro! 'Aere!

Tangi'ia.   'Oa ta korua tama'ine, 'e apinga tikai tona 'u'a te ra'i. E 'oke
                   mai koe na te ra kopu 'e 'oni'oni.

   [Kata te matakitaki]

Mama & Papa.   Aue toe e, aue toe.
   [Tangi te ka'ara]

Papa 3.   Aue toe Ma e.

Mama 3.   E a'a atu ra 'oki ta taua ravenga?

[Tangi atu rai te ka'ara e motu]

Papa 3.   E Ma!

Mama 3.   E ou e Pa!

Papa 3.   Tuku mai 'i ta taua tama'ine ka 'apai 'ei 'ariki atu 'i te ta'ae.

Mama 3.   Te tangi nei 'oa au.

Papa 3.   'Are a taua ravenga.

Mama 3.   E a'a atu ra 'oki te ravenga?

Papa 3.   Me kore taua 'e 'apai 'i ta taua tama'ine 'o taua rai te 'openga ka
               mate.

Mama 3.   'Are ['e] kino e Pa te 'akatika nei au. Te ra mai, 'aere ra
               'apaina.

[Tangi te ka'ara]

               Aue. Aue.

[Motu te tangi ka'ara]

               Aue. Aue. 'Aere ra 'e ta'u tama'ine.

Papa 3.   Aue toe e te tangi i ta'u tama'ine e. Mania e ia. Tangi'ia 'ei!

Tangi'ia   'Ou! 'Ia koi mai.

Papa 3.   Teia 'oa ta'u tama'ine 'ei kai na'au 'i teia avatea.

Tangi'ia.   'Ia koi e koe 'ua raparapa ta'u kopu. Taviviki mai.

Papa 3.   E a'a.

Tangi'ia.   Taviviki mai.
Papa 3.   'Are koe.

Tangi'ia.   E ia, 'ua raparapa ta'u kopu a kainga [kai i nga] atu koe e au.

[Kata te matakitaki]

Papa 3.   E a'a.

Tangi'ia.   Tukua mai.

Papa 3.   Tera mai.

[Kata te matakitaki]

[Tangi te ka'ara]

Papa 3.   Aue te tangi 'i ta'u tama'ine e. Aue toe toe.

['Akamutu te tangi ka'ara]

Tangi'ia.   Teia nei 'ua 'akarongo au e 'e te no'ora [no'o a ra] teta'i tangata
                     tei karanga 'ia tona 'ingoa 'e ko Marere. E 'apinga tikai tona
                     tama'ine no te taurekareka 'i te va'apiro atu. 'Are 'e kino te tere
                     atu nei au 'i te kimi 'i a ia. E Marere ee . . . i! E Marere! E
                     Marere ee . . . i! E Marere!

Va'ine.   E Marere!

Marere.   E 'ou.

Va'ine.   Te 'akarongo'ra ['akarongo a ra] koe 'i tera reo.

Tangi'ia.   E Marere! E Marere!

Va'ine.   Tei te mareva.

Tangi'ia.   E Marere! E Marere!

Marere.   A! 'Ua rongo au.

[Kata te matakitaki]

Tangi'ia.   E Marere! E Marere!

Marere.   E ou!

Tangi'ia.   E 'aere mai nei au e karanga 'i a 'au 'ia 'apai ake koe 'i ta korua
                     tama'ine potakataka, te taurekareka, te 'u'a 'i te kikokiko, 'i
                     runga 'i ta'u ko'atu 'ei etieti atu naku.

Marere.   Kare 'e tika 'i aku ['i a aku].

Tangi'ia.   Me kare koe 'e 'apai ake, ko koe 'e ta'au va'ine 'e ta korua tama'ine 'akaperepere ka katikati katoatoa 'ia kotou 'e 'aku.

Marere.   A-u-e. A-u-e.

Va'ine.   E Marere!

Marere.   E ou.

Va'ine.   E a'a tena tara 'ou.

Marere.   Tera ake ta'ae 'oki.   'Ua 'inangaro 'i ta taua tama'ine potakataka.

    [Kata te matakitaki]

Va'ine.   Aue-e-Marere.

Marere.   'Ua 'inangaro 'oa ei va'amura na 'ana.

Va'ine.   Aue! 'Are koe 'i 'akaari atu ana 'i tera 'apinga.

    [Kata te matakitaki]

Marere.   'Are rai 'oki ona pu'apinga. Ka mate. 'I kakaro ra 'e 'a 'o 'ona rima.

Va'ine.   'Are koe 'i 'akaari atu.

Marere.   No te a'a.

    [Kata te matakitaki]

Va'ine.   E a'a?

Marere.   Me 'are ake a 'au ravenga 'e mate ei 'ia taua teia ta'ae.

Va'ine.   No te a'a.

Marere.   Mena! Mena!

Va'ine.   E 'aere atu koe 'i te Raei.

Marere.   E a'a?

Va'ine.   E koi mai koe 'i te ora.

Marere.   'Ae.

Va'ine.   'Eke ake koe na Tua'ati.

Marere.   'Ae.

Va'ine.   Tei reira nga pukupuku 'utu.

Marere.   'Oia.

Va'ine.   Rave mai koe, 'apai mai koe 'i to taua ngutu'are,

Marere.   A-a-a-a! A-a-a-a!

Va'ine.   Ka ropa taua.

   [Tangi ka'ara: tangi ka'ara 'oro'oro]

Marere.   'Ua oti 'oa.

Va'ine.   'Ia koi, 'ia koi.

Marere.   'A! 'Ua oti, te rere nei au.

Va'ine.   'Are 'e kino, me 'aere koe, 'are koe nei 'i te ora ta'i nga'uru ma
                     varu ka kite 'aia 'i teta'i 'apinga ka pera 'aia.

Imene.   **Tera, te tama a Marere**
                     Aue, te tangi
                     Tera tu kino nei
                     Te mamae nei 'a roto 'i taku ngakau.

Va'ine.   Aue taku tama'ine 'akaperepere.
                     Tera, te tama a Marere.

Tangi'ia.   Te roa 'i ta'u katikati
                     Aue, te tangi
                     Teia tu kino nei
                     Te mamae nei 'a roto 'i taku ngakau.

Va'ine.   Aue, aue, aue.

'Aere, 'aere, 'aere ra 'e taku tama'ine
Pure ki te 'Atu, kia ora mai koe
'Aere, 'aere, 'aere ra 'e taku tama'ine
Pure ki te 'Atu, kia ora mai koe.

Marere. No'o ake ra. E pure ki te Atua no taua 'e ta taua tama'ine.

Va'ine. Mai 'ia 'ongi 'i a atu.

Marere. Tera mai.

Va'ine. Aue taku tama'ine 'akaperepere e! Aue taku tama'ine 'akaperepere e! 'Aere ra 'e taku tama'ine.
'Aere, 'aere, 'aere ra 'e taku tama'ine
Pure ki te 'Atu, kia ora mai koe.

Va'ine. Aue taku tama'ine 'akaperepere e
'Aere, 'aere, 'aere ra 'e taku tama'ine
Pure ki te 'Atu, kia ora mai koe.

[Motu te imene]

Va'ine. Aue taku tama'ine e. 'Aere ra 'e taku tama'ine na te Atua koe 'e tauturu.

Marere. 'Oi!

Tangi'ia. 'Oe [e ou]!

Marere. Teia mai nei au.

Tangi'ia. A'a'a.

Marere. 'E 'akatika 'i to manako.

Tangi'ia. I!

Marere. Teta'i na'au manga mea 'ei va'apiro na'au.

Tangi'ia. Mmm?

Marere. E a'a ara?

Tangi'ia. 'Oa 'e te taeake tona 'u'a, 'ua potakataka. Aaaa, Aaaa.

Marere.   E' [E ia], E' [e ia]!

Tangi'ia.   E a'a tena.

Marere.   E pati'anga teia 'i a 'au. Me ka 'ariki mai koe, 'o te reira ia.

Tangi'ia.   E tara ana 'oki koe na mua.

Marere.   'O te kai 'are 'o te mea pu'apinga te reira. Na mua ana taua 'ia
                 tongi ana koe 'i ta'u unuunu a . . .

Tangi'ia.   A'a?

Marere.   E unuunu 'a, 'a kava Maori.

Tangi'ia.   A 'a 'a. 'Ua tano tena 'ia kakai rava atu au 'i to tama'ine. 'I na
                 ake 'e ia ['i te tama'ine]. E ia paia to mea.

Marere.   Ae. Aae.

Tangi'ia.   'Ia koi. Mai' ['omai]. Mmm. Ki te koe 'e te taeake 'i to mea
                 ta'i rai kapu 'ua veravera ta'u rape taringa.

Marere.   A'a'a, 'ua tano tena.

Tangi'ia.   Mai 'aka'ou teta'i 'ia tano reka.

   [Kata te tangata]

Marere.   E a'a?

Tangi'ia.   Mai' ['omai], Mai' ['omai].

Marere.   E a'a?

Tangi'ia.   Kite koe 'e te taeake e ta'i, e rua kapu 'ua konakona [Name]*,
                 [*Name—tangata rongonui no te kaikava]. 'E ia, takia mai, ka
                 kai au . . . ['ua kona].

Marere.   'Are koe 'e 'inangaro kapu 'aka'ou.

Tangi'ia.   No te a'a, ma'ani mai koe, 'ua kapu.

Marere.   'Ei.

Tangi'ia.	'Ua kapu, 'ua kapu, 'Ua konakona. Kite koe 'e te taeake 'ua anini ta'u pauru. 'Are 'e kino ka 'aere au 'i ko 'i ta'u va'ine. No'o ake koe 'e te taeake.

[Paku]

Aaa! Aaa!

Marere.	E kai ra! [Paku!] E kai ra! [Paku!] E kai ra 'i to kutukutu.
Tangi'ia.	Aaaa! Aaaa! [Mate a Tangi'ia]

Va'ine
a Tangi'ia.   Kua roa ake nei te au ra 'i topa ki muri. 'Are rai taku 'ereiti 'i 'oki mai ake 'i to maua ngutu'are. 'Ua 'uke ta'u umu, 'ua tiaki au 'ia 'oki mai ake 'i tena puku tiromi. E te manako nei au ka 'aere atu au ka kimi 'aere e tei 'ia 'aia te ngai 'i 'aere ai. Aue koe 'e taku 'ereiti 'e Tangi'ia e. Aue, aue.

Marere.	A'a'a! A'a'a!

Va'ine
a Tangi'ia.   Aue, aue.

'Imene 'openga.

**Tukuna 'ia te tama 'a Marere, 'e Tangi'ia Pe'au e
'I kai toto ana koe tama 'i Tamarua e
Tera te 'openga 'ua inu koe 'i te kava konakona tukerai
Aue ko te mate 'e tama kare 'e tangi mai e
Tukuna 'ia te tama 'a Marere, 'e Tangi'ia Pe'au e
'I kai toto ana koe tama 'i Tamarua e
Tera te 'openga 'ua inu koe 'i te kava konakona tukerai
Aue ko te mate 'e tama kare 'e tangi mai e
Me 'aere 'aere 'aere 'aere 'ua e
To vaerua kino 'e Tangi'ia
Tiri ei koe ('i) to va'ine
Me 'aere 'aere 'aere 'aere 'ua e
To vaerua kino 'e Tangi'ia
Tiri ei koe ('i) to va'ine
Me ta taua tama'ine
'Oro mai ra 'e 'ine 'ia 'ongi pakakina 'uake taua e
Me ta taua tama'ine
'Oro mai ra 'e 'ine 'ia 'ongi pakakina 'uake taua e
Mauria 'ia ra te 'au 'o te Mesia e Marere**

Nana 'e tuku mai te ora
Mauria 'ia ra te 'au 'o te Mesia e Marere
Nana 'e tuku mai te ora
No ta taua tama'ine purotu
Te mamae nei 'a roto 'i taku ngakau
No ta taua tama'ine purotu
Te mamae nei 'a roto 'i taku ngakau.

WINGED TANGI'IA

Performed by the Oneroa Church Group

Main Characters

Mataora Harry	*Tangi'ia*
Torotoro Kimipiiti	*1st man*
'Apaina Kareroa	*1st woman*
Kite-'i-te-kata Harry	*2nd man*
?	*2nd woman*
Ata'aere Papatua	*3rd man*
?	*3rd woman*
Area'i Ngairua	*Marere*
Mareva No'oroa	*Marere's wife*
Metu Samuel	*Tangi'ia's wife*

To our people. This story is written 15 years after the performance actually took place. If anyone is slighted or offended we sincerely apologize for that.

[Sound of drums]

Master of Ceremonies.

> Now, Oneroa will begin their legend. This is the story about Winged Tangi'ia. He is one of the terrible ones who arrived on our island. Thank you very much, ladies and gentlemen.

Introductory song

> Tangi'ia who has flown here through space,
> Tangi'ia who has flown here through space,

Your arms are birds' wings that have brought you here.
Tangi'ia who has flown here is the most feared and
terrible in the world.
Your arms are birds' wings that have brought you here.
Tangi'ia who has flown here is the most feared and
terrible in the world.
Tangi'ia who has flown here through space,
Tangi'ia who has flown here through space,
Your arms are birds' wings that have brought you here.
Tangi'ia who has flown here is the most feared and
terrible in the world.

An audience view of the area where the Tangi'ia drama was enacted.
Two lines of seated dancers, backed by the village chorus, await the actors.
Photo: Marivee McMath

Tangi'ia.   I am the terrible one who has traveled here through space, whom everyone calls Tangi'ia Pe'au. He arrived at Kiriapi in Tamarua. He lived with a woman from the district of Veitatei.[9]

---

[9] In this monologue Tangi'ia introduces himself to the audience, speaking of himself part of the time in the third person. Mangaians recognize this as a technique whereby an actor, while acting his or her part, can also opt briefly and in an informer role to tell the audience about something of particular importance.

| Tangi'ia. | Oh, I am so hungry. I am hungry for a child, I feel like nibbling one. Now I will go out and find a child to nibble.[10] |

[The sound of drums signaling a change of scenery]

| 1st man. | Dear! |

| 1st woman. | Yes, Pa! |

| 1st man. | Could you find out what the sound of the drums is about? |

| 1st woman. | Alas, dear, it's tragic news. |

| 1st man. | What is it, Ma? Its arrival is untimely, for my wings have been broken in battle. |

| 1st woman. | Have courage, my partner. |

| Tangi'ia. | Hello, household! |

| 1st man. | Yes, what is the purpose of your visit to my house? |

| Tangi'ia. | I have come to get a child. |

[The audience laughs at his deliberate pronunciation and his accompanying facial expressions, which indicate that great strain is involved in producing each word in this sepulchral tone.]

| 1st man. | You see, feared one, we have no children. The two of us live alone here. Our job is feeding pigs. |

| 1st woman. | Alas, Pa. |

| Tangi'ia. | Don't make a mistake! If you are lying to me, I will eat you all: you, your wife, and all your children. |

| 1st woman. | Alas Pa, work out how we can run away, alas. |

| 1st man. | Very well, feared one, for you have arrived while my wings are broken. So, go. If you had arrived when I was still healthy and strong, I would have pierced you with my spear. |

---

[10] Tangi'ia's desire to eat a child in a playful manner, nibbling at his meal without fear of attackers, reflects his arrogance and position of strength.

[Drums signal Tangi'ia's exit]

	Ma?
1st woman.	Yes, Pa.
1st man.	You have heard what the feared one said?
1st woman.	Alas it is so tragic, alas!
1st man.	Look here, I am weak. If we have to run to Tava'enga, his wings.
1st woman.	Oh, alas, you are right.
1st man.	And so we have to bear it. I love our children too. Life has only given us two . . . .

[The audience laughs uproariously, for this implies they were unable to have more children. Being infertile is like being a cripple; it is something to be joked about.]

	So we have to agree to what the feared one asked. Our first-born will have to go.
1st woman.	Alas, our children, alas!
1st man.	You see, our children will have to go so the feared one's purpose is served.

[Drums signal Tangi'ia's entry and again bring fear]

1st woman.	Alas, alas.
1st man.	Bear this, dear. Because my leg is broken I have to let our child go. I love you, my child. If only my leg were not broken.
1st woman.	Alas, alas.

[Drumming which persists, then suddenly stops, reinforcing the feeling of fear]

1st man.	Tangi'ia, Tangi'ia! I am here to bring your "hunger satisfier."
Tangi'ia.	Haaa, haaa! Yum, yum!

1st man.   You are lucky, because you have asked while my wing is
                    broken.

Tangi'ia.   Ahahaha, ahahaha! Yeum, yeum!

1st man.   And now I'm letting my child go to satisfy your hunger.

Tangi'ia.   Hurry up you, give it here! Chomp, chomp!

[The audience laughs, applauding the fact that the father has offered some
resistance. Drumming begins, and continues throughout the speech that
follows.]

1st man.   Alas, my child is being eaten by the feared one. People of the
                    district! There is a man in Tamarua, he eats humans!
                    Households, beware!

Tangi'ia.   It's been a while, and my stomach has gone down.

2nd woman.   Pa!

2nd man.   Yes, Ma!

2nd woman.   I'm going to feed our children.

2nd man.   Feed them.

Tangi'ia.   And now I'm thinking I will go out again to find another fat
                    child so my stomach will get even bigger.

2nd woman.   Children, come here and eat.

[Drums signal a change of scene, then persist. At first loud, they gradually get
softer, then suddenly stop, creating a feeling of fear.]

                    Alas, alas, oh alas!

2nd man.   Ma, don't make too much noise! [slap, slap!] Don't make so
                    much noise! [slap, slap!]

[The audience laughs because the husband was hitting the woman's bottom to
stop her wailing. People are laughing at this public imitation of a husband
hitting his wife. By church law, mainly, husbands are not allowed to hit their
wives, so this act is perhaps being seen as a humorous act of defiance of that
law.]

2nd woman.	Alas, alas, alas!
Tangi'ia.	Hello, household!
2nd man.	Sit down there.
Tangi'ia.	I have come...
2nd man.	What for?
Tangi'ia.	To get your fattest daughter, not the skinny one but the roundest one, so I can eat her.
2nd woman.	Alas, alas.

[The audience is laughing. The drums signal Tangi'ia's exit and the audience continues to laugh as the woman wails and writhes on the ground.]

2nd man.	Ma!
2nd woman.	Yes, alas.
2nd man.	I don't allow it [the noise his wife is making].
2nd woman.	O Pa, alas, alas, alas! It is so tragic [that words cannot properly express it]!
2nd man.	But the trouble is, if we don't agree we will be eaten and so will all our children.
2nd woman.	Alas,

[Audience laughs at the woman's crying and wailing]

What else can be done?

2nd man.	And so we have to agree to what the feared one wants.
2nd woman.	Alas, my children! What else, alas! Well, take one so we can live, and so can the rest of our children. Alas!
2nd man.	Ma!

[Drums signal Tangi'ia's entry]

2nd woman.   Alas, alas our children! Alas, this is tragic for the children. Here comes that pig of a feared one.

[Audience laughs]

2nd man.   Alas, alas.

2nd woman.   Alas, my child. Get out of the way so I can see my child disappear into his stomach. Alas.

[Audience laughs]

Tangi'ia.   Aha. Now I know I am the most feared one on this land of A'u A'u [an ancient name for Mangaia].

2nd woman.   Alas, go my child, all the way into the stomach of that stupid man, alas!

Tangi'ia.   Ah! Your daughter is ravishing, just like the flesh of a fat, rich sea egg. Hurry up you, hurry! Ah. [Chomp. Chomp.][11]

[The audience laughs]

2nd man and
  woman.   Alas!

[Drums signal another episode]

Tangi'ia.   Oh, this is lovely. And now I am going out again to eat another child.

[Sound of drums]

3rd man.   Housewife![12]

3rd woman.   Yes, Pa!

3rd man.   Here comes that brown-spotted ghost.

---

[11] When the children were delivered to Tangi'ia, he "ate" them by engulfing them in his wings. One of the minor actors in the play explained that Tangi'ia took a child into his wings first (like a hen gathering her chicks underneath her wing), then after a short pause ate her.

[12] The word *'arerau* is here an image referring to the man's wife (*'are* = house + *rau* = leaves = thatched house).

Tangi'ia.	Oi!
3rd man.	How terrifying, alas!
Tangi'ia.	Oi!
3rd man and woman.	Alas, alas.
3rd man.	Go away.
Tangi'ia.	I have come...
3rd man.	What do you want? Go away!
Tangi'ia.	Your daughter's thighs are fat.[13] Give her to me so I can be satisfied!

[The audience laughs at the double entendre]

3rd man and woman.	Alas, alas.

[The drums sound, and continue through the next two lines]

3rd man.	Alas, Ma!
3rd woman.	What else can we do?
3rd man.	Ma!
3rd woman.	Yes, Pa!
3rd man.	Let me have our daughter so I can offer her to the feared one.
3rd woman.	I dread this.
3rd man.	But we can't do anything else.
3rd woman.	Well, what else can we do?
3rd man.	If we don't take our daughter it is the end for both of us.

---

13 As well as a reference to their culinary potential, there is a sexual implication here: the girl has shapely, attractive legs.

3rd woman.   Okay Pa, I agree. Here, go and take her.

[Sound of drums]

               Alas, alas.

[Drums suddenly stop]

               Alas, alas. Go, my daughter.

3rd man.   Alas, I love you, my daughter. [To his wife, who is still
               wailing] Shut up, you. Tangi'ia!

Tangi'ia.   Yes, hurry up!

3rd man.   Here is my daughter for you to eat this afternoon.

Tangi'ia.   Hurry up, you, my stomach is empty. Hurry it up.

3rd man.   What?

Tangi'ia.   Hurry.

3rd man.   Aren't you...

Tangi'ia.   Here, my stomach is empty—or I'll eat...

   [The audience laughs at the man's playing dumb as a way of delaying Tangi'ia]

3rd man.   What?

Tangi'ia.   Let her go!

3rd man.   Here you are.

   [The audience laughs. The sound of drums indicates Tangi'ia's authority as he
   takes the child as his meal.]

3rd man.   Alas, my lovely daughter, alas.

   [Drums stop, indicating a change of scene]

Tangi'ia.   Now, I have heard there lives a man called Marere. His daughter is very beautiful to eat,[14] so I will go and find him. Marere, Marere! Marere, Marere!

M's wife.	Marere!
Marere.	Yes.
M's wife.	Can you hear that call?
Tangi'ia.	Marere, Marere!
M's wife.	It's far away.
Tangi'ia.	Marere, Marere!
Marere.	Ah, I can hear it.

[Marere and his wife have been playing dumb, pretending they don't hear Tangi'ia. The audience laughs at this.]

Tangi'ia.	Marere, Marere!
Marere.	Yes!
Tangi'ia.	I have come to tell you about your daughter who is plump and beautiful, whose thighs are nice, and to demand you bring her onto my altar so I can tear her up.
Marere.	I won't agree.
Tangi'ia.	If you don't bring her—you, your wife, and your dear daughter—I will eat you up.
Marere.	Alas, alas.
M's wife.	Marere!
Marere.	Yes!
M's wife.	What's the news?
Marere.	Only that feared one. He desires our plump daughter.

---

[14] The word *taurekareka*, "beautiful" or "pretty," is not a word normally applied to something you are going to eat.

[The audience laughs at the double entendre]

M's wife.   Alas, Marere!

Marere.   He wants to devour her.

M's wife.   Alas, you didn't show him this? [She shows her biceps, flexing her arm upwards]

[She is small and has little muscle, so draws quite a laugh from the audience]

Marere.   Well, they're useless, they will be overcome. Well, look, he has four arms! [He is twice as strong and Marere's muscles will be useless]

M's wife.   But, you didn't show [your muscle to him]?

Marere.   Oh, yes.

[The audience laughs, knowing he has little strength]

M's wife.   What?

Marere.   Have you no other plan for killing this ferocious creature?

M's wife.   Oh, yes.

Marere.   Let's have it, let's have it!

M's wife.   You go over to the Raei . . . [a particularly barren part of the makatea, an ancient uplifted coral reef]

Marere.   What for?

M's wife.   To collect some *ora papua* [poisonous roots of the vine (*Derris malaccensis*)].15

Marere.   And?

M's wife.   You climb down at Tua-ati,

Marere.   And?

---

15 This is a poisonous plant occasionally used to kill fish. When its roots are crushed and mixed with water, they make a lethally poisonous brew.

M's wife.	There you will find some fruit of the '*utu*' [*Barringtonia asiatica*].16
Marere.	Yes, all right.
M's wife.	Get them and bring them to our home,
Marere.	Aaaah, aaaah! [A sigh of satisfaction]
M's wife.	And we will prepare them.

[While the drums sound, Marere goes out looking for the poisonous plant materials. Meanwhile the two lines of young women perform hand actions (*kapa rima*) which mime the making of *kava*.]

Marere.	It's finished.
M's wife.	Hurry, hurry!
Marere.	Ah, that's enough. I'm going.
M's wife.	Okay. When you're gone, you won't be gone for the hour eighteen before he feels something. He'll be like this....17

Song [interspersed with dialogue]

> **There is Marere's child.**
> **Alas, it is so sad,**
> **This terrible event.**
> **My heart hurts so much.**

M's wife.	Alas, my dear daughter.
	There is Marere's child.
Tangi'ia.	My dinner has taken a while.
	Alas, it is so sad,

---

16 This fruit is also crushed and used to poison fish. Tangi'ia is so strong that Marere and his wife are going to give him two poisons, a double dose.

17 The exaggeration of time in the idiom "the hour eighteen" indicates that it will not take long for the poison to act.

This terrible event.
My heart hurts so much.

M's wife.   Alas, alas, alas.

Go, go, go, my daughter,
Pray to God you will be saved.
Go, go, go, my daughter,
Pray to God you will be saved.

Marere.   You stay here. Pray to God for us and our daughter.

M's wife.   Let me kiss her goodbye.

Marere.   Here.

M's wife.   Alas, my dear daughter, alas, my dear daughter! Go then, my
                   daughter.

Go, go, go, my daughter,
Pray to God you will be saved.

M's wife.   Alas, my dear daughter.

Go, go, go, my daughter.
Pray to God you will be saved.

                   Alas, my daughter. Go, my daughter, and God will help you.

Marere.   Ohi!

Tangi'ia.   Oh, yeah!

Marere.   Here I have come.

Tangi'ia.   Ahahaha!

Marere.   To satisfy your wishes.

Tangi'ia.   Hi!

Marere.   [Offering the *kava*] Just a little something to satisfy you.

Tangi'ia.   Mmm?

Marere.   And now what?

Tangi'ia.   Oh my friend, her legs are plump and shapely. Ahaha, ahaha!

Marere.   Hey, hey!

Tangi'ia.   What is it now?

Marere.   I beg of you, if you would allow me—if not, that's all right. . .

Tangi'ia.   You say it first.

Marere.   Food is not the most important thing. Let us, if we may, taste my drink of...

Tangi'ia.   Of what?

Marere.   A drink of *kava maori*.[18]

Tangi'ia.   Ahaha, that's right, so I can really enjoy eating your daughter. You [to the girl], get out of the way. You [to Marere], do your thing! [in other words, let's get on with the drinking].

Marere.   Yes, yes.

Tangi'ia.   Hurry up, give it here. Mmm . . . [drinking the *kava*]. Oh, your drink, my friend, wow, one cup and my ears are warm already.

Marere.   Ahaha, that's good.

Tangi'ia.   Give me another one, just to get the feeling.

[The audience laughs. While drinking the *kava* Tangi'ia has become steadily more drunk; he is slurring his speech and staggering about, all the while accompanied by the laughter of the audience. This public display of drunkenness flouts current opinion whereby according to some it is immoral to drink, let alone get drunk, in public.]

Marere.   How is it?

Tangi'ia.   Here, give it here!

---

[18] The expression *kava maori* refers to the poisoned brew, but is also an implicit reference to Mangaian bush beer.

Marere.	How now?
Tangi'ia.	You see my friend, one or two cups and [Name]* is drunk.[19] Here, pass it over. I. . . will drink. [Tangi'ia is getting very drunk now and is really slurring his words.]
Marere.	You don't want another cup?
Tangi'ia.	Oh, yes, make it, serve it up.[20]
Marere.	Here.
Tangi'ia.	Serve it up, serve it up. I'm drunk. Well, my friend, my head is spinning. Never mind, I have to go to my wife. I'll leave you, my friend. [Falls to the ground]. Aaah, aaah!
Marere.	Take this! [Thumps him] Take this! [Killing him] You've got what you deserved.
Tangi'ia.	Aaah, aaah! [Dies]
Tangi'ia's wife.	It's been days now and my dear one has not returned to our home. The oven is ready and I have waited, but he has not returned for his *puku tiromi* [a special dish of mashed taro] and his *kou poke* [another special dish of mashed taro in coconut sauce]. And now I think I have to go out and find where he's gone. Alas, my dear one Tangi'ia. Alas, alas.
Marere.	Ahaha! Ahaha!
Tangi'ia's wife.	Alas, alas.

Ending song.[21]

> **Tangi'ia Pe'au let go of Marere's child!**
> **He has been a blood-sucker in Tamarua,**

---

[19] A well known local drinker from the village of Tamarua was named here. He is said to drink a lot of bush beer, but not quite to be an alcoholic.

[20] The word *ma'ani*, ("make") is Rarotongan, not Mangaian. One wonders if this may be a reference to the long rivalry between Mangaia and Rarotonga, the implication being "drunk, like a silly Rarotongan."

[21] The final song, which summarizes the story and highlights its themes, is an important feature of the *peu tupuna*.

But in the end he drank a different drink.
Alas, death does not pity anyone.
Tangi'ia Pe'au let go of Marere's child!
He has been a blood-sucker in Tamarua,
But in the end he drank a different drink.
Alas, death does not pity anyone.
Wandering, wandering, wandering, wandering—
Your evil spirit, Tangi'ia! [an allusion to spirit possession]
And you left your wife.
Wandering, wandering, wandering, wandering—
Your evil spirit, Tangi'ia!
And you left your wife.
Oh, our daughter!
Come on girl, give us a big kiss.
Oh, our daughter!
Come on girl, give us a big kiss.
Hold the peace of the Messiah, Marere,
He will give peace.
Hold the peace of the Messiah, Marere,
He will give peace.[22]
For our beautiful daughter
My heart aches,
For our beautiful daughter
My heart aches.

Concluding Remarks

We have seen that in W. W. Gill's earlier version of the story, Tangi'ia was a god who spoke through a priest of the same name. In the 1973 performance, Tangi'ia is not presented as a priest but rather as a demonic being with remarkable powers: unlike Gill's Tangi'ia he has wings, which have enabled him to fly to the island. He does, however, resemble the priest in the older story in many ways. In both versions, he devours children but ends up being poisoned by Marere.

Before looking at some possible interpretations it is useful to consider certain aspects of Mangaian history and culture. According to one version of Mangaian history, the eldest children of the primal parents, Vatea and Papa, were the original gods of Mangaia and were, in this order, five males: the twins Tangaroa

---

[22] These lines, which thank the Messiah for the peace they have attained, also convey a direct message to the audience that they remain Christians.

and Rongo, and Tongaiti, Tane-Papa-Kai, and Tangi'ia.[23] Tangaroa went to live at Rarotonga, leaving Rongo as the supreme god at Mangaia. In addition, the descendants of each of the children of Vatea and Papa chose their own tribal gods, usually the one from whom they claimed descent. However, Rongo's descendants, the Ngariki, adopted Motoro for their god (W. W. Gill 1876a:19, 25-28). In this kind of social system, senior individuals or lineages have authority over junior. Power and control is intimately related to such social groupings; although defined according to kinship, they are also political groupings. One way in which dominance is expressed is in the control and allocation of the resources, especially the prized taro lands; another is in exacting tribute, for example by confiscating land. According to Mangaian history, which revolved around continual struggles for supremacy and the right to control these resources, any established order was subject to challenge.

In order to consult the tribal gods, a food gift of *kava*, taro, and fish was presented to the priest, through whom the god spoke (W. W. Gill 1876a:35). When a priest might occasionally demand a human sacrifice in place of the usual offering, the victims would ordinarily be taken from one of the other tribes which had been defeated in war.[24] There is a conceptual equivalence between land, food, and certain classes of people such that those in power could demand land, food, or people as tribute from those over whom they exercised control. Tangi'ia, as the fourth son of Vatea and Papa, was said to have been the most junior and least significant of the gods (*ibid*.:28), and his followers were included among those who were eligible for sacrifice to Motoro (36-37). However, Tangi'ia's demands for a sacrificial offering from Marere indicate that Marere, and therefore the Ngariki and their god Motoro, are inferior to Tangi'ia. So at one level, the story may be seen (cf. Clerk 1985) as an expression of conflict between tribes. It culminates, in both versions, in eventual Ngariki victory, although in 1973 the Messiah, rather than Motoro, was credited with helping Marere achieve this victory.

Tangi'ia's eating children, and his boasting of his power, are consistent with a whole range of ideas about power and dominance, in this case expressed through the metaphor of human sacrifice. In addition, a rule of exogamy meant that marriage partners were, in theory at least, potential sacrificial victims to their partner's gods. The plays on words about eating that provide sexual double entendres are consistent with these ideas, and in an interesting departure from

---

[23] The version of Mangaian history used here comes from Buck 1934:23. There are other versions; for example, W. W. Gill indicates not the birth order Tangaroa and Rongo, Tonga'iti, Tangi'ia, and Tane, but the political order: Tangaroa and Rongo, Tonga'iti, Tane, and Tangi'ia (1876a:11, 28). In still another version, a Tonga'iti version, the order of seniority is changed even more markedly in that Tonga'iti is said to be Papa's husband (*ibid*.:44-45; Clerk 1985).

[24] It was common in many parts of Polynesia to refer to sacrificial human victims as fish. See, for example, Clerk's discussion (1985:237ff) about Mangaian symbolism and the conceptual equivalence of land, food, and people.

Gill's version (wherein Marere's son was the specified victim), Tangi'ia devours/marries the female children of his opponents.[25] This may have been a device to facilitate humor via the sexual double entendres, but perhaps it also reflects changes in Mangaian society: with the cessation of warfare, marriage has become an even more important means of acquiring (devouring) land and consolidating political power.

Some other interpretations are also possible. For example, the sexual double entendres, the husband's hitting his wife, and the public display of drinking and drunkenness all poke fun at rules that have been imposed by the church. These incidents and expressions reflect contemporary social and political differences on Mangaia, where post-contact history has been marked by continued resistance to many of the controls various church leaders have attempted to impose. In 1973 few people knew of the *kava* plant or how it had been used, and the word was used to denote alcoholic beverages in general; *kava maori* was a term for "bush beer," a home brew which is locally, regularly, and illegally produced. Yet the hand actions performed by the two lines of dancers accurately mimed its preparation, and it retains its earlier place in the story. On the one hand, there is a historical element, in that Tangi'ia's image as a powerful, priestly figure is reinforced when he is served a chiefly drink and, that being so, must drink it before he eats the child. On the other hand, the behavioral and verbal references to bush beer relate to recent history and modern practices.

In the 1973 play Motoro has been replaced by the Christian God, and Tangi'ia appears at first glance to have been transformed into a particularly sinister winged figure suggestive of the fallen archangel, Lucifer. Yet even here we have precedents in Mangaian culture. Unlike the other Mangaian gods, Motoro was not one of the sons of Vatea and Papa; he came to Mangaia from Rarotonga when the Ngariki requested a replacement for their earlier god, Tane, with whom they had become dissatisfied. Motoro's replacement by the Messiah is therefore consistent with a Mangaian cultural pattern. Even Tangi'ia's wings may be nothing new, since there is also in Mangaian oral tradition a winged figure known as Tangi'ia-ka-rere who flies in and devours the sun (W. W. Gill 1876a:47).

The performance itself, including such elements as the costuming, the special effects, the selection of a story by a group of "appropriate people," and the consensus approach to the performance, provides evidence of the continuity of a dramatic tradition. The form of the *peu tupuna* appears to be the same as that involved in the presentations described by W. W. Gill (1876a:225-50, 1894:243-58). The 1973 Nuku was itself an interesting example of the syncretism evident in contemporary Mangaian society; the Tangi'ia play presented on this occasion constitutes another example. Where some types of Mangaian oral tradition appear to resist change, the *peu tupuna* is an extraordinarily flexible art form that readily

---

[25] Land confiscated from those defeated in war was land "eaten" by the victors. Land can also be acquired (devoured) by trade or through adoption or marriage arrangements, so by the act of substitution we come to an equivalence between devouring and marrying.

incorporates new elements. Although syncretism may be evident, the performance was indisputedly Mangaian. But above all it was fun, and can be accepted as just that. One doesn't have to know history to enjoy good entertainment.

A biblical pageant at the 1973 Nuku.
Here, actors wear biblically derived garments made of modern materials.
Photo: Marivee McMath

References

Buck   *See* Hiroa, Te Rangi.

Caillot 1914   A.C. Caillot. *Mythes légendes et traditions des Polynésiens.* Paris: Ernest Leroux.

Clerk 1985   Christian Clerk. "The Fish of Rongo: Some Readings of a Polynesian Myth." *Folklore,* 96:234-42.

W. Gill 1856   William Gill. *Gems from the Coral Islands: or Incidents of Contrast between Savage and Christian Life of the South Sea Islanders.* vol. 2: *Eastern Polynesia: Comprising the Rarotonga Groups, Penrhyn Islands, and Savage Island.* London: Ward.

W. Gill 1880   _____. *Selections from the Autobiography of the Rev. William Gill; being chiefly a Record of his Life as a*

                        Missionary in the South Sea Islands. London: Yates
                        and Alexander.

W. W. Gill 1876a   _____. William W. Gill. *Myths and Songs from the
                        South Pacific.* London: Henry S. King.

W. W. Gill 1876b   _____. *Life in the Southern Isles: or, Scenes and
                        Incidents in the South Pacific and New Guinea.*
                        London: The Religious Tract Society.

W. W. Gill 1894   _____. *From Darkness to Light in Polynesia, with
                        Illustrative Clan Songs.* London: Religious Tract
                        Society.

Hiroa 1934   Te Rangi Hiroa. *Mangaian Society.* Honolulu,
                        Hawaii: Bernice P. Bishop Museum, Bulletin 122.

Hiroa 1939   _____. *Anthropology and Religion.* New Haven:
                        Yale University Press.

Hiroa n.d.   _____. "Advent of Christianity in the Cook Islands."
                        Ms. in the Buck Collection, Group 3, Box 7.5.
                        Bernice P. Bishop Museum, Honolulu, Hawaii.

Loomis 1984   Terence Loomis. "The Politics of Cook Island
                        Culture-troupe Performance." In *Tauiwi: Racism and
                        Ethnicity in New Zealand.* Ed. by P. Spoonley, C.
                        MacPherson, D. Pearson, and C. Sedgwick.
                        Palmerston North, New Zealand: Dunmore Press. pp.
                        128-41.

Mark 1976   M. V. Mark (née McMath). "The Relationship
                        between Ecology and Myth in Mangaia." Unpublished
                        M. A. thesis, University of Otago, Dunedin, New
                        Zealand.

Sykes 1980   W. R. Sykes. "Botanical Science." In *Bibliography
                        of Research on the Cook Islands.* Compiled by W. R.
                        Sykes et al. New Zealand Soil Bureau, DSIR, for the
                        New Zealand National Commission for UNESCO.
                        pp. 9-67.

Contributors

JAMES and ACHSAH CARRIER studied Ponam Island society in 1979 and returned to the island repeatedly in 1980 and 1986, when they were teaching at the University of Papua New Guinea. They have written extensively on many aspects of Ponam society, and their *Wage, Trade and Exchange: A Manus Society in the Modern State* was recently published by the University of California Press.

CHRISTIAN CLERK teaches social anthropology for the extramural services of London University and City University. His special interests lie in the anthropology and history of Polynesia. He carried out field research in the Cook Islands for his doctoral thesis, *The Animal World of the Mangaians* (University of London, 1981), and has published articles on ethnozoology and on myth. He is Secretary of the Pacific Islands Society of the United Kingdom and Ireland, for which he has recently prepared the *UK and Ireland Pacific Research Register*.

STEVEN FELD is Director of the Center for Intercultural Studies in Folklore and Ethnomusicology at the University of Texas at Austin. His research on the intersection of verbal and musical genres among the Kaluli people of Papua New Guinea is discussed in *Sound and Sentiment: Birds, Weeping, Poetics, and Song in Kaluli Expression*, which appeared in a second revised edition in 1990, and in numerous articles.

RUTH FINNEGAN is Professor in Comparative Social Institutions at the Open University, England, and former editor of the anthropological journal *Man*. Her main publications are in the comparative anthropology/sociology of art (particularly of verbal art/oral literature and of music) and include *Limba Stories and Story-telling*, *Oral Literature in Africa*, *Oral Poetry*, and (ed. with Raymond Pillai) *Essays on Pacific Literature*. Her most recent research on local musicians in an English town is published by Cambridge University Press as *The Hidden Musicians*.

RAYMOND FIRTH is Emeritus Professor of Anthropology at the University of London. He collected songs and other traditional oral material on his first expedition to Tikopia in the Solomon Islands in 1928-29, and on several subsequent visits. He has published about a half-dozen volumes and many articles on aspects of Tikopia ethnography, incorporating much oral tradition, and has recently completed a general book on Tikopia songs to be published by Cambridge University Press.

JUDITH HUNTSMAN is Associate Professor in the Department of Anthropology at the University of Auckland and former editor of the *Journal of the Polynesian Society*. Her research involvement with Tokelau and Tokelauans spans over 20 years, and, in collaboration with Antony Hooper, she has published numerous historical and ethnographic articles about these tiny Polynesian atolls. A historical ethnography of Tokelau is now in preparation which combines local traditions (or accounts) and the writings of outsiders with ethnographic research to probe the differences among the three atolls, and their relations with one another and the world beyond.

MARIVEE McMATH, an independent scholar with an interest in Mangaian culture and history, spent ten months on Mangaia in 1971 and 1973-74 as a graduate student at the University of Otago, researching the relationship between ecology and myth. Since this time she has had a close relationship with the Cook Islands community in New Zealand.

MARGARET ORBELL is Reader in the Department of Maori at the University of Canterbury. She specializes in Maori and other Polynesian poetry, imagery, and mythology. Her most recent works are *The Natural World of the Maori* (1985) and *Hawaiki: A New Approach to Maori Tradition* (1985).

TEAEA PARIMA is Mangaian and has lived on the island for most of his life. He is currently completing a Bachelor of Science degree and teaching at a high school on Mangaia.

WENDY POND has been translating Tongan poetry for twenty years, working with Tupou Posesi Fanua and other poets in Tonga and in New Zealand, where there is a large resident Tongan population. She has been a guest editor of Tonga's literary magazine, *Faikava*. An independent scholar, she is currently attached to the Stout Research Centre at Victoria University of Wellington, discerning systematic principles of Maori and Austronesian classification of the insect fauna.

ALLAN THOMAS (School of Music, Victoria University of Wellington) is an ethnomusicologist whose work encompasses Asian and Pacific research, teaching, and performance. Since 1980 he has been researching the traditional music of the Tokelau community in New Zealand and in the Tokelau Islands.

INELEO TUIA was until recently Community Officer for the Tokelau Research Project of the Epidemiology Unit, Wellington Hospital. As a leader in the Tokelau community, he has done much to ensure the continuing vitality of Tokelau traditional arts in New Zealand.

JOHN D. WAIKO is Director of the Institute of Applied Social and Economic Research, a position to which he is seconded as Professor of History from the University of Papua New Guinea. His publications include studies of Binandere tradition and its textual analysis, and of the history and politics of Papua New Guinea.

Index

Note: Non-Western names are given in the order cited in the book.

Aloisio Kave Ineleo: 127n7, 128-32, 153-55
Amerindian Brazil: 95
Apache: 102-3
Ariki Kafika: 75-76
Baddely, J.: 162-64
Bakhtin, Mikhail: 90
Basso, Keith: 102-3
Bauman, Richard: 174
Biblical stories: 14
Binandere: general: 9, 177-94; lament (ji tari) in, 185-86; and oral tradition: 179-82; oral tradition and art forms in, 182-88; sirawa (fish-trap) in, 179-82; song/dance (ya jiwari) in, 186-87; standardized song/dance (guru) in, 187-88
Boas, Franz: 155-56
Bourdieu, Pierre: 197
Buck, Peter: See Te Rangi Hiroa
Carrier, Achsah: 27, 195-214
Carrier, James: 27, 195-214
Chenoweth, V.: 178
Clerk, Christian: 26, 161-76
Comparative theory: 11
Composition: 11, 16-18, 86, 96-98, 116-18
Cook Islands: 9, 161-76. See also Mangaia, Spirit narratives
Cultural context: 21-24, 124n1
Emic vs. etic: 192
Ethnohistory: 195
Ethnopoetics: 195
Extratextual context: 1, 11, 124n1
Feld, Stephen: 25, 85-108
Finnegan, Ruth: 1-5, 6-29, 30, 96-98
Firth, Raymond: 25, 64-84
Foley, John Miles: 20, 21, 31
Fox, James J.: 155-56
Gell, Alfred: 198
Genre-dependence: 31
Gill, William Wyatt: 162, 215, 251
Hawaii: 8n2
Huhane, Vīvī: 57-61

Huntsman, Judith: 26, 112, 124-60
Ihaia Puka (Tokelau poet): 8n3, 9, 14, 17, 18, 109-23; repertoire of, 118-19
Individual and tradition: 11, 16-18, 46-47, 85, 109, 124, 162, 206-11
Intertextuality: 90-104, 106
Ioane Toma: 127n7, 157
Kaluli: boundaries of speech and song, 85-86, 95-96; composition in performance in, 86, 96-98; emotion in, 86, 98-100; gender and genre in, 86, 100-02; general, 9, 85-108; intertextuality in, 90-104, 105-6; "lift-up-over-sounding" (dulugu ganalan), 88-90; placenames in, 102-4; polyphony and heterophony in, 88-90, 105-6; rituals of transition and renewal in, 86; "sung-texted-weeping" (sa-yalab), 86, 87-88
Kavakiua (Pa Vangatau): 68-69
Kiribati (Gilbert Islands): 9
Kitione Mamata: 53-57, 61
Lili Fakaalofa: 127n7, 145-53, 153-55
Loketi Lapuka: 51-53, 61
Lord, Albert B.: 16, 18, 20, 24, 30, 96-98
Mangaia: dramatic tradition in, 218-19, 253-54; festivals in, 217-18; general: 215-55; history and culture in, 251-53; the nuku in, 219-22, 253; syncretism in, 216-17, 253-54. See also "Winged Tangi'ia."
Manuele Palehau Leone: 127n7, 132-45, 153-55, 158
Maori: general, 9; poetic conventions in, 37-45, 45-47; society and poetic genres, 33-37; texts in, 31-33; women's songs in, 30-48
Maranda, E.K.: 161
McMath, Marivee: 27, 215-55
Melanesia: 8
Micronesia: 8n3
Mika Tinilau: 127n7, 156-57
Miller, J.C.: 182
Neu, Jerome: 98-100
New Zealand: 8n2
New Guinea: See Papua New Guinea

Niua Islands, Tonga: colonization of, 50-51; general, 49-63; Niuafo'ou, 53-57; Niuatoputapu, 51-53, 57; Tafahi, 57-61

Nonverbal features: 1, 18-20. *See also* Oral tradition: visual aspects

O'Hanlon, Michael: 197

Ong, Walter J.: 31

Oral tradition: concept of, 105; variety of, 1, 12-16, 16-17, 21; visual alternatives to, 195-214; visual aspects of, 11, 20-21. *See also* Individual and tradition

Oral Tradition (the journal): 3, 11, 12*n*5

Oral-Formulaic Theory: 18, 31, 96-98

Orality: 12

Orbell, Margaret: 1-5, 24-25, 30-48

Pacific region: neglect of oral traditions, 6-8

Papua New Guinea: 9, 177-94. *See also* Binandere

Parima, Teaea: 27, 215-55

Parry, Milman: 16, 20, 31, 96-98

Performance: as concept, 18-20, 124*n*1; features, 1, 11

Pike, Kenneth L.: 192

Polynesia: 8

Ponam: 9, 195-214

Pond, Wendy: 25, 49-63

Propp, Vladimir: 85

Reflexivity: 2

Sahlins, M.: 173-74

Shortland, Edward: 41

Societies (islands): 8n2

Solomon Islands: *See* Tikopia

South Slavic epic: 16, 24, 30

Spirit narratives: actions and reactions in, 171-73; bodily sensations in, 168; general: 161-76; smells in, 169; sounds in, 167-68; spirits and place in, 170-71; spirits and time in, 169-70; users of, 173; visible forms in, 164-67

Strathern, Andrew and Marilyn: 197

"Taetagaloa, Story of": 127-53

Te Rangi Hiroa (Peter Buck): 216

Thomas, Allan: 25-26, 109-23

Tikopia: dance songs (*mako*), 65-66; general, 64-84; insults in, 77-83; laments (*fuatanga*), 65; sex in, 67-70; sexual imagery in, 70-75

Tokelau Islands: "account" (*tala*) in, 125-26, 153-55, 155-57; "action song" (*fatele*) in, 113ff.; change and continuity in song, 113-16; "choral song" (*pehelagilagi*) in, 113, 115; composition in, 116-18; degeneration and creation in, 155-57; general, 109-23; Ihaia Puka's songs described, 118-19; "love song" (*mako*) in, 113, 114-15; narrative in, 124-60; ownership and anonymity in, 119-22; poet (*pulotu*) in, 109ff.; "tale" (*kakai*) in, 125-26, 153-55, 155-57. *See also* Ihaia Puka

Tonga: *See* Niua Islands, Tonga

Tradition: changes in, 188-92; concept of, 1, 11, 12-16

Tradition-dependence: 31

Tuia, Ineleo: 25-26, 109-23

Urban, Greg: 95, 105

Urban legend: 161

Visual aspects: *See* Oral Tradition

Waiko, John: 26, 177-94

"Winged Tangi'ia: general: 215-55; performance of, 220-21, 253-54; story of, 220; transcript of, 221-22, 222-36; translation of, 221-22, 236-51

Writing and speaking: 195-96